FENG-SHUI AND DESTIN

FENG-SHUI AND DESTINY

Raymond Lo

Tynron Press, England

© *Raymond Lo, 1992*

First published in 1992 by
Tynron Press
Unit 3 Turnpike Close
Lutterworth
Leicestershire LE17 4JA
England

ISBN 1-85646-026-6
All rights reserved

Reprinted 1994

Typeset in Singapore by Points Prepress
Printed in Singapore by Express Printers

Contents

Preface ix

Part 1

1. Unravelling the *Feng-shui* Mystery 1
2. The Five Elements: The First Law of *Feng-shui* 3
3. Cycles: The Age of the Magnificent Seven 5
4. The Magic Tortoise of the River Lo and The Flying Stars 7
5. *Feng-shui* Appraisal 11
6. Physical *Shars* 14
7. The Art of Placement: Health and Wealth 16
8. *Feng-shui* Tools: Fish, Mirror and Wind Chime 20
9. *Lo Pan:* The *Feng-shui* Compass 22
10. The Eight Houses *Feng-shui* Theory 24
11. Your Home: Good and Bad Locations 26
12. Prosperity: Keeping a Way Open 27
13. Putting Your House in Order 29
14. The Flying Star School of *Feng-shui* 31
15. Joy and Sorrow: Cyclical Changes 32
16. The Prosperity of Hong Kong: The Dragon's Lair 35
17. Bank of China: Concentration of Benevolent Forces 36
18. World Wide House: Escalators as a Source of Wealth 39
19. The Governor's House: Hong Kong's Future 42

20.	The Hongkong Bank Building	44
21.	*Feng-shui* and the Supernatural	48
22.	Charting Murder and Mishaps by the Flying Stars	51
23.	8/8/88 and the Art of Selecting an Auspicious Date	57
24.	Landscape and the Fortune of Hong Kong	59
25.	The Chinese Birth Chart and Your Fortune	64

Part 2

26.	The Four Pillars of Destiny	71
27.	Hu Yaobang: The Destiny of a Reformer	74
28.	The Ups and Downs of Zhao Ziyang	78
29.	In Search of the Birth Data of Deng Xiaoping	82
30.	The Rise and Fall of Margaret Thatcher	85
31.	Paul Chung: Suicide of a Star	89
32.	Marilyn Monroe: Murder or Suicide?	93
33.	John Lennon: Tragic Death of a Great Talent	96
34.	Karen Carpenter: Death by Uncommon Disease	98
35.	Bruce Lee's Mysterious Death	100
36.	Richard Nixon and Watergate	103
37.	How Ronald Reagan Survived Assassination	105
38.	Corazon Aquino: From Housewife to President	109
39.	Nicolae Ceausescu: The Fall of a Dictator	112
40.	Mikhail Gorbachev and the Future of Perestroika	116

41.	Nelson Mandela's 27 Years of Imprisonment	121
42.	Mike Tyson vs James Douglas	123
43.	Stefan Edberg vs Michael Chang	129
44.	President George Bush's Victory in the Gulf	133
45.	The Destiny of Saddam Hussein	135
46.	Operation Desert Storm	139
47.	The Destiny of Wars	141
48.	The Collapse of the Stock Market, October 13, 1989	143
49.	The *I Ching* Oracle and Chinese Politics	145
50.	The *Kua* of Hong Kong's Economy	150
51.	The *I Ching* and Perestroika	152
52.	The *I Ching* View of the Gulf Crisis	154
53.	Conclusion: Destiny and Free Will	157
Glossary		161
The 120 Years Basic Element Components Table		164

Preface

My interest in the occult began when I was a young boy puzzled by the meaning of life and phenomena not explainable by science. Educated in the English College, I started to find out more about the mystery of life by reading books on Western astrology and found great fun in trying out its principles on the characters and behaviour of my friends. The accuracy of astrology in describing human character increased my belief in the "will of heaven" and in destiny. Soon I developed an appetite for other branches of occult studies as well, particularly Chinese metaphysics.

The first field I ventured into was *feng-shui*. I recall one particular year when I found myself running into a series of misfortunes immediately after moving into a new flat. Mysterious illnesses and mishaps happened one after another and there could not be any logical explanation except that I had just changed my living environment. So I decided to study *feng-shui* to see if it could offer me some clues. And it was in *feng-shui* that I discovered the enormous treasures of Chinese cosmology and metaphysics.

Chinese fortune-telling is an ancient art. It is so vast and rich that I think no man can, in a single lifetime, master even a small fraction of it. However, these subjects are so interesting that, once someone is attracted to them, they will easily become a lifelong engagement. And I must add that the sense of satisfaction and achievement is a never-ending reward.

There are three branches in Chinese fortune-telling which stand out as the most useful and well-organised systems for revealing the future. *Feng-shui* is a study of the influence of the environment on human fortune and it will help us fully to utilise the laws of nature to exploit the potentials in our destinies and to avoid and minimise misfortunes. The Four Pillars of Destiny is a code used by the ancient Chinese to reveal the cosmic components of each person. Destiny and fortune can be revealed by analysing the interaction between such components. The *I Ching* oracle is an art which seeks answers from the Divine to specific questions about the future. It can be employed as a supplement to *feng-shui* and the Four Pillars of Destiny.

As these techniques address directly the perennial question of destiny and human existence, they are certainly not easy subjects. In order to acquire a fair mastery of the skills of fortune-telling, one has to put in a great deal of effort, and one must have faith and courage. However, as they are able to cast light on the vast mystery of life, I consider such "investments" worthwhile and the reward is the satisfaction of painfully acquired knowledge and the joy of feeling the truth about life.

In 1988, because of a series of successes in fortune-telling, I became firmly convinced of the validity and value of such skills. The existence of a pattern of predictable destiny became proven truth to me and I thought such great treasure should be shared with others, especially English speakers who do not have easy access to ancient Chinese culture.

It was at this time that I started to write about *feng-shui* in English. This book is an entirely new revision of the articles which I contributed to the *Hong Kong Standard*'s *feng-shui* column from October 1988 to June 1990. I begin with the elementary techniques and then go on to the applications of such techniques to controversial and interesting topics of current interest. During the year of great changes, turbulence and revolutions in 1989, the articles presented to readers fresh ideas about the nature of such changes, viewed from a metaphysical point of view. These articles are unique in that they are commentaries on events based on the objective laws of the cosmos. It is my hope that they will be able to stimulate new thinking and present a different view of what is happening around us.

While putting the finishing touches to this book, the Gulf crisis broke out and threw the world into disharmony with the Iraqi invasion of Kuwait in August 1990. This crisis developed into a full-scale war in early 1991. The quick and decisive victory of the Allied Forces brought in a new world order. Throughout the progress of the crisis I have applied the techniques of *feng-shui,* the Four Pillars of Destiny and the *I Ching* oracle to forecast the crisis. Readers of the *Hong Kong Standard* were kept up-to-date on the Gulf situation and I am gratified that the predictions were fairly accurate. Many of the analyses appeared as early as September 1990 and are genuine predictions rather than reviews after the event.

Besides giving interesting explanations and predictions about people and happenings, this book also teaches you many skills commonly employed by practitioners of Chinese fortune-telling, and most of the techniques introduced are not easily available to English readers. Many of the techniques have never been presented in English before. For this reason I have made my own translation of some *feng-shui* and fortune-telling terms. However, I have tried to keep technical jargon to a minimum. Hopefully, you will enjoy reading this book and by the time you put it down, your entire view of life and the universe may have changed radically.

I am grateful to Master Lam Kwok Hung who introduced me to *feng-shui* and I am indebted to my teacher, Master Suen Tai Chuen, who not only generously shared his vast knowledge and experience with me, but also showed me the right attitude towards *feng-shui.* Thanks are due to the *Hong Kong Standard* for providing me the opportunity to publish my articles. I am also grateful to Mr Sara who brings the articles to life with his superb portraits of prominent persons.

My wife, Maureen, has been most supportive in the months of writing. Without her, none of what follows would have been written.

Raymond Lo

PART ONE

1. Unravelling the *Feng-shui* Mystery

Anyone who has ever come into contact with Chinese society must have come across the term *feng-shui*. He will have encountered some mysterious *feng-shui* terms and practices which are unique to the East. An imaginative Westerner may be interested to find out what *feng-shui* is all about. However, he will always find the door to such knowledge blocked — not only by the language barrier, but also by the large variety of *feng-shui* schools and methods.

Let us assume you know how to read and write Chinese and you are fortunate enough to find a good teacher. Even so, it requires many years of study and experience before you can be sufficiently equipped to practise *feng-shui*. For Westerners who do not know any Chinese, there is practically no way to study the subject because both lectures on *feng-shui* and learning material in English are rare. This book is intended as a first step in bridging the gap between English speakers and *feng-shui*. I hope at least to provide the rudiments of *feng-shui* by answering some common questions, by correcting some misconceptions and, most important of all, by providing a direction for further study.

Let us start by looking at the words *feng-shui*. When considering the various influences upon the quality of life, the Chinese have a quintessential saying: "First, destiny; second, luck; third, *feng-shui*; fourth, philanthropy; fifth, education ...".

This shows how important an influence *feng-shui* has on Chinese beliefs.

So what is *feng-shui*? Literally, *feng* means wind or air and *shui* means water. In a much broader sense, *shui* has wider applications and also embraces physical circumstances, including mountains and landscape. In modern cities, it also refers to roads, streets, flyovers, buildings — the concrete jungle. So *shui* embraces the tangible, physical environment. *Feng* is harder to explain. It does not merely refer to wind and air but also to something abstract and intangible. It is some invisible force which the naked eye cannot see. Hence the study of *feng-shui* is the study of environmental influences on human life. Such influences are divided into two categories — the tangible, physical environment and the intangible, invisible forces.

What are these invisible forces? They are still a mystery as so far, no systematic scientific research has been conducted to determine their nature. Magnetism? Cosmic waves? Radioactivity? We are still very far from any conclusive findings. However, just as it is not necessary to understand computer programming before you can use a computer, *feng-shui* can be understood — and the Chinese have made good use of it for centuries – without being able scientifically to verify its existence.

Ancient Chinese tradition indicated that the invisible forces are "directional". Different forces are associated with different directions. Also, these forces are not static but move according to a predictable pattern. They interact with the physical environs to exert influences on people. An understanding of the moving pattern and influences of the directional forces not only enables you to select a house or site with good *feng-shui* but also to predict events that may take place there.

The ancient Chinese applied *feng-shui* methods to the selection of grave sites, called *yin* houses or houses for the dead. The Chinese believe that the influence of *feng-shui* forces on the grave sites of ancestors will have a great bearing on the well-being of their descendants.

For example, a rather famous Hong Kong merchant in the construction business was jailed for corruption a few years ago. *Feng-shui* experts found that the grave of his ancestors, located in Guangdong province in China, was badly located and surrounded by lychee trees which symbolise imprisonment.

As time went on, the art of selection of *yin* houses was also applied to *yang* houses – houses for the living. Besides, to choose a good *yin* house is a very costly exercise and is not so popular in a crowded modern city where land is scarce and expensive. The *feng-shui* technique was first applied to the construction of temples and palaces – it is now a household tool to stimulate good fortune and avoid evil influences.

Let us see how a *yang* house study is done and what evaluation you can expect from a *feng-shui* man. If you invite a *feng-shui* man to look at your flat, he will first look around the building and establish its direction by means of a *lo pan* – a complicated Chinese compass. Then he will check the age of the building. There is a big difference in *feng-shui* terms between a house built in 1984 and one built a year earlier. With this information, he will be able to draw up a plan of the intangible forces affecting the building from all directions and in a particular time span. This plan is like a birth chart for a building, similar to the natal chart in Western astrology.

He will also look at the physical aspects, and observe the surroundings of your flat. He will view the landscape, see if there are any unusually shaped objects nearby or in sight, determine the direction and curve of surrounding roads, flyovers, the travelling direction of cars, and so on. In short, he will establish the influence of the physical environment.

He will then look at the interior arrangement of your flat: how it is divided into rooms; how the doors are located; where the oven, the beds, the toilets, the plants are; what can be seen from each window.

A *feng-shui* expert will also check the birth date of at least the bread earner – as different people receive different influences.

There are thousands of small things of paramount importance in *feng-shui*. Only by an accurate study of the interaction of both the physical environment and intangible forces, can he make a proper evaluation and accurate predictions.

After collecting all this information, he will be able to offer advice. Such advice will usually include the following items:

1. A general comment on the building, with reference to riches and health.
2. A general comment on your flat regarding the chance of getting rich or getting sick.
3. Which are the best and worst locations in your flat and how to use or avoid them.
4. What type of person is most suitable or unsuitable to live in your flat.
5. What are the suitable and unsuitable colours and objects for decorating your flat.
6. Whether you should redecorate or rearrange your flat, or sell it to the first interested buyer as soon as possible.
7. How to dissolve bad influences by the placement of certain objects.
8. The prediction of some specific events – for example, a man living in the southeast bedroom (Fig. 1) will be sick during a given period.

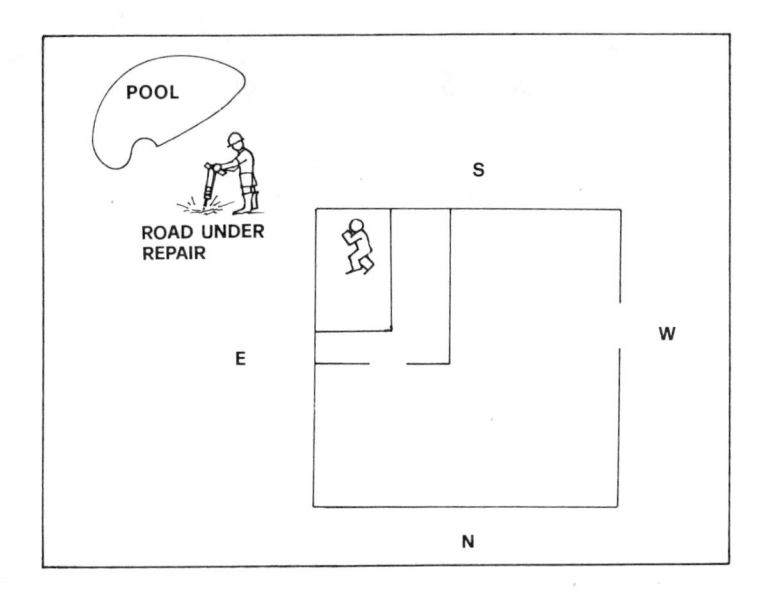

Fig. 1. Feng-shui can predict that the man in the southeast room will be sick in October 1988.

Experts with reasonably good training will be able to predict events correctly. Sometimes the nature of certain diseases can also be reflected by *feng-shui* study. But remember that there is a large variety of *feng-shui* schools and methods, so do not be surprised if your *feng-shui* man makes the study in a different manner.

These methods can also be applied on a wider scale to larger environs, from the choosing of a good grave site to the fortune and prosperity of a city or a country. For example, why is business so poor in one shopping complex while another nearby is thriving? Why are some numbers luckier than others? Why has there been an upsurge of women leaders and female power in the recent years since 1984? In the following chapters I will attempt to provide some answers long held by *feng-shui* masters.

2. The Five Elements: The First Law of Feng-shui

The philosophical basis of *feng-shui* and Chinese fortune-telling is the theory of the five elements. These elements — metal, wood, water, fire and earth — are believed to embrace, and are constituents of, all matter in the universe, and influence daily life greatly.

Everything on earth can be classified using this theory. For example, a lion is metal, a tiger is earth, a baby boy born in 1988 is wood, and so on. Since the five elements constitute the five basic forces in the universe, everyone (except deities) is influenced. We should always bear in mind that the names of these elements have a significance far beyond the limitations of their syntactical meaning. However, for the beginner, there is no harm in considering just the physical attributes of any particular element. For example, under the category wood we find trees, plants, the colour green. By extension, wood needs water to survive and connotes prosperity in spring. The same can be applied to the other four elements.

Natural rules exist to govern the interaction of the five elements. A clear understanding of this interaction is the starting point in the study of *feng-shui*. Fig. 2 illustrates the cyclic relationship between these elements, also called the cycle of birth. The arrows show the direction of birth. For example, metal gives birth to water. Like a mother giving birth to a child, the energy of metal is exhausted by giving birth to water, so water becomes stronger and metal is weakened in the process.

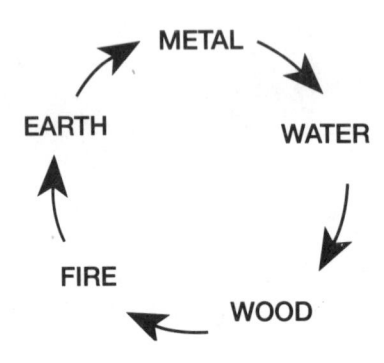

Fig. 2. The Cycle of Birth.

A *feng-shui* expert often advises clients to place certain objects at certain locations to dissolve unwelcome bad forces. If he advises you to place a red carpet beneath your favourite chair, it means that the bad influence acting on the location of the chair must be of the wood category. The colour red belongs to the fire element and draws away the wood energy, reducing its evil power.

The law of birth can be demonstrated by another example. Imagine the house directly opposite yours has a fierce-looking statue of a tiger and when you leave for work each morning, you feel uneasy about the tiger staring at you. A *feng-shui* master will advise you to put the picture of a lion on your front door to challenge the tiger. Using the law of birth, the lion will be victorious because the tiger belongs to earth and the lion, metal. The tiger's earth energy is drawn away by giving birth to the metal lion.

This law is also commonly applied to colours. Metal is equated with gold or white; wood, green or brown; water, blue, black or the various shades of grey; fire, red or purple; and earth, yellow. If a *feng-shui* master advises you to add more red to your room, he is in fact saying that your natal chart indicates that you belong to the earth element and need fire (red) to make you stronger.

There is also a corresponding cycle of destruction (Fig. 3).

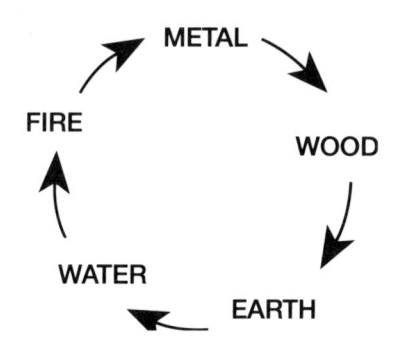

Fig. 3. The Cycle of Destruction.

The arrows show that metal controls or destroys wood and wood controls or destroys earth. However, as this cycle is antagonistic and disrupts harmony, it is not recommended for use when there is a need to dissolve bad influences. In brief, then, the cycle of birth is harmonious, like a mother and child relationship, and problems can be solved peacefully using this method. The reverse is true of the cycle of destruction — it is usually the cause of problems.

3. Cycles: The Age of the Magnificent Seven

In chapter 1 we examined the tangible and intangible forces in *feng-shui*. These influences have a space dimension in terms of direction and location. They also have a time dimension as they move in a certain fixed cyclic pattern through time. To understand the moving pattern of the intangible forces, we must be familiar with the time dimension — the concept of time cycles in *feng-shui*.

In Western astrology, time is divided according to the 12 sun signs of the zodiac; we are now reaching the Age of Aquarius which will last for 2,000 years. There is a similar cyclic time concept in *feng-shui,* but the divisions are more refined. Instead of dividing time according to the constellations, the Chinese system divides time into nine ages, each lasting 20 years. Three 20-year ages make up one period. So it takes a total of 180 years to complete a full cycle. Each period is assigned a number, from one to nine, always in ascending order (Fig. 4). Such a division of time has its origins in a mysterious mathematical arrangement called the *lo shu* diagram, as well as in the eight *kua* (trigrams) of the *I Ching (The Book of Changes).*

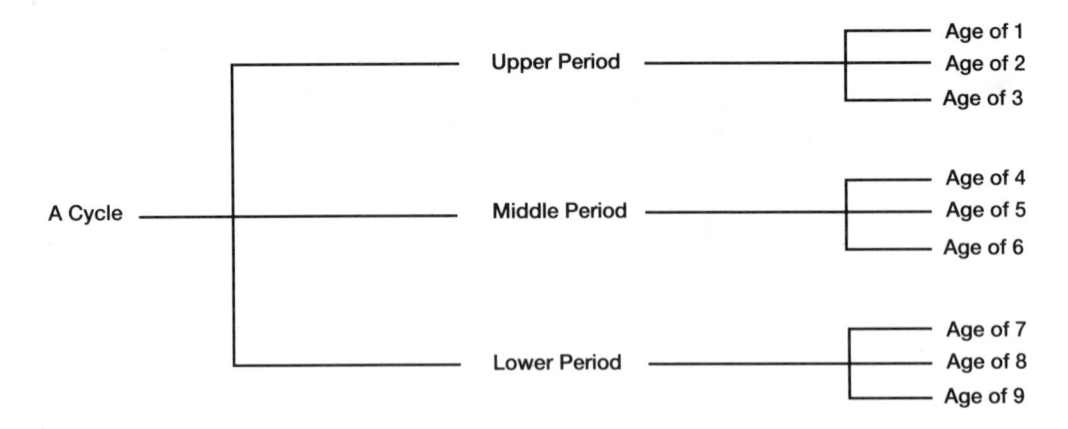

Fig. 4. The feng-shui system of cycles and ages.

(Major differences aside, there is a curious similarity between the Western and Eastern systems: the Chinese 20-year age system is close to, but does not coincide with, the alignment of the planets Jupiter and Saturn which occurs once every 20 years. There is a difference of four years. For example, the last Jupiter-Saturn alignment took place in 1980 but the Chinese Age of Seven started in 1984. The eight *kua*, the *lo shu* diagram and the influence of the Jupiter-Saturn alignment will be treated in detail later in the book.)

Let us take a look at the present age. Since 1984, we have been in the Age of Seven which will last until 2003. The number seven can also be represented by one of the eight trigrams (*kua*), in symbolic form: ☱

This trigram, in very simplified and generalised terms, contains useful information:

Direction — west
Object — gold, metal
Person — young girl, female
Occupation — entertainment, fortune-telling, matters spiritual
Action — speaking, sex, demolition and rebuilding
Body — mouth

So the Age of Seven naturally represents the prosperity of activities associated with a combination of the items above. The recent upsurge of women in leadership positions, the flourishing fortune-telling business, the popularity of the supernatural and the spiritual, the growing interest in religion, the glamour of the entertainment business, sexual liberation, the great advances in technology — all these are obvious examples of the influence of the number seven. This trend will continue and is not likely to wane until the year 2003. (It is also worth remembering that houses completed between 1964 and 1983 are houses belonging to the Age of Six, and those completed between 1984 and 2003 belong to the Age of Seven.)

Living as we do in the Age of Seven, this number is generally considered the reigning number and represents prosperity and good luck. If the number is related to personal things — telephone number, identity card number, house number, car number, and other numbers containing a seven — it can be regarded as an indication of very good luck.

The next best number after seven is eight. The Age of Eight will not arrive until 2004, so at present eight signifies good fortune in the not too distant future; it represents growth and hope. Furthermore, eight belongs to the earth category and seven belongs to metal. Therefore eight will give birth to seven and strengthen its prosperity. A lucky number combination would be 87.

4. The Magic Tortoise of the River Lo and the Flying Stars

The numerology in *feng-shui* has its origins in a mysterious mathematical arrangement called the *lo shu* diagram. According to ancient Chinese legends, a giant tortoise surfaced in the River Lo in central China about 6,000 years ago. On the back of the tortoise shell the ancients discovered a pattern (Fig. 5). This pattern was the basis of Chinese numerology and, in time, became the famous plan of the nine squares (Fig. 6).

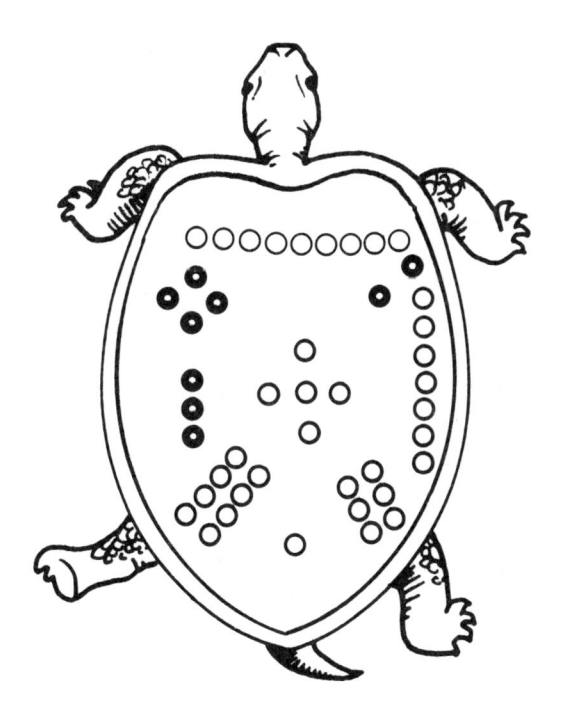

Fig. 5. The magic tortoise of the River Lo.

8   Feng-shui and Destiny

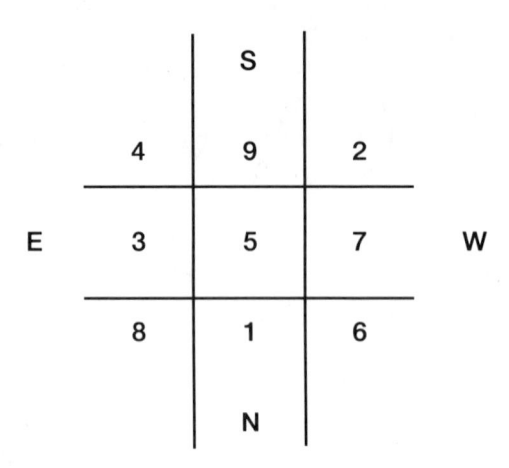

```
              S
        |           |
    4   |   9   |   2
        |           |
   -----+-------+-----
        |           |
E   3   |   5   |   7   W
        |           |
   -----+-------+-----
        |           |
    8   |   1   |   6
        |           |
              N
```

Fig. 6. Lo shu diagram – the original nine square plan.

Each square represents a direction and contains a number. This is called the *lo shu* diagram or the original plan and is the foundation of the flying star school of *feng-shui*. One interesting aspect of the nine-square plan is that you can add up any three numbers in a straight line in any direction – up, down, across or diagonal — and you always get a total of 15.

It is said that a perspicacious Chinese emperor (Emperor Chou), after making extensive studies, incorporated the eight *kua* of the *I Ching* into this plan. This amalgamation gradually developed into a practical numerology and *feng-shui* system. The *lo shu* diagram — eight *kua* combination is the foundation of Chinese numerology. As the eight *kua* is believed to embrace the whole universe, the nine numbers of the *lo shu* diagram have considerable fortune-telling significance. It is therefore worthwhile spending a little time memorising the significance of each number.

One (water), six (metal) and eight (earth) are generally good numbers. Of the three, eight is the best as it signifies hope and prosperity (see chapter 3). Six represents riches and prosperity in the Age of Six (1964 to 1983). When seven "took over" in 1984, the good influence of six began to wane. Nine belongs to the fire element. Since this age will not arrive until 2024, it represents good luck in the distant future and is not significant in the present age. However, its fire nature can cause harm to seven which belongs to the metal element. Two and five are unlucky numbers: two usually brings about ill health and five represents authoritarian aspect of power. Two and five together can bring about trouble. Three is equated with anger and agitation. Four represents romance, literature, education and sex. (Seven was discussed in the previous chapter.)

Even traditional Chinese are often surprised by the associations discussed above. For example, the Cantonese have a preferance for two because pronounced in Cantonese, it sounds like "easy"; the same goes for eight which sounds like "prosperity". Four is taboo because it sounds like "die". But in *feng-shui*, two and five are to be avoided at all costs. Four is not necessarily bad and can bring about romance and promotion. Eight enjoys a lucky place in *feng-shui* and traditional Chinese beliefs. The unique numerical arrangement taken from the shell of the mysterious tortoise, called the *lo shu* diagram, holds a very significant position in *feng-shui* as it is believed that the pattern of the numbers 1 to 9 as revealed by the plan actually shows the moving pattern of *feng-shui* intangible forces.

The intangible forces in *feng-shui* are not static; they are dynamic and move in a fixed pattern through time. The pattern of movement is shown by the nine-square plan. The nine squares represent eight directions and a centre. It should be noted that the nine squares (derived from the *lo shu* diagram) always have the directions upside down, i.e. with south in the position of north (right on top). If you intend to take up the study of *feng-shui* seriously, it is recommended that you get thoroughly familiar with this directional pattern as it is the original *lo shu* way and appears frequently in *feng-shui* literature.

Fig. 6 shows the *lo shu* diagram with the number five in the centre. This is also called the original plan because it is an exact copy of the plan on the shell of the giant tortoise in the River Lo. It is from this plan that we derive the moving pattern of the intangible forces.

If you start from five in the centre and go through the numbers one by one in ascending order, you will discover the following pattern: centre — 5; northwest(NW) — 6; west(W) — 7; northeast(NE) — 8; south(S) — 9; north(N) — 1; southwest(SW) — 2; east(E) — 3; southeast(SE) — 4. Five is called the reigning number and represents the reigning Age. So the *lo shu* diagram in fact coincides with the plan for the Age of Five. In the present Age of Seven, the number seven goes to the centre and all other numbers will change their positions accordingly.

The plan for the Age of Seven is shown in Fig. 7. This plan gives a rough indication of how the intangible forces are distributed between 1984 and 2003, and is the basic guide for drawing up a birth chart of any house completed in this Age.

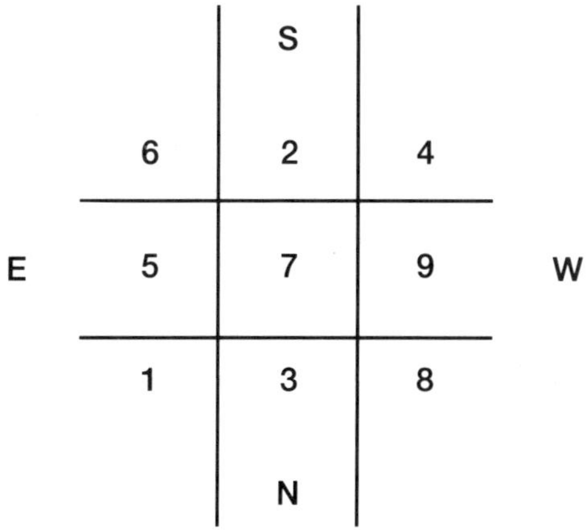

		S		
	6	2	4	
E	5	7	9	W
	1	3	8	
		N		

Fig. 7. Intangible forces 1984 — 2003 (Age of Seven).

10   Feng-shui and Destiny

Similar plans can also be drawn up for every year with the reigning number in the centre changing from year to year, month to month — even day to day. For example, three is the reigning number in 1988 and six is the reigning number for October of the same year. Put together, we get a plan showing a distribution of the intangible forces for October 1988 (Fig. 8). Such a plan can be used to compare with the birth chart of a house and to determine the events that will take place in October 1988.

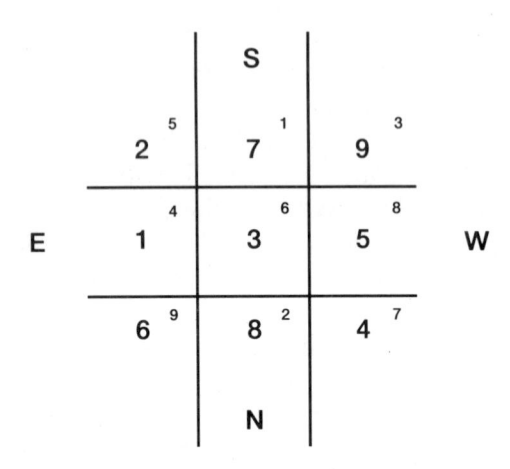

	S	
5 2	1 7	3 9
4 E 1	6 3	8 5 W
9 6	2 8	7 4
	N	

Fig. 8. Intangible forces in October 1988.

We have seen previously that two and five are unlucky numbers. Fig. 8 shows that two and five are located in the southeast in October 1988. So unless the house has other favourable *feng-shui* forces, something unhappy is likely to happen to the person living in the SE room in October 1988. Of course the nature and intensity of such unhappiness will be subject to a number of factors. These include the actual birth chart of the house, the birth data of the person affected, the furnishings and arrangement of the affected area, the external environs, and so on.

This method of appraising houses on the basis of the moving pattern of the intangible forces is called the flying star school of *feng-shui* and is popular with many *feng-shui* experts in Hong Kong and Taiwan. (The intangible forces — represented by numbers – are called the flying stars because they fly through time and space.)

The example given above is a simple one. We now take a look at a more complex example. Fig. 9 shows the plan of the flying stars in June 1988. One, six and eight are good numbers and they tend towards east, northeast and north respectively. A house which enjoys such a configuration is considered lucky. One of my friends has a flat that enjoys just such an auspicious directional pull. The entrance of the flat is located in the north, the cooking stove in the north-east and her bedroom in the east. In June 1988 she gave birth to a healthy boy.

```
          S
      9       5       7
   2       7       9
      8       1       3
E  1       3       5    W
      4       6       2
   6       8       4

NE        N
```

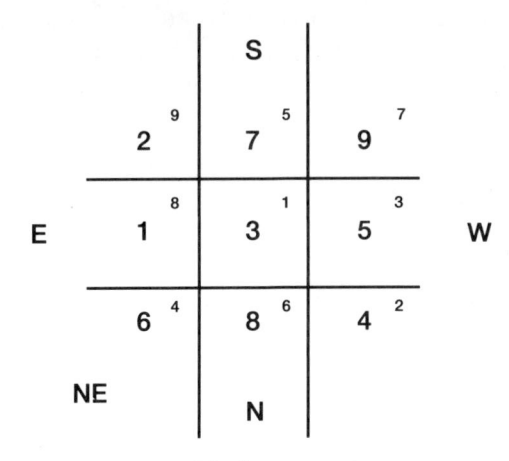

Fig. 9. Intangible forces in June 1988.

5. *Feng-shui* Appraisal

It is a common belief among the Chinese that you do not need a *feng-shui* appraisal if you live comfortably. As with all folklore this is only part of the truth. A lucky person always comes by a house with good *feng-shui* by pure chance simply because he is in luck. On the other hand, an unlucky man is not likely to find such a house even if he is a *feng-shui* expert, which explains why not all *feng-shui* masters are millionaires.

However, destiny and luck aside, it is advisable to have a *feng-shui* appraisal at least once a year. It will be clear from earlier chapters that the influence of *feng-shui* on a house changes from time to time. Particularly noteworthy are the bad forces — called *shar* because it sounds like "kill" in Mandarin – which change location yearly, monthly, even daily. Fig. 10 shows the location of the major *shars* and flying stars in 1991 – the Year of the Ram.

```
             S
      8      4      6
                   GRAND DUKE
                   THREE SHARS
E     7      9      2      W
                      SHAR
      3      5      1
           SHAR
             N
```

Fig. 10. The feng-shui influences in 1991

Each of the squares represents a direction and each figure within each square symbolises a star – meaning a type of *feng-shui* influence. I have, in the last chapter, explained the meaning of each of the nine numerical stars but for readers' easy reference, I now briefly list the essentials again:

1 – Water, long gone prosperity
2 – Earth, sickness (a *shar*)
3 – Wood, disputes, conflict
4 – Wood, education, romance, scandal
5 – Earth, misfortune, sickness (a *shar*)
6 – Metal, faded prosperity
7 – Metal, current prosperity
8 – Earth, prosperity of the near future
9 – Fire, future prosperity

From the above chart, the *feng-shui* man of the flying star school can easily tell the general fortune of a house that one can expect in the Year of the Ram. The nature of the mishap and its intensity will vary depending on the layout of the building, the interior arrangements and decorations, the external circumstances and the luck of the occupants. It is usually recommended that a metal wind chime be placed in any major north locations coming under the influence of the star five, as it is believed that the wind chime will generate the noise of metal which will help dissolve the star five, a *shar* in the category of earth, as metal will exhaust energy generated by the earth element.

To introduce some more complications, besides the yearly flying stars, there is also another set of monthly flying stars which change positions every month. It is these monthly flying stars that provide the *feng-shui* expert with the clues for predicting the timing of events. For example, the yearly star chart shows that the location north is potentially dangerous with the bad star five situated there in the Year of the Ram. This is a potential threat but we do not know in which month the mishap is likely to occur. The pattern of the monthly stars will provide an approximate answer. It is anticipated that the months of July and October will be most vulnerable as the monthly stars of five and two, meaning mishap and sickness, will also arrive at the north location and intensify the danger.

The next bad star or *shar* to watch is the star two, often associated with sickness. Such a star is found in the west location in the Year of the Ram. If your doors or bedrooms are located in the west of your house, the month of April will be the time to take extra care as the monthly star five also arrives at the west to intensify the bad effects. A common way to dissolve the star two is to hang a string of six metal coins at the west locations.

The number nine, representing fire, goes to the centre in 1991 and is the reigning star. So the element fire will feature prominently in the Year of the Ram. We have already seen the burning of the oil wells in Kuwait during the Gulf War, causing grave environmental consequences for the world. It is interesting to note that the fire started around February when the monthly star five, the trouble maker, also went to the centre position. The combined forces of the stars five and nine in February indicate misfortunes caused by the fire will occur in the middle area between the East and the West. This points quite accurately to the fire disaster in Kuwait, located in the Middle East. Also, it will not be surprising if we found ourselves or our family members more susceptible to diseases related to the eyes, the heart, the lips, blood pressure, etc. as these parts of the body are associated with the fire element.

Besides the notorious stars five and two, we should also note the position of the planet Jupiter which the Chinese respectfully regard as The Grand Duke of the Year. So high a regard is accorded this planet that they also name the year after the position of Jupiter. For example, the Ram in fact refers to the direction southwest which is supposed to be the position of Jupiter in the Year of the Ram. Traditionally, it is believed that sitting at the position opposite the Grand Duke (Jupiter) or facing the Grand Duke will bring misfortune. Ancient Chinese warlords made it a policy to avoid advancing towards the Grand Duke and prefer fighting with Jupiter at their back. It is interesting to note that in the Gulf War, the Iraqi soldiers fought facing the southwest – the position of Saudi Arabia in relation to Kuwait and the direction of Jupiter in 1991. However, the Allies advanced towards the northeast with the Grand Duke behind their back. Therefore the direction of advance of the Allies was more favourable in terms of *feng-shui* and, viewed in these terms, their victory was inevitable.

It is also generally believed that the location of the Grand Duke should be left in peace and no major construction work should be carried out in its direction. Disturbing the earth in the Grand Duke location, the southwest, is normally regarded as "disturbing earth on the head of the Grand Duke" and will lead to misfortune.

Chinese office workers are particularly concerned about a location called the three *shars*, which is the direction in conflict with the Grand Duke. The three *shars* are found in the west in 1991 and the right west direction is regarded as sitting on the three *shars* and will attract trouble and exert pressure in the Year of the Ram.

So much for bad influences. Let us now consider some good *feng-shui* spots. As we are now in the *feng-shui* phase called the age of Seven, the number seven in the yearly *feng-shui* chart reflects prosperity and will bring wealth and success. The lucky star seven is found in the east in 1991 and will be most beneficial if it falls on areas of open space and activities. For example, if the main entrance of your house or office is in the east location, or your living room is located in the east, then you may benefit from the lucky star of seven. Some activities in these locations, such as a clock with a pendulum, if placed in these east locations, will help to activate the beneficial influences and bring good fortune.

All the same, we should note that the impact of the yearly stars is also very much dependent on the primary *feng-shui* of the house which is represented by a basic *feng-shui* chart drawn up according to the age and the direction of a particular building. So different houses having different *feng-shui* charts will be affected differently by the yearly stars.

The yearly star has to interact with the primary *feng-shui* of a house for events, whether good or bad, to take place. For example, if we examine the primary *feng-shui* chart of a house and find the star eight in the east location, and if this east location is an area of activity allowing the free flow of intangible *feng-shui* forces, then we can expect prosperity in the Year of the Ram as the star eight, symbolising future prosperity, is in the earth category and so is in harmonious relationship with the metal star seven, which happens to arrive in the east in 1991. On the other hand, if the basic star of your house in the east is not eight but one, symbolising prosperity that is long gone and belongs to the element water, the yearly lucky star seven will not be able to generate prosperity as the water element will exhaust the metal power. This may even cause financial loss in the Year of the Ram.

So we can see all these *shars* and flying stars change their seats yearly and monthly and are believed to exert bad influence if not properly handled. (That is why the study of *feng-shui* is a lifelong exercise.) Owing to the shifting influence of these *shars* and stars, a *feng-shui* appraisal once a year is recommended. The beginning of spring (or around February) is the best time because this is when the lunar year starts and all *shars* change positions.

Aside from the yearly appraisal, there are other occasions for which a *feng-shui* consultation should be sought. Buying a new house or office and designing or renovating it are important events for which a *feng-shui* appraisal is recommended. When things seem to go wrong and there seems to be no reasonable explanation, a *feng-shui* expert is able to determine whether you are under the influence of any bad *shar*. Major environmental disturbances such as construction and demolition may disturb the positions of the *shars* and cause misfortune. This is another occasion when a *feng-shui* expert should be consulted.

6. Physical *Shars*

Bad *feng-shui* or intangible *shars* influence have their counterparts in tangible "physical" *shars*. Collectively, these refer to the physical surroundings, landscape, constructions or buildings; in fact any structure that will exert bad *feng-shui* influence on people. There are three main types of physical *shars*.

The first type refers to structures that may pose real environmental danger, for example pollution or problems of hygiene. More specific examples would be chemical factories and warehouses storing explosive materials or weapons.

Physical *shars* of the second kind refer to buildings and structures of a special nature or for a special purpose which may have a spiritual effect on the surrounding atmosphere. Graveyards, funeral parlours and hospitals are unhappy places associated with sickness and death. Such structures are believed to emanate inauspicious elements into the environs. Police stations, though necessitated by the good of all, also fall within this category because firearms are believed to disrupt harmony, aside from their association with crime and vice.

Temples exert a unique spiritual influence and it is not advisable to live near one. Old temples are usually built on well-chosen *feng-shui* sites and absorb all the energy from their surroundings. Houses in the vicinity of temples will contribute to the prosperity of temples by losing *feng-shui* energy to them. Another reason is that religious structures are usually guarded by spiritual forces which create a kind of shield against alien, hostile influence. Such shields protect the temple but may have an adverse effect on the houses nearby.

The third kind of physical *shar*, and the most important, embraces structures that pose some kind of psychological threat. The most common *shar* in this category is a sharp point or edge (Fig. 11a). For example, the controversial shape of the Bank of China building in Hong Kong is said to have cast a sharp-edged *shar* on the surrounding buildings. Another common *shar* is the "bow-shaped water" or road (Fig. 11b). If the bow-shaped road is a flyover, it is often compared to a sharp blade threatening to cut through a house facing the curvature.

Straight roads with traffic rushing towards a house create another kind of physical *shar*, like an arrow aimed at a person's heart. The intensity of the *shar* increases if the traffic runs downhill from a slope (Fig. 11c). Houses built on the junction of crossroads, especially those on the right north-south direction or east-west direction, with traffic rushing towards it at right angles, are believed to be susceptible to scandals of a sexual nature. The two joined roads are believed to represent a woman's legs (Fig. 11d).

Figs. 11a – 11d. Four types of physical shars.

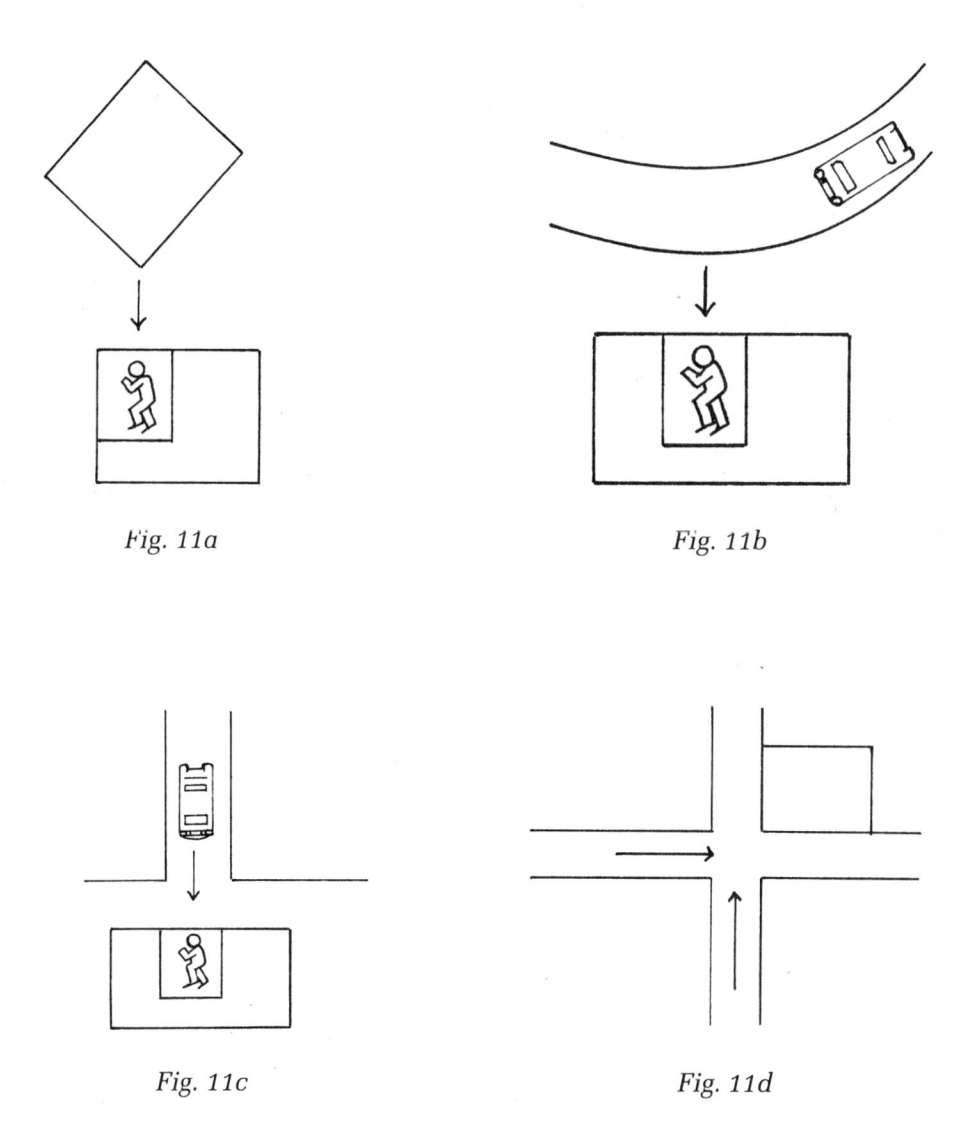

Fig. 11a

Fig. 11b

Fig. 11c

Fig. 11d

16 Feng-shui and Destiny

There are hundreds of examples of physical *shars* recorded in ancient *feng-shui* books. Each *shar* creates a special threat and can be dissolved by a special *feng-shui* method. However, it must be stressed that physical *shars* only pose a threat. Of themselves they cannot harm without being triggered off by bad intangible forces. Real misfortune only occurs when a bad intangible force, or bad flying star, happens to be in the same location as that of the physical *shar*.

As the intangible forces change positions through time, a physical *shar* is like a time bomb and will explode into misfortune when the intangible *shar* or flying star reaches its location. This is why *feng-shui* experts usually advise against coming into contact with physical *shars*.

7. The Art of Placement: Health and Wealth

In one of the few modern works in English, *Feng-shui: the Chinese Art of Placement* by Sarah Rossbach, the author appropriately describes *feng-shui* as "the art of placement". Indeed, the object of studying *feng-shui* is to be able to place objects, ranging from the remains of our ancestors to decorative items, in the most auspicious positions. This will ensure harmony because well-placed objects "receive" the best possible intangible forces.

Just as external environmental *shar* can have a bad influence, the interior arrangements of a house may induce the presence of unwelcome influence. Such interior *shars* can be divided into three categories.

The first kind is related to the shape of the house. It is generally believed that, other things being equal, a symmetrical floor plan, such as a square or a rectangle, has better *feng-shui* than an asymmetrical one. Figs. 12a – 12c are examples of inauspiciously-shaped houses. The basis of whether a house is well-shaped goes back to the ancient Chinese way of measuring and indicating directions. It is based on a circle divided into eight

Figs. 12a – 12b. Houses of irregular shapes.

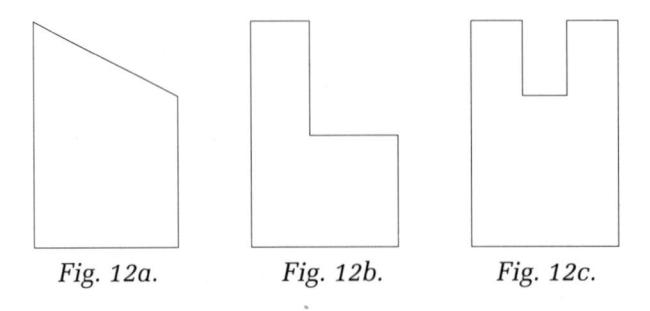

Fig. 12a.   *Fig. 12b.*   *Fig. 12c.*

equal sectors of 45 degrees. Each sector is called a *kua* or trigram and each *kua* represents many things. Irregularly shaped houses are not auspicious because they cannot receive all the intangible directional forces in a balanced manner (Figs. 13a – 13c). A square or a rectangle has equal opposite sides and are therefore "balanced" recipients of intangible forces.

Figs. 13a – 13c. Division of feng-shui influences into 8 kua.

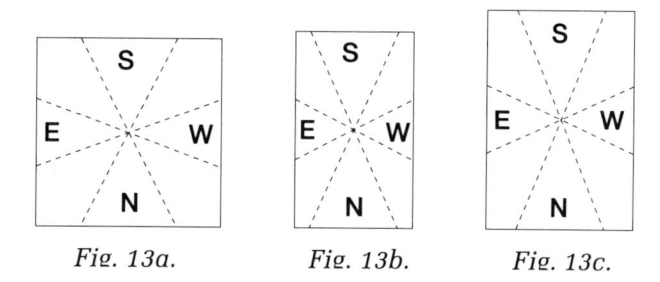

Fig. 13a.   *Fig. 13b.*   *Fig. 13c.*

A narrow rectangular house cannot accomodate all the eight *kuas* in equal proportions. If a house is irregularly shaped, it will lose some directional influence. Each *kua* represents one categogy of people. If even one *kua* is missing, misfortune may visit a member of the family.

The second type of interior *shar* refers to the floor arrangements and partitions (bedrooms, living room, toilets, kitchen, etc.). For example, a harmonious house should not have living rooms smaller than any one bedroom. The theory is that the bedroom is *yin* (female) and the living room is *yang* (male). The male should always be stronger (Fig. 14a). Also, the front entrance should not face a toilet directly. The front door is the main recipient of intangible forces and any good influence coming through the door will be drained down the toilet (Fig. 14b). Similarly, the front door should not face a window directly (Fig. 14c.)

There should not be any window on the longest diagonal line drawn from the door, as corners are often thought to be the gathering places from which intangible forces circulate the house. An open window will draw away good forces before they have time to get round the house. Such corners are commonly called the locations of wealth (Fig. 14d).

Figs. 14c – 14d. Floor plans of unfavourable feng-shui

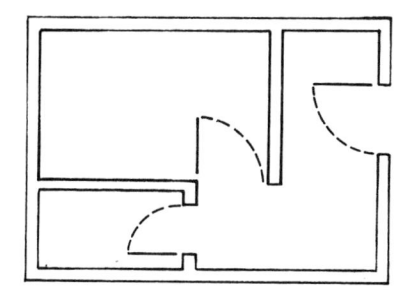

Fig. 14a. 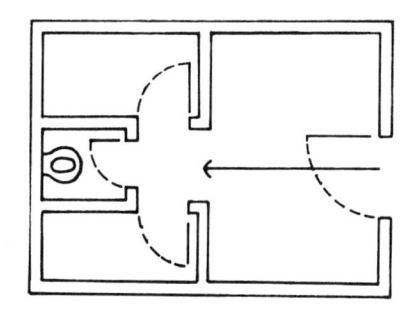   *Fig. 14b.*

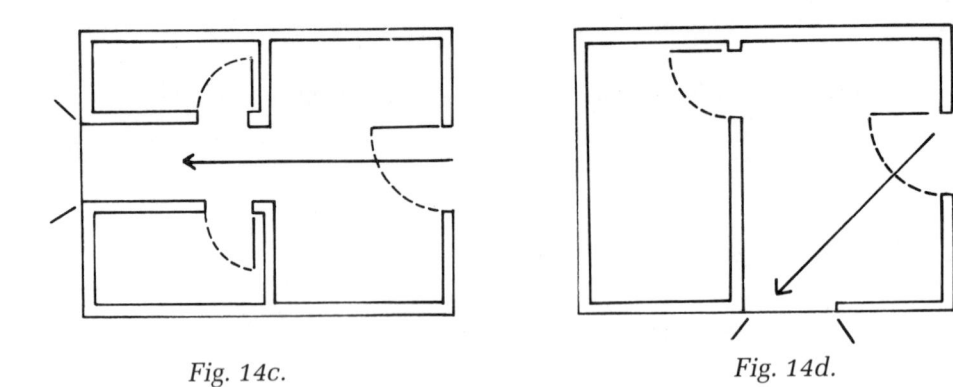

Fig. 14c. *Fig. 14d.*

The third category of physical *shars* in the house refers to the arrangement of furniture and household objects. For example, you should not put your bed or desk directly under heavy concrete beams as they will exert "pressure" on the person working or sleeping under it (Fig. 15a). Sceptics may dismiss such "pressure" as merely psychological. However, there is reason to believe that some kind of magnetic force does exist in heavy masses. Students of *feng-shui* are often puzzled by the phenomenon of long buildings. Although it is known that the entire building is along a straight line (so that every point is in the same direction), the compass often indicates different directions when, for example, the readings from both ends of the building and the centre are measured. A reasonable explanation seems to be that there is some kind of imbalance in the concrete mass, hence the different readings. So a person who often sits or sleeps under concrete beams may be subject to magnetic influences.

It is taboo to place big mirrors at the foot of a bed. Should you wake in the middle of the night, you may get quite a fright from looking at your mirror image. However, there is also a spiritual basis to this: a person's mirror image is *yin* (female), similar to "soul". Therefore a mirror at the foot of the bed would "hold" and expose the image during the hours of sleep (Fig. 15b).

The cooking stove is of great importance in *feng-shui*. It should not face outwards in the direction of the front door. It is closely connected with the health and prosperity of the family. It should therefore face the centre of the house to intensify the family's prosperity (Fig. 15c).

Figs. 15a – 15e. Unfavourable interior arrangement of furniture and household objects.

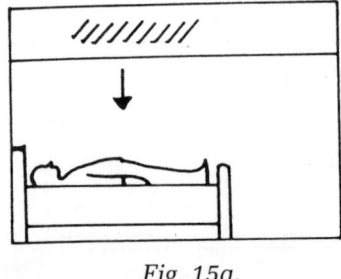

Fig. 15a. 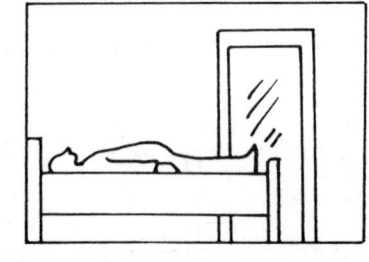 *Fig. 15b.*

Fig. 15c.

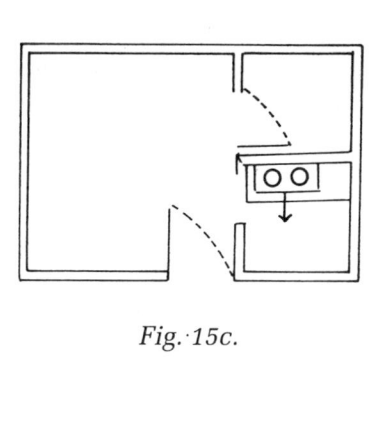

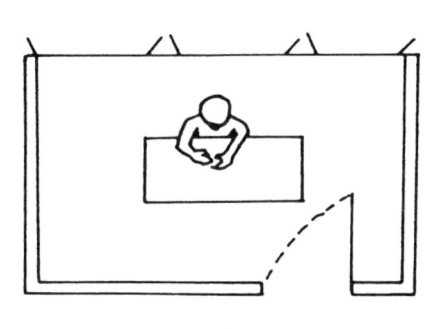

Fig. 15d.

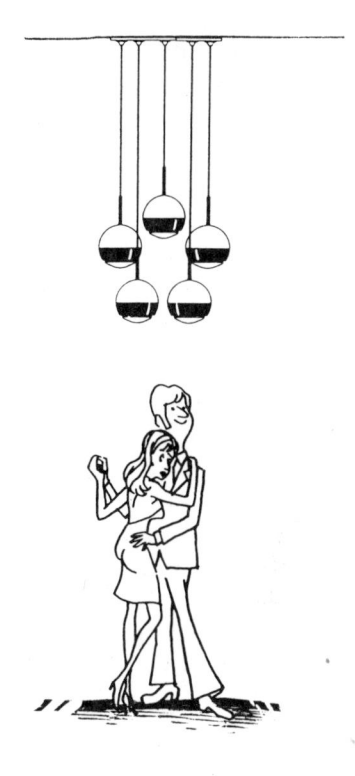

Fig. 15e.

The desk or bed should not be placed in the middle of a room without a wall to support it, especially if the room is wide and rectangular in shape (Fig. 15d). The theory is that a person in authority needs some firm backing, and a desk in the middle of the room "floats" in the air, lacking the firm support of the surroundings. The origins of this belief can be traced to the old days when Chinese villagers usually placed the coffins of deceased relatives in the yard of a temple (while a suitable burial site was being chosen). The coffins were often placed in the middle of the yard without the support of a wall. So placing a bed or desk in this manner is often called the "coffin" arrangement.

As was mentioned earlier, the *shar* of five should not be disturbed. It is therefore advisable to avoid ceiling lamps that have five bulbs. A five-bulb lamp can represent such a *shar* and activities under it may cause disturbances in the atmosphere and consequently, bring about misfortune (Fig. 15e).

Like the external *shars*, interior *shars* will not cause much harm without the bad intangible forces. All the same, the "rules" in *feng-shui* often work in harmony with comfort and environmental hygiene. It is therefore recommended that we should observe these rules, not only because of its *feng-shui* implications, but also for the sake of a more orderly, comfortable and harmonious home.

8. Feng-shui Tools: Fish, Mirror and Wind Chime

The most useful tool in *feng-shui* is the *lo pan,* a very sophisticated Chinese compass. It consists of concentric rings of Chinese characters and symbols, with a delicate magnetic needle in the centre. Each circle serves a particular function. The *lo pan* is so complex an instrument that it is virtually impossible to set down all its applications in writing. The subject will be dealt with in a later chapter.

There are, however, other less complex tools. Goldfish in a tank is often used as a "drawer" of wealth and prosperity (Fig. 16a). The tank and goldfish symbolise moving water and is often compared to the flow of money. It is advisable to place the tank at the point of wealth and prosperity (this is indicated by the directional forces generated by the layout of the house). A *feng-shui* expert will also advise you on the right number of fish the tank should contain. Six is the most common number as it belongs to the metal category and gives birth to water which usually symbolises wealth. For the purpose of stimulating wealth, putting nine goldfishes in a tank is also acceptable, as the number nine is the largest odd number, or *yang* number, symbolising full capacity and completeness. The fish tank can also be used to ward off *shars* or bad *feng-shui* influence. In this case the *feng-shui* expert may advise you to place the tank containing six black fish in a direction opposite a sharp-edged or sharp-point *shar.*

Another tool commonly used in *feng-shui* is the mirror. There are different kinds of mirror and each serves a different purpose. An ordinary mirror can be used to draw a distant image into the house. This is necessary when a *feng-shui* expert detects good influence at a distant location and uses the mirror to bring it nearer. The eight *kua* mirrors (little octagonal mirrors encircled by the eight *kua*) are often seen hanging on the lintel of a Chinese home (Fig. 16b). They deflect evil influence. Such mirrors should only be used if there is a real *shar* threat. A concave mirror which produces an inverted image is also commonly used to "challenge" a *shar* and cause it to change direction.

All mirrors belong to the metal categoy. Therefore a tank of black fish, representing water, can dissolve the threat of an eight-*kua* mirror if a selfish neighbour should choose to use it to deflect all bad forces in the direction of your house.

Wind chimes are used to dissolve the *shar* of five which can cause misfortune (Fig. 16c). If this tool is used, you should pay heed to the *feng-shui* expert's advice regarding its location because if hung in the wrong location, it may attract ghosts or spirits. A grandfather clock with its moving pendulum or a string of coins can often be used to dissolve the bad influence of the *shar* of five and two. These *shars* belong to the earth element which will lose their evil energy by giving birth to metal. A red lamp, properly used, can have the effect of resolving sex scandals or disputes. Porcelain ware belongs to the earth category and can be used to avoid fire as it draws away fire energy.

Figs. 16a – 16c. Feng-shui tools.

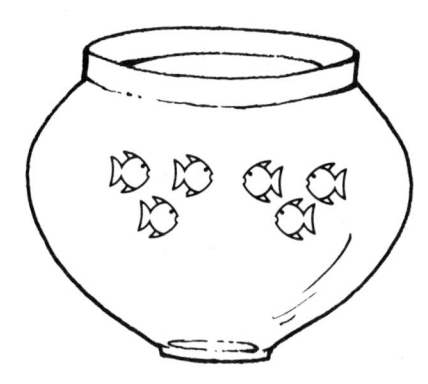

Fig. 16a.

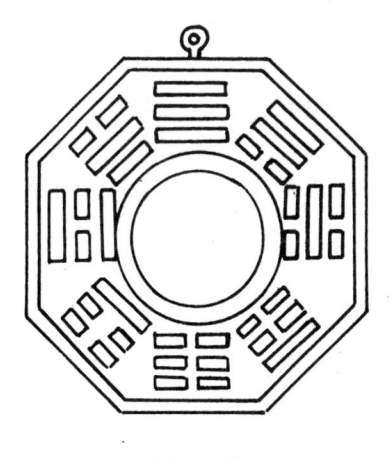

Fig. 16b.

Fig. 16c.

Feng-shui experts sometimes advise placing animal figures to balance the birth data of the household. For example, the figure of a horse will intensify the fire element and will thus bring luck to the house if fire is in harmony with the household's birth data.

These methods of dissolving bad influence are based on the interaction theory of the five elements. The basic principle is that *shars* and bad influence can be classified under the five basic elements — metal, wood, water, fire and earth — and so can be dissolved using objects which symbolise their offspring according to the cycle of birth (see chapter 2).

9. Lo Pan: The *Feng-shui* Compass

The origins of this indispensable tool in the study of *feng-shui* goes back to ancient Chinese mythology. It is believed that the Yellow Emperor obtained the magnetic compass from a goddess and the tool assisted him in winning his heroic battle against a sorcerer chief around 26th century BC.

Over time, the *lo pan* has been modified and refined. The modern *lo pan* is usually a square and red in colour, with a delicate magnetic needle in the centre which is surrounded by concentric rings of Chinese symbols and characters. In Hong Kong and Taiwan, there are basically three types of *lo pan* — The Three Ages Compass, The Three Combination Compass and The Mixed Compass. The differences lie in the Chinese characters and symbols found on each *lo pan*. Such differences, however, become more significant when you appraise *yin* houses (grave sites). For beginners, any of the three types will do equally well.

Like the ordinary compass, the main function of the *lo pan* is to indicate direction. The intangible forces of *feng-shui* are directional in nature and even a light variation in the direction of an object can have serious implications. Therefore the computation of directions must be very accurate.

The first step in learning how to use the *lo pan* is to familiarise yourself with the directional readings. In *feng-shui* a circle is divided into eight major directions. The difficult part is instead of calling these directions north, south, east, west, and their sub-divisions, they are represented by the eight *kua* (trigrams), which is shown as a combination of continuous and broken lines. Such a representation is necessary because the eight *kua* embrace the whole universe and each *kua* has implications far beyond that of directional bearings. Table 1 shows simplified versions of each *kua*:

Table 1. The eight kua (trigrams).

☰	northwest, metal, old man, heaven
☵	north, water, middle-aged man, ear, winter
☶	northeast, earth, stop, hands, youngest son, mountain
☳	east, eldest son, wood, foot, thunder, spring
☴	southeast, wind, wood, eldest daughter, buttocks

☲	south, fire, middle-aged woman, eyes, summer
☷	southwest, earth, old woman, stomach
☱	west, metal, young girl, mouth, autumn

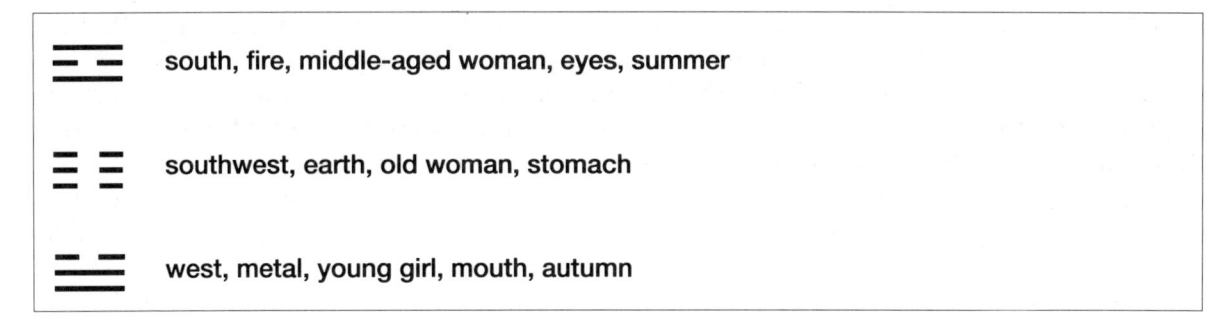

To divide a circle into eight sectors is not accurate enough. Thus each *kua* has three sub-divisions. In total there are 24 sub-divisions and these are commonly known as "twenty-four mountains".

Each mountain occupies 15 degrees. Fig. 17 shows the ring of the 24 mountains on the *lo pan* with their corresponding directional implications. The magnetic needle is carefully cased in a round transparent box called "heaven's pool". It usually rests on a white background with a thin red diameter. The square of the compass is bound by two pieces of nylon string forming a cross exactly on the centre of "heaven's pool".

Fig. 17. The 24 mountains on a lo pan

When measuring the direction of an object, first hold the *lo pan* horizontally so that the needle can swing freely, then point the nylon string towards the object in a straight line. Then use both thumbs to rotate the circular board until the magnetic needle and the red diameter on the "heaven's pool" are in allignment. The characters directly below the nylon string indicate the directional reading of the object.

Lo pans are available in different sizes, ranging from three inches to 12 inches in diameter. The small ones are handy but the magnetic needle is too light and can be easily affected by metal objects in the surroundings, and you may have a hard time trying to find a steady directional reading. The larger ones with a heavier needle are more accurate. For beginners, a 6.2 inch *lo pan* is recommended.

10. The Eight Houses *Feng-shui* Theory

There are many schools of *feng-shui* but the two most popular in Hong Kong and Taiwan are the eight houses and the flying stars. The main difference between these two schools is that the former is considered static while the latter can be described as dynamic as it attaches more weight to the yearly and monthly changes of the intangible forces in *feng-shui*. A comparison of the merits and demerits of these two schools is a sensitive subject. Each school has its supporters but it should be stressed that the serious *feng-shui* student should be familiar with both techniques as each is useful to particular circumstances.

The eight houses refer to the eight *kua* of the *I Ching* (see chapter 9). As the eight *kua* represent eight directions, in the eight houses school, all houses are divided into eight categories according to their directions. For example, a house sitting with its back to the northwest and facing southeast is called a *chien* house.

It should be noted, however, that a house is classified according to the direction its back faces. Table 2 shows how houses are grouped under the eight *kua*. It shows that the eight houses are divided into two major types: the "east four houses" and the "west four houses". The former belong to water, wood and fire and the latter belong to metal and earth. As water gives birth to wood and wood in turn gives birth to fire, the east four houses are therefore in a mother-and-child relationship and so are in harmony. In the same way, the west four houses are also in a harmonious relationship as earth gives birth to metal (see chapter 2).

On the other hand, any one of the east four houses will not be in harmony with any of the west four houses. For example, a *chen* house (east) belongs to wood, a *tui* house belongs to metal, and as metal destroys wood, they are not in harmony.

THE WEST FOUR HOUSES				
House name	Symbol	Back	Front	Element
Chien	☰	NW	SE	Metal
Kun	☷	SW	NE	Earth
Ken	☶	NE	SW	Earth
Tui	☱	W	E	Metal
THE EAST FOUR HOUSES				
Li	☲	S	N	Fire
Hum	☵	N	S	Water
Chen	☳	E	W	Wood
Sun	☴	SE	NW	Wood

Table 2. West four houses and east four houses.

The interactions between the eight *kua* become more complex when we consider the fate of a human being because in this case, we have to include the year of his or her birth. Like the eight houses, people are divided into east and west and are referred to as the "east four persons" and the "west four persons". The important thing to remember in the eight houses school is that the west four houses suit the west four persons and the east four persons are in harmony with the east four houses. For example, if you are a man born in 1952, you are of the *chen kua* and belong to the east. (See Table 3.) The house most suited to you is an east four house, such as a house with its back to the south and its front to the north.

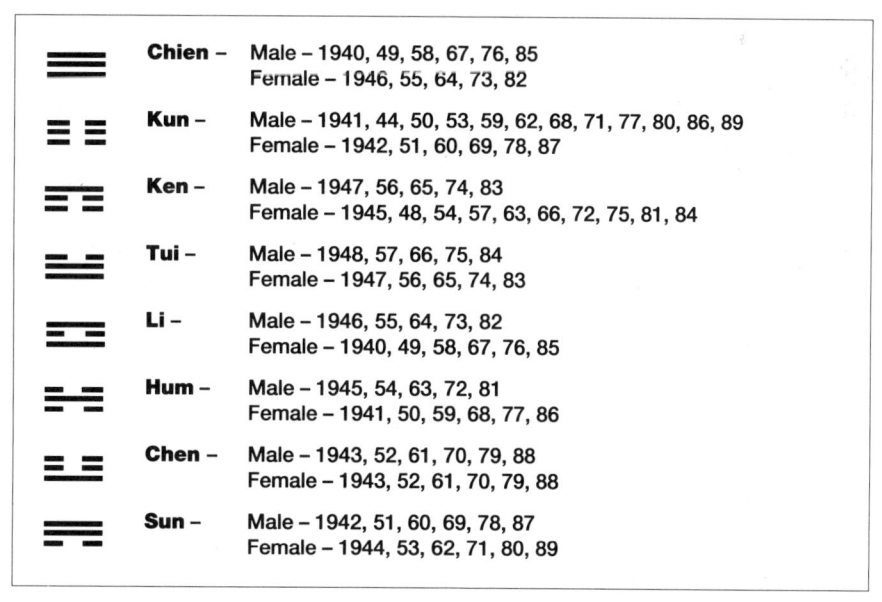

Symbol	Kua	Birth years
☰	Chien –	Male – 1940, 49, 58, 67, 76, 85 Female – 1946, 55, 64, 73, 82
☷	Kun –	Male – 1941, 44, 50, 53, 59, 62, 68, 71, 77, 80, 86, 89 Female – 1942, 51, 60, 69, 78, 87
☶	Ken –	Male – 1947, 56, 65, 74, 83 Female – 1945, 48, 54, 57, 63, 66, 72, 75, 81, 84
☱	Tui –	Male – 1948, 57, 66, 75, 84 Female – 1947, 56, 65, 74, 83
☲	Li –	Male – 1946, 55, 64, 73, 82 Female – 1940, 49, 58, 67, 76, 85
☵	Hum –	Male – 1945, 54, 63, 72, 81 Female – 1941, 50, 59, 68, 77, 86
☳	Chen –	Male – 1943, 52, 61, 70, 79, 88 Female – 1943, 52, 61, 70, 79, 88
☴	Sun –	Male – 1942, 51, 60, 69, 78, 87 Female – 1944, 53, 62, 71, 80, 89

Table 3. Personal kua according to birth year

26 Feng-shui and Destiny

The next most important item to consider is the front door. It is also preferable for an east person to open an east four door. So the entrance of the house should face north, which is *hum,* an east four direction. A difficult question is this: if a family has both east and west members, then how can they choose a house which suits both types? The compromise is to choose a house which suits the head of the family best and use the interior arrangement to suit each individual. The head of the family is the bread-earner, usually the father, but the head can also be anyone who contributes most to the family income.

11. Your Home: Good and Bad Locations

Having found a house with directions which complements a person's *kua,* the next step is to make the most suitable interior arrangements. In the eight houses school of *feng-shui* the interior of each house can be divided into eight locations according to each of the *kua* directions. Each location is given a name; it represents good or bad influence in the house. The following is a list of the eight locations with their respective significance:

1. **The prime location** — good. It has the same direction as the back of the house and is suitable for beds, doors and religious statues. The cooking stove should be placed in a direction opposite the prime location.
2. **The death location** — bad. It signifies accidents, poor health, misfortune and loss and is suitable for the toilet.
3. **The health location** — good. It brings good health and strength and is good for beds, doors, the master bedroom and the dining table.
4. **The disaster location** — bad. It signifies disputes, quarrels, anger, legal entanglements and irritation. It is suitable for a storeroom or toilet.
5. **The six *shar* location** — bad. It refers to loss, laziness, sex scandals, and is suitable for the toilet or kitchen.
6. **The longevity location** — good. It brings health, harmony and peace, and is good for beds, the dining table, bedrooms of old people and the location of the dining room.
7. **The five ghosts location** — bad. It refers to theft, robbery, financial loss and fire hazards, and is suitable for a storeroom or a toilet.
8. **The prosperity location** — good. This is the best location, representing prosperity, strength, energy, riches and promotion, and is the most auspicious place for the front door, room doors, the kitchen door, beds, working desks and other objects associated with health and prosperity.

To find these eight locations in your house, the first step is to establish the *kua* of the house according to its directions. (For example, if your house has its back to the north and its front facing south, then it is called a *hum* house.) Having done this, you can look up the suitable locations in Table 4. There is, however, an easier way to find a good location. If your house is an east four house, i.e. with its back facing south, north, east, or southeast, then all the east four directions are good locations and all the other directions — west, southwest, northwest, northeast (west four directions) — are bad locations.

House	Chien (NW)	Kun (SW)	Ken (NE)	Tui (W)	Li (S)	Hum (N)	Chen (E)	Sun (SE)
Location								
Prime	NW	SW	NE	W	S	N	E	SE
Death	S	N	SE	E	NW	SW	W	NE
Health	NE	W	NW	SW	SE	E	N	S
Disaster	SE	E	S	N	NE	W	SW	NW
6 Zar	N	S	E	SE	SW	NW	NE	W
Longevity	SW	NW	W	NE	N	S	SE	E
5 Ghosts	E	SE	N	S	W	NE	NW	SW
Prosperity	W	NE	SW	NW	E	SE	S	N

Table 4. Eight houses theory — Table of good and bad locations

As always, the five elements should be borne in mind. For example, the best location in a *hum* house (north-water) is southeast (wood) because water gives birth to wood. The worst location is in the southeast (earth) because earth destroys water. Then have a floor plan drawn to scale, with its appropriate centre and then draw a circle and divide it into eight sectors. Using Table 4 you will be able to assess the location of your flat according to the eight houses school of *feng-shui*.

The basis of the eight houses theory of arrangement in a house is that you should utilise the good directions for your bedrooms, beds, seats, desks and doors, and the bad locations for the toilet, kitchen and storeroom. The cooking stove should be placed in a bad location with its knobs facing an auspicious direction.

12. Prosperity: Keeping a Way Open

Having dealt with the theoretical aspects of the eight houses school of *feng-shui,* we will now address some of its practical difficulties. The first problem is the direction of the house. As this forms the basis of all *feng-shui* appraisals, any mistake in this first step will nullify the effects of subsequent evaluations. Therefore, the accurate judgement of the direction of a house is of the utmost importance.

In the past, finding the front and back entrances of a house was easy because houses had obvious front and back entrances. This is not so in today's high-rise buildings. Modern apartments do not have prominent front and back "sides"; for example, big commercial buildings have three or four side entrances and it is difficult to determine which is the front entrance. Other buildings are diamond-shaped, Y-shaped, X-shaped, and so on, with several entrances and many front and back "sides". Even *feng-shui* masters often find it difficult to establish the proper direction and hence the direction of the building. Experience is invaluable but there are some general pointers which can help the beginner.

1. The eight houses theory was formulated at a time when houses were built at the foot of a mountain and by the side of a river. Mountains (synonymous with dragons) and rivers are believed to affect intangible forces. Roughly speaking, mountains and rivers affect health and prosperity. In the old days, a house with a mountain at its back and water in front was therefore considered a typically well-sited house. The entrance of such a house often faced the river, welcoming the prosperous intangible forces, and such a house was named by the direction of the mountain at its back. In modern cities, mountains are replaced by tall buildings and rivers by roads. Hence, very often the direction of the building facing a main road is considered the front of the house and the opposite side its back. The house is thus named by the direction its back faces. For example, in Fig. 18 the house with its back against the south is called a *li* (south) house.

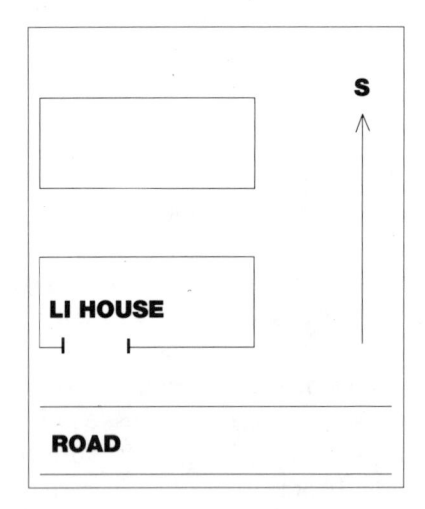

Fig. 18. A li house with its back against the south.

2. The front of the house is often the side of the building from which the intangible forces gather, concentrate and enter. It usually has an open space called the "bright hall" which induces intangible forces to concentrate before entering the house. Such a bright hall can be a main road, a park or just an open area.
3. It is advisable to look at the main entrance first. For many buildings, the main entrance is the side facing a main road but this is not always the case. If the main entrance faces a narrow side street, it does not necessarily mean that the front of the house is at the side street as there is no bright hall for the intangible forces to gather and concentrate.
4. In the case of a Y-shaped or X-shaped building, each arm or block of the building should be considered an independent building and needs to be appraised separately as there is no common front or back representing all blocks.

5. If a building has entrances and bright halls on all sides, it means the house is receiving intangible forces from several directions. In such cases, if it is still not possible to establish the front and back of the building applying the principles mentioned here, the intangible forces can be very mixed. What needs to be done is to check the front and back of an apartment of your choice, taking the entrance as the front and the opposite side as its back.
6. It should be remembered that in the eight houses theory, the direction of the back of a house determines its *kua* assessment. A common error among beginners is making an appraisal by just looking at the front without reference to the back (Fig. 19). If only the front is assessed, it is easy to mistake it as a *chien* house with its back against the northwest. In fact it is a *hum* house with its back against the north. The direction of locations inside the house should be taken from the centre. For example, the door of the *li* house in Fig. 18 is considered a *kan* (northeast) door because it has an opening at the northeast of the house although it faces north.

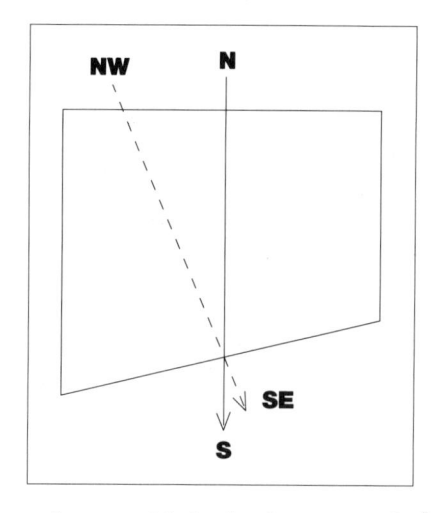

Fig. 19. A hum house with its back against the north.

13. Putting Your House in Order

After accurately locating the *kua* of your house, you should then compare it with the *kua* of the year of your birth and see if they are compatible. A good instance of compatibility is when both belong to the west four group of *kua* — for example, a *tui* house (back against the west) and a *chien* man (for example, born in 1949). The next step is to check the doors and locations of beds, desks, etc. to see if they are appropriately placed in the west four locations. You should also ensure that the toilets, storeroom and cooking stove are situated at the east four locations.

When measuring the eight locations of a house, it is advisable to draw a diagram of the floor plan (the diagram must be drawn to scale). Then find its centre, draw a full circle, divide it into eight equal sectors and label each according to the compass reading which gives both

30   Feng-shui and Destiny

direction and location. You are likely to encounter problems if your house is not symmetrical in shape and the centre is found outside the floor plan (Fig. 20a). If this happens you should divide the apartment into sectors and measure the eight locations from the centre of each sector. If the centre remains within the apartment (Fig. 20b), draw dotted lines to form a symmetrically-shaped figure and look for the location from the centre. In this case, the locations are not evenly distributed and some portions will occupy a greater area than others.

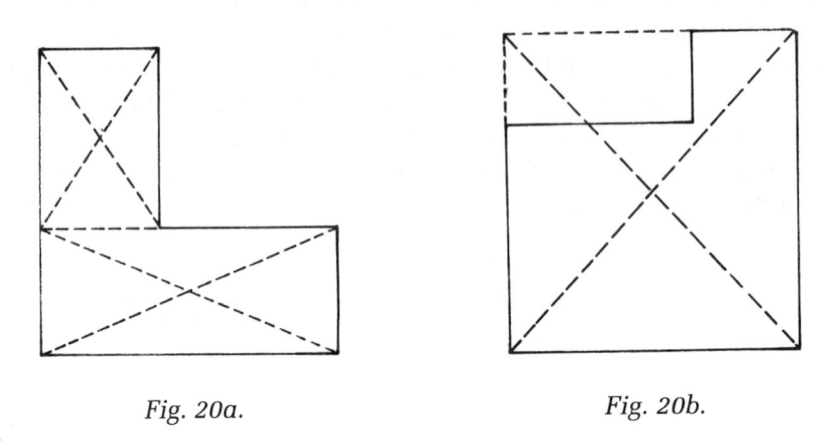

Fig. 20a.   *Fig. 20b.*

Figs. 20a - 20b. To find the centre of your house for marking feng-shui locations.

The influences that *feng-shui* exert are directional, so there is no space restriction in the application of *feng-shui* theories. They can be applied to a country (big *tai chi*) or to a bedroom (small *tai chi*). In this way you can determine the eight locations within your bedroom or study room by finding the centre of each room and dividing them into eight portions.

The above are ideal situations. In real life it is common for an east four *kua* person to live in a house which belongs to the west four *kua* and there are very good reasons against moving to another house. It would be impossible to move out immediately or move at all. Such situations call for a compromise. For example, if you are an east four person living in a west four house, you can improve the *feng-shui* by altering the arrangement of furnishings according to your personal *kua* and disregard the *kua* of the house. All the same, you should determine the eight locations of your *kua* (not the house *kua*) and use good locations (prime, prosperity, health and longevity) and bad locations (death, disaster, six *shar*, five ghosts) as guides for placing the furnishings. For example, if you are a *li* (east four) person living in a *chien* (west four) house, you cannot change the house into an east four house to suit your *kua*. What you can do is to make the arrangement of furnishings in your house to suit you. The eight locations of a *li* person are: prime — south; health — southeast; longevity — north; prosperity — east; death — northwest; disaster — northeast; six *shar* — southwest; ghosts — west. You should then use the east location for your bedroom and the northwest for the toilet, etc.

One drawback of the eight houses school of *feng-shui* is the difficulty of avoiding the four bad locations as it is virtually impossible to place all beds or seats at the four good locations;

nor is it possible to open all doors on them. However, it should be noted that the location of the door, bed and stove is vital as these are the three most important items in a house. In his classic *A Bible for Houses,* the *feng-shui* master, Ng Zee Ching, recommends that a cooking stove should face the prime location as this arrangement will bring children; or if you feel wealth is more important, the stove should face the prosperity location as this will bring wealth. In cases where husband and wife have different *kua,* Ng recommends that the bed and bedroom door should face the good location of the wife, while the cooking stove should face the good location of the husband.

14. The Flying Star School of *Feng-shui*

The eight houses school of *feng-shui* emphasises the direction and interior of a house and how these suit people born in particular years. However, a complete *feng-shui* evaluation should take into account both the time and space elements. Such factors can have practical implications. For example, if a *feng-shui* expert, using the eight houses school method, chooses an "excellent" grave site, does it mean that the descendents of the deceased will enjoy prosperity forever? The obvious answer is "no". The history of China demonstrates that dynasties rise and fall. There is obviously a time element involved.

The flying star school of *feng-shui* incorporates this by dividing time into 20-year periods, called ages. Each age has a ruling star or *kua* which is expressed in numbers. For example, the period 1984 to 2003 is called the Age of Seven and the ruling *kua* is *tui*, represented by the number 7 (see chapter 3).

A birth chart of a house can be drawn up on the basis of its direction and the age during which the building is constructed. Such a "natal" chart shows the distribution of intangible *feng-shui* influence in relation to the house. Fig. 21 shows the birth chart of a house completed in 1985. The front and back of the house face east and west respectively. Each square represents a direction. There are three numbers in each square. The larger number in the middle is derived from the age of the building, the other two smaller numbers represent intangible *feng-shui* influence the house will receive from a particular direction. Such numbers are commonly called "stars" although they do not have any direct relation to the stars and planets in the universe. The star on the left is the "mountain star" and that on the right is the "water star". They are derived from the direction of the back and front of the building respectively. In general, mountain stars influence human health and water stars wealth and prosperity.

One very important principle to note is that a benevolent mountain star can be "activated" to exert good influence only if it is placed "on the mountain", i.e. its location should be a wall or objects that are closed, still, high or solid in nature. On the other hand, a good water star can only bring wealth and prosperity when it is located at places that are open, fluid, active or in a state of flux. In our sample birth chart of the house built in 1985, as we are presently in the Age of Seven, the stars of seven symbolise the most prosperous *feng-shui* influences. From Fig. 21 we can see that the mountain star seven is located in the west and the water star seven is located in the east.

```
             S
  1   6   5   1   3   8
    6       2       4
  ─────────────────────
  2   7   9   5   7   3
E   5       7       9   W
  ─────────────────────
  6   2   4   9   8   4
    1       3       8
             N
```

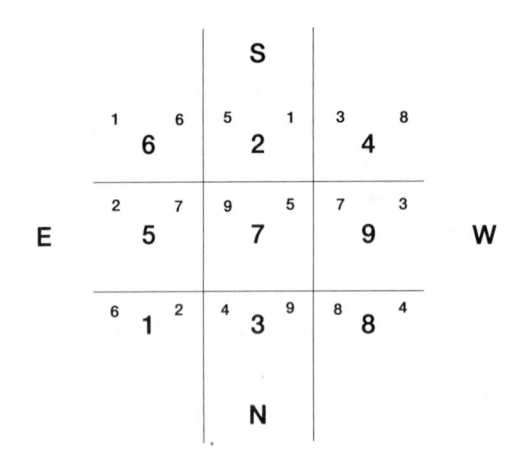

Fig. 21. Birth chart of a house completed in 1985 in east-west direction.

So it is best to have your bedroom located in the west as it is an enclosed, private area most suitable of the mountain star. The entrance of the house is best located in the east as the door lets in air which is considered fluid and open, allowing the water star to bring in prosperity. If the arrangements are reversed, then we have a configuration called "water star goes up the mountain, mountain star falls into the water". This is very bad *feng-shui* and will have adverse effects on wealth and health.

It should be noted, however, that the intangible forces have to interact with the actual physical surroundings for them to exert any influence. Hence even a poor natal chart can be exploited to exert benevolent influence if the physical surroundings and the interior arrangement of the house are good.

15. Joy and Sorrow: Cyclical Changes

Joy and sorrow, ups and downs are the norm of our daily life. There may be good health and prosperity in one year and nothing but anxiety and sickness in another. Or a businessman may be puzzled that despite increased efforts, he keeps making losses. In *feng-shui* such changes are considered periodic, not random, and the flying star school addresses this phenomenon by incorporating the time element.

Intangible forces are dynamic and changes all the time. Such changes are cyclic and follow a fixed pattern. In this school there are altogether nine stars (1 to 9) and each star has its peculiar quality and implications, and occupies one location (direction) on the nine-square chart. The periodic changes have certain time scales: the 20-year age, the yearly, the monthly and the daily cycles. In theory, it is possible to establish an hourly cycle but because its practical implications are slight and the undertaking tedious, it is seldom used.

The 20-year age cycle is often used to predict the *feng-shui* on a macro scale: the fortune of countries, cities and regions. It is also used to draw up the birth chart of a house. For

Joy and Sorrow: Cyclical Changes 33

fluctuations in a person's wealth and health, the yearly and monthly cycles are more useful as short term changes are often the cause of the ups and downs in our lives.

The pattern of movements in the flying stars school has its origins in the *lo shu* diagram (see chapter 4). It takes three triangular movements to trace completely all the nine numbers. This pattern is still very much a mystery and according to the *feng-shui* classic *A New Edition for the Fortune of Houses,* the triangle symbolises an ancient "three-level" philosophy which predates the dualistic *yin-yang* theory. For example, all matter can be divided into upper, middle and lower levels. Again, matter has three states: solid, fluid and gaseous. The concept of heaven, earth, man is another example of this three-level philosophy. It is interesting to note that the triangle often features prominently in many theories of the occult. In astrology we have a trine relationship with three stars forming the three points of a triangle. A similar triangular configuration is found in the Four Pillars of Destiny and *Zeiwei* fortune-telling. Interesting though this concept is, it remains a mystery and is not necessary for the practical applications of *feng-shui*.

In Fig. 22 the number in the centre of each square represents the intangible forces for 1989. The smaller numbers at the corners are the monthly intangible forces for February 1989. Because the monthly and yearly numbers are the same for February, the intensity of the intangible forces are strengthened in this month. For example, there are two fives in the square on the lower left. This means the *shar* of five is concentrated in the northeast direction.

In order to to determine how the *shar* of five will affect household items in the northeast direction, the year and month in the *feng-shui* chart is superimposed onto the birth chart of the house (Fig. 23). Fig. 24 shows the floor plan of the house. The natal chart indicates that the number two (the star of sickness) is found in the northeast which is the location of the main entrance. The number five in the centre functions as a water star and in the south as a mountain star. It can be clearly seen that the man's bed is wrongly placed at the

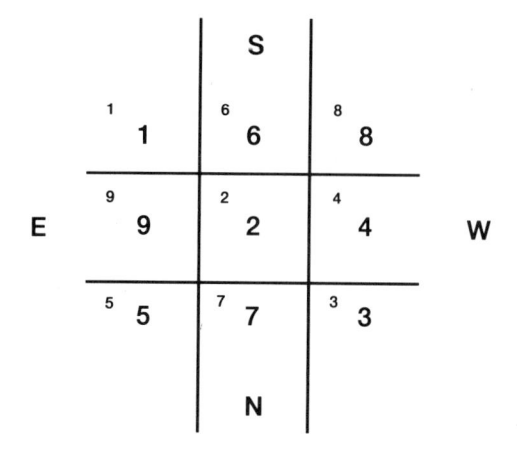

Fig. 22. Feng-shui influences in February 1989.

34   *Feng-shui and Destiny*

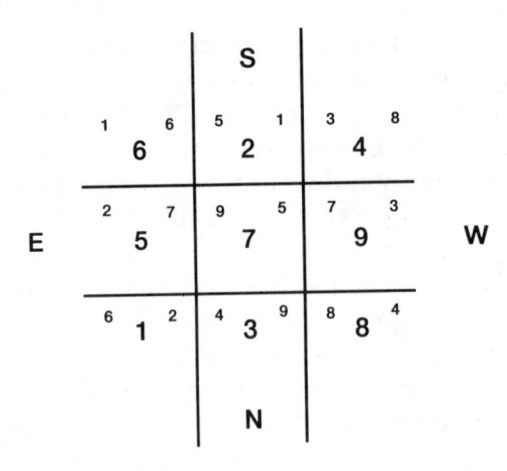

```
           1    6 | 5    1 | 3    8
              6  |    2   |    4
           ------+--------+------
           2    7 | 9    5 | 7    3
     E        5  |    7   |    9      W
           ------+--------+------
           6    2 | 4    9 | 8    4
              1  |    3   |    8
```

Fig. 23. Birth chart of house.

south and receives the direct bad influence of the twos and fives. In February 1989, the two and five are intensified with the monthly and yearly five at the entrance and the two concentrated in the middle passage (Fig. 24). All these contributed to mishaps and grave illness in the house in February.

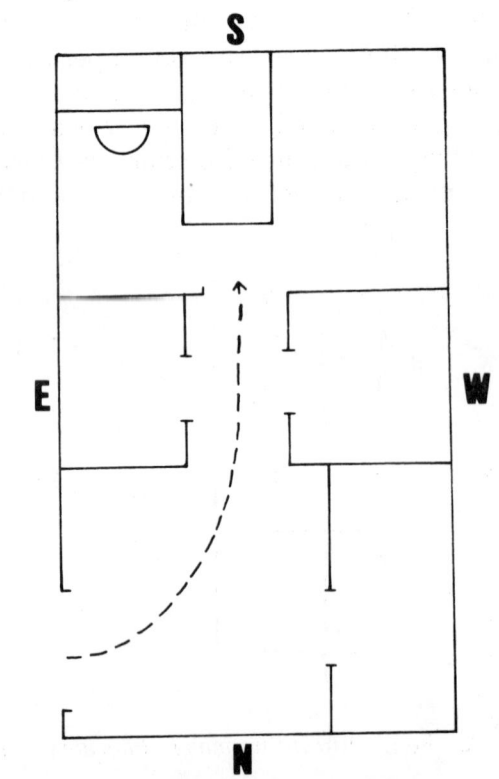

Fig. 24. Floor plan of house.

16. The Prosperity of Hong Kong: The Dragon's Lair

Landscape in *feng-shui* is made up of mountains, plains and rivers. Mountain ranges are called dragons and the influence is essential in evaluating *yin* houses (grave sites) as well as in assessing macro *feng-shui* (the fortune of cities and countries).

Mountain ridges are called dragons' veins and these rise and fall to form landscape on their way to the sea. Occasionally, a dragon falls in a valley, a small plain or plateau. This is known as the dragon's lair and is the place where the intangible forces of the dragon (*qi*) are believed to concentrate. If such a lair is well-sheltered at the back and at both sides, and there is water and a protective "hill" situated favourably in front, the landscape is considered a well-guarded throne. This makes a very good grave site and will bring long-lasting prosperity to the descendents of the person buried there. Such *yin* house *feng-shui* techniques can be used to evaluate the fortune of a country or a grave site.

The dragons of Hong Kong have their origins in the Kun Lun Range in western China. This gigantic mountain range with its many branches passes through thousands of miles in China, stretching eastwards. One of its arms extends into the New Territories (the northern part of Kowloon). It is generally believed that the Tai Mo Shan is a far extension of the Kun Lun Range and the mountain ends at the Kowloon Peninsula with a plain before the land strip dips into Victoria Harbour. The dragon dives into the sea and rises up again to form Hong Kong Island and Victoria Peak.

The Governer's House, the Plantation Garden and the Hongkong Bank building are believed to be sitting on the dragon's lair. The technical term used to describe the landscape of Victoria Peak is "dragon turning its head towards the ancestors" and this is considered good *feng-shui* contributing to the prosperity of Hong Kong. The philosophy behind this lies in the *tai chi* (the universe). *Tai chi* is divided into the female (*yin*) and male (*yang*) principles.

A balanced relationship between *yin* and *yang* brings harmony. For example, the mountain is *yin,* the plain *yang* and the place where a mountain descends smoothly into a plain is the place where *yin* and *yang* meet. Hence the *feng-shui* of this area is good. The Kowloon Peninsula and the northern part of Hong Kong Island are good examples of such areas. This is one reason for Hong Kong's economic prosperity. Futhermore, the Kowloon Peninsula forms a plain before it dips into the sea and the shape of Victoria Harbour surrounding Kowloon is auspiciously-shaped. Across the water, Hong Kong Island (with Victoria Peak) turns its "head" towards Kowloon, forming a protective mole hill. Such a topographical configuration harmonises well with the *yin* house *feng-shui* theory. The prosperity of Tsim Sha Tsui, Mong Kok and central Hong Kong is not a coincidence. These locations have good *feng-shui* influences.

The theory of *tai-chi* and *yin* and *yang* can also be adapted for the evaluation of districts within a city. For example, Yau Yat Chuen, Waterloo Hill and Kadoorie Hills in Kowloon are slightly higher in altitude and are locations where one finds the *yin* within the *yang*.

A more simple way of appraising the *feng-shui* of Hong Kong is to find the direction and location of her dragons and compare these with the *lo shu* diagram (Fig. 6 reproduced here).

```
            S
    ┌───┬───┬───┐
    │ 4 │ 9 │ 2 │
    ├───┼───┼───┤
  E │ 3 │ 5 │ 7 │ W
    ├───┼───┼───┤
    │ 8 │ 1 │ 6 │
    └───┴───┴───┘
            N
```

Like the intangible forces that affect a *yang* house, the influences of a dragon's veins also change with time and space. For example, taking Kowloon and central Hong Kong as the town centre, the dragons of Hong Kong are most prominent in the northwest, i.e. Tai Mo Shan. Using the *lo shu* diagram, we can find that the number in the northwest is six which belongs to the period 1964 to 1983. This 20-year period saw Hong Kong's economy prospering by leaps and bounds.

17. Bank of China: Concentration of Benevolent Forces

The interesting shape of the new Bank of China Building has caused some controversy recently. Discussions generally centre round the sharp edges of the upper corners of the building. Some *feng-shui* experts thought these edges created a *shar*, threatening the surrounding area. The discussions, however, were confined to the external appearance of the bank building and little was mentioned about the site and directions of the bank. Having received quite a number of requests to appraise the *feng-shui* of the building, I decided to make an academic study of the building, adopting the technique of the flying star school of *feng-shui*.

When I arrived at the tram stop opposite the building, I was a little surprised to see that it looks more pleasant when viewed from the front. The building, when seen from a distance or when viewed sideways, appears a bit odd but the front view is rectangular with the lower block designed in the magnificent shape of the Great Wall of China. It is a modern building, blending Western architecture and the gracefulness of traditional Chinese motifs.

As mentioned before, the first step in evaluating a building is to take a careful look at its physical surroundings, that is, the landscape. One should pay special attention to the mountains (buildings), water (roads), traffic, adjacent buildings and any unusual structures that may impose a *shar* on the building in question.

Fig. 25 is a rough sketch showing the surrounding area of the new Bank of China building.

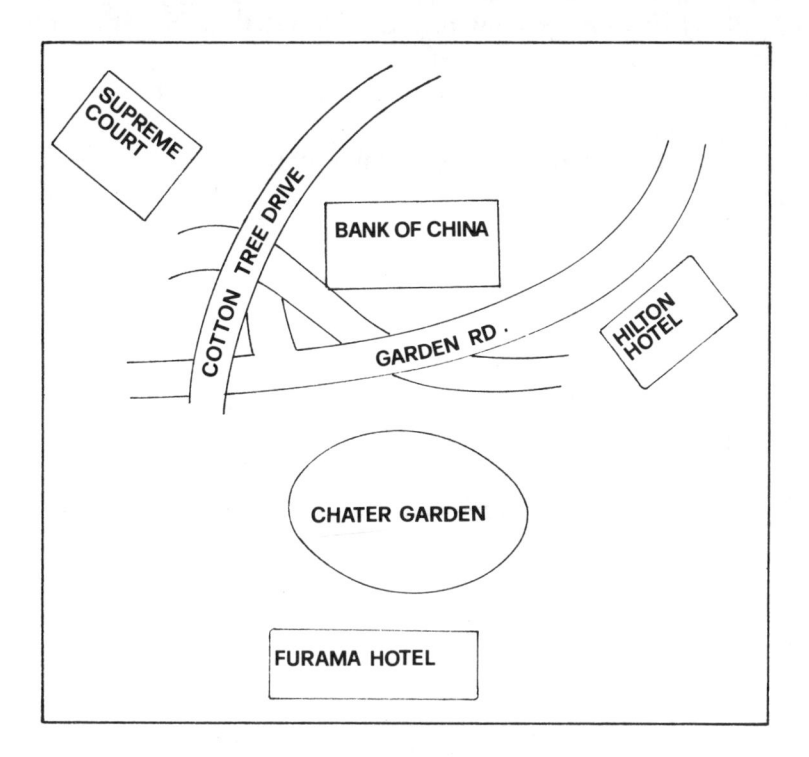

Fig. 25. Location of the Bank of China building.

The front of the bank faces north; its back faces south, with the Hilton Hotel and the Supreme Court on either side. In *feng-shui* terminology, they are called the dragon arm and tiger arm. These terms are derived from the traditional Chinese use of the dragon to symbolise the left and the east, and the tiger to symbolise the right and the west. In the same way, the phoenix represents the front and south, and the tortoise stands for back and north.

The building is sited in an area of busy traffic and several flyovers on Garden Road, Cotton Tree Drive and Queensway cross its front and back. In *feng-shui* appraisal, roads and flyovers in cities are considered flowing water. One should observe the curves and shapes of the roads and flyovers. If the curve of these structures bends towards the building, it is compared to the blade of a knife or a bow with an arrow pointing at the building. On the other hand, if the curve "embraces" the building or meanders round it, the site is considered auspicious. Such a configuration means the roads (water) surround the building in an "affectionate" manner and exert a benevolent influence.

The flyovers and traffic come round the Bank of China building from at least four directions and, surprisingly enough, none of the roads has a sharp curve pointing towards it. This is a classic arrangement known as "greeted and embraced by multiple waters with affection". Fast-moving traffic will carry the intangible forces away, but the apparent slow flow of the traffic due to the many traffic lights in the area contributes to the concentration of benevolent intangible forces (*qi*).

Opposite the bank building is an open space — Chater Garden. This garden constitutes what is called a "bright hall" in *feng-shui,* meaning an area open to the accumulation and

38   *Feng-shui and Destiny*

concentration of intangible forces. Beyond Chater Garden is the Furama Hotel. This structure may block the sea view a little but one should note its role as a shield which prevents *qi* from dispersing, so it can be regarded as a "greeting mountain from afar" in the *yin* houses theory of *feng-shui*.

If we compare the physical surroundings of the new Bank of China Building with that of the Hongkong Bank building, we can easily observe similarities. Each has a bright hall: the Hongkong Bank has Statue Square and the Bank of China has Chater Garden, and each sits in an auspicious south-north direction. There is, however, one difference: the Bank of China has the Furama Hotel as a shield which the Hongkong Bank seems to be lacking, with the low Star Ferry Pier in front.

We have so far concentrated on the physical environs of the Bank of China building. Now let us look at how it fits in with the distribution of intangible forces. By measuring the front of the bank building, my *lo pan* pointed to a south-north direction, meaning the bank is sitting with its back against the south and its front entrance absorbs the intangible forces directly from the north. The building is constructed in the Age of Seven so the birth chart (Fig. 26) can be drawn up:

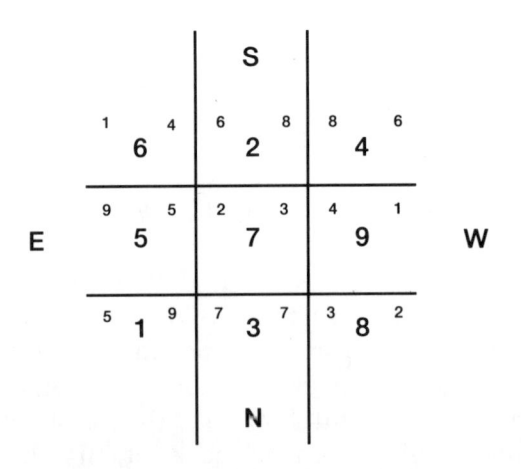

```
                       S
           |           |           |
        1     4     6     8     8     6
           6           2           4
       ____|_____|_____|____
           |           |           |
        9     5     2     3     4     1
  E        5           7           9        W
       ____|_____|_____|____
           |           |           |
        5     9     7     7     3     2
           1           3           8
           |           |           |
                       N
```

Fig. 26. Birth chart of Bank of China building.

From the chart, one can see that the building has the prosperous double sevens right at the front entrance. The seven at the right is a water star for which an open, fluid direction is most suitable as it conducts wealth and prosperity. The environs in front of the bank building serves this purpose remarkably well. The meandering traffic, the roads and flyovers, Chater Garden (the bright hall) — all fit in well with the water star of seven and intensify its prosperous influence. The other seven on the left is the mountain star. In theory, a mountain star located on the front side means an arrangement called the "mountain star falls into the water" and is not a good configuration for human health and human resources. Fortunately, the tall Furama Hotel building situated directly in front can be regarded as a remedy by "putting the mountain star back on the mountain".

The next star to examine is the number eight which is found in the south as a water star. The number eight is significant as it refers to prosperity of the immediate future. To allow this water star to bring in prosperity, it is necessary to keep the location open and fluid. In addition, there is no tall building to block the "water flow" at the building's back. So future prosperity is also safeguarded.

Observed from the exterior of the building, its birth chart indicates that the best "seating arrangement" for offices in this building is to sit at the southwest with the back against the mountain star eight, with the main office entrance at the north to welcome the prosperous water star seven. The inauspicious locations are in the east and northeast where the *shar* of five is found. The east location should be used for enclosed rooms with less activity whereas the location northeast could be used as a reception area, a concourse, or halls. Office entrances can also open to the northeast as this location fits in with the castle gate theory and is comparable to the north direction in terms of prosperity.

One more credit found in the birth chart is that the water stars and the age figures (centre numbers) all add up to a total of 10 in all the nine squares. This will also contribute to prosperity. (The castle gate theory and the theory of 10 belong to the more advanced levels of *feng-shui*.)

One ancient principle of classical *feng-shui* is that prominent water features on the landscape will enhance the place as an economic centre. On the other hand, if mountain features are the main characteristic, it is suitable as a political centre. The Bank of China building sits on a superb site in the midst of benevolent water influences and is one of the best economic locations in Hong Kong. The arrival of the yearly star of seven at the north main entrance also coincided with the grand opening in 1989 — this auspicious star augurs well for the Bank of China.

18. World Wide House: Escalators as a Source of Wealth

World Wide House shopping arcade in the central district of Hong Kong has been a controversial building in property circles. Its disappointing occupancy rate in the early years created much speculation. Such a building is naturally a good subject for a thorough *feng-shui* appraisal.

Measuring the direction of World Wide House from the side of Connaught Road, the *lo pan* points to the southwest/ northeast direction. World Wide House was constructed between 1964 and 1983, so its birth chart is drawn on the basis of a building belonging to the Age of Six. Figs. 27 and 28 show a sketch of the building and its birth chart.

The first thing we should look for is the number six which is found in the southwest direction as a mountain star and in the northeast direction as a water star. Such a configuration means both the prosperous stars are in the right positions, with the mountain star on the mountain and water star in the water. The influence of the prosperous water star is intensified by Victoria Harbour and the traffic flow of Pedder Street and Connaught Road from the northeast to the north. Such a building should be prosperous, enjoying success both in terms of money and human resources. So what is wrong with this building?

Most *feng-shui* enthusiasts argue that the physical layout of the building does not provide a proper main entrance for the reception of good intangible forces and that there is no bright

40   *Feng-shui and Destiny*

hall at the entrance to allow the intangible forces to concentrate and circulate. In fact, the entrance from Des Voeux Road leads straight back out onto Connaught Road. The inability to retain good influences means failure to keep one's wealth. Also, there are two MTR (subway station) outlets underneath the building on both Des Voeux Road and Connaught Road. The busy escalators only convey people in and out of the MTR station and do not bring prople into World Wide House.

Such outlets are comparable to the outflow of water and again symbolise the leakage of water and wealth, and people running away from the building. The escalator leading to the shopping arcade is situated in the southwest of the building and the birth chart shows the mountain star six is located there. As the entrance of a house is considered an air inlet and water inflow, putting an escalator at the location of a prosperous mountain star means "mountain star falls into water". As a mountain star affects human resources, such a

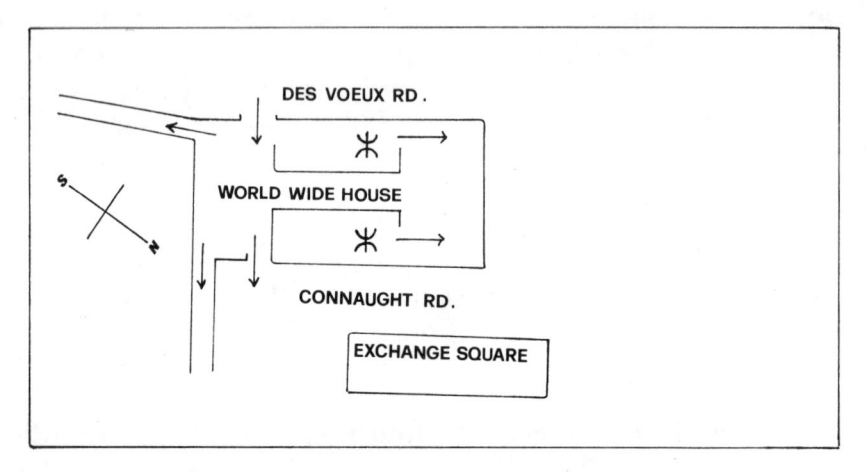

Fig. 27. Location of World Wide House.

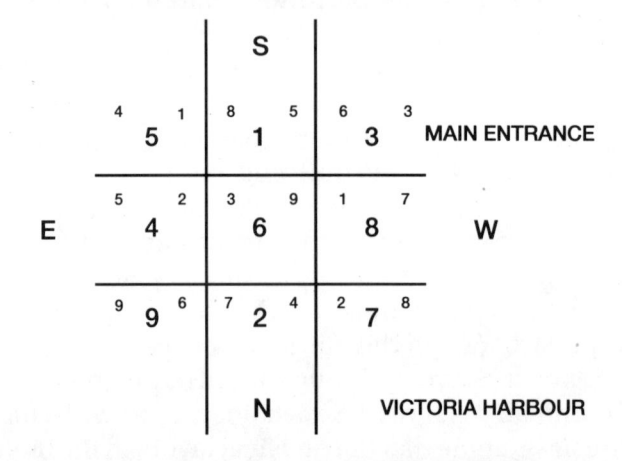

Fig. 28. Birth chart of World Wide House.

configuration means a lack of shoppers, especially before 1984 (Age of Six). The same adverse effect is also found in the south, where the mountain star eight falls into water as there is a bridge connecting World Wide House with Swire House.

However, it is interesting to observe that after 1984 and in the subsequent years, the popularity of the shopping arcade has improved to almost full occupancy. In recent years, the arcade has become a very popular spot for Filipino maids and white-collar workers in the central district.

The flying star school of *feng-shui* offers answers to this sudden surge in popularity. There was a change of *feng-shui* after 1984 (the Age of Seven) and the influence of the moving star six on the birth chart declined, with the number seven taking precedence. The water star seven is found in the west and the busy traffic flow on Des Voeux Road from west to east enhances its influence to bring in more money. The mountain star seven is in the north direction where, before 1984, one could only find Blake Pier and Victoria Harbour, meaning the mountain star "fell" into water. However, after 1984, the prosperous mountain star seven was "put back" onto the mountain with the appearance of the huge Exchange Square building sitting in the north and acting as a mountain to bring in human prosperity to World Wide House. Those who prefer not to rely on mysterious moving stars can also interpret it as improved popularity due to more people using the bridge through World Wide House to Exchange Square, thus bringing in more visitors and shoppers. Still, this is a classic example of how *feng-shui* affects the prosperity of a shopping arcade.

We shall now look in greater detail at how *feng-shui* theories affect the modern city and, in particular, such features as entrances and escalators. A modern complex with a large number of shopping lots is a recent phenomenon and one cannot expect to find any guiding examples in classic *feng-shui* books.

From the outside, a modern complex has many entrances and it is difficult to tell which is the main direction accepting the major intangible influences. Inside, the shops are arranged in a maze and one can hardly identify how each one lot receives its directional *feng-shui* influences. Judging from the failure of many shopping arcades, one can imagine that investing in a shop within a big complex is quite a risky business and one must be careful to choose a good arcade and a good shop site.

The first thing to note is the birth chart of the building. The shopping arcade is part of a big building. The prosperity of the building itself is of course the prerequisite for a popular arcade. For example, the birth chart of World Wide House in the central district is a prosperous one after all, with mountain stars and water stars well-positioned to receive the prosperous influences.

The second step is to see if the floor plan is designed in such a way that the shopping arcade is in a position to receive the best intangible influences. Returning to the example of World Wide House, one should note that despite the entrance at the ground floor being in the southwest location, the escalator in fact brings people up to the west location when they reach the first floor. Therefore, the main entrance of the World Wide House shopping arcade is in fact in the west location with the presence of the prosperous water star seven, which will have a good effect after 1984 when the Age of Seven is in the ascendant.

As shoppers are most important to a shopping arcade, one should check whether the mountain stars of the birth chart, meaning human prosperity, are well located, and there is no incidence of "mountain star falls into water". Such an occurrence actually contributed to the lack of popularity of World Wide House before 1984 as the mountain star six fell into the main entrance, the mountain star seven fell into Victoria Harbour and the mountain star eight fell onto the bridge connecting Swire House in the south.

If you are satisfied with the external surroundings and physical layout , you should then check the interior design. One prerequisite is smooth traffic flow in the arcade. It must be designed in such a way that shoppers should be able to go round most of the shops without coming to a dead end. Inconvenient traffic flow often reduces popularity and prosperity.

The arrangement of escalators is also an essential feature of the traffic flow affecting an arcade's prosperity potential. "Up-and-down" escalators, located far apart, encourage shoppers to walk round the arcade and visit all shops, thus bringing the intangible forces to all corners on their path.

There is a famous arcade in Mong Kok which was converted into a big shopping centre in recent years after the closure of a big department store. This shopping centre has three floors and the third floor is occupied by a Chinese restaurant. The up-and-down escalators are situated in the same location, bringing people straight up to the third floor restaurant and straight down from the restaurant to the main entrance. Such an escalator arrangement does not encourage people to visit the shopping arcade on the first and second floors. Despite the fact that the building is in a prime location in Mong Kok with popular shopping centres, restaurants and a cinema in the vicinity, many shops in this arcade are suffering losses and are closing down one by one. However, the Chinese restaurant on the third floor is enjoying huge prosperity as it receives all the intangible influences right from the main entrance up the escalator to the third floor. It is also interesting to note that shops located immediately next to the escalator are doing well as they are able to receive intangible influences which spill over from the escalator. Those down in the heart of the arcade appear to be in trouble.

19. The Governor's House: Hong Kong's Future

The Governor's residence at Garden Road can be considered the heart of Hong Kong. It is said to have been designed by renowned *feng-shui* experts. The *feng-shui* of the Governor's House directly affects the Governor's wellbeing and so can have a direct bearing on the fortune of Hong Kong.

The prestigious building is situated in the "dragon's lair" of Victoria Peak. When measured with a *lo pan* at the main gate on Garden Road, the house is found to stand with its front to the southwest and its back to the northeast. So instead of leaning against the mountain like many conventional Chinese buildings, it leans towards Victoria Harbour and faces Victoria Peak. This is a unique *feng-shui* configuration called "sitting empty, facing solid".

The house was first constructed in 1855 which was in the Age of Nine. However, it was substantially renovated and extended in 1890, the Age of Two. Therefore, it is more appropriate to draw a birth chart on the basis of the renovation year (Fig. 29).

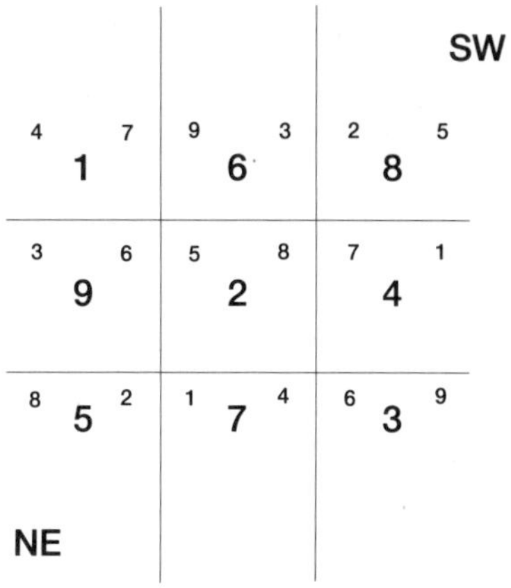

		SW
4　　7 　1	9　　3 　6	2　　5 　8
3　　6 　9	5　　8 　2	7　　1 　4
8　　2 　5	1　　4 　7	6　　9 　3

NE

Fig. 29. Birth chart of the Governor's House.

As the building belongs to the Age of Two, we should focus our attention on the number two in the chart which is the most prosperous star of the age. The number two is found as a water star in the northeast and as a mountain star in the southwest. To recapitulate, a prosperous mountain star should be placed on the mountain and a prosperous water star should be placed on the water. The Governor's House has such a configuration as it has Victoria Peak in the southwest and Victoria Harbour in the northeast. This reflects the possible involvement of *feng-shui* experts in the selection of the site and the directional planning of the house and also explains why the configuration "sitting empty, facing solid" was chosen.

Going through the history of Hong Kong, it is very interesting to find that the *feng-shui* of the Governor's House seems to reflect the ups and downs of the city. If we evaluate by ages, we observe that between 1964 and 1983, the 20 years in the Age of Six were very prosperous for Hong Kong as the water star (six) is located in the east, and the east of the Governor's house overlooks Victoria Harbour, a practical demonstration of the auspicious principle "prosperous water star falls in water".

I have conducted a small statistical survey to see if the yearly changes in intangible *feng-shui* influences at the house's entrance and at its back could have some bearing on the fortune of Hong Kong. I find that whenever the Governor's House came under the influence of the *shar* of five or the *shar* of two, there were unfortunate happenings in Hong Kong.

In 1941, the year when Hong Kong surrendered to Japanese invaders, the *shar* of two was at the house entrance. In 1956, a year of riots, the *shar* of five was at the entrance. In February 1965, the year and month of an economic crisis, the yearly *shar* of five was found at the entrance and the monthly *shar* of two was at the back. In August 1971, 120 people died when ferries sank in a severe typhoon. At that time the yearly *shar* of five was at the back and the monthly *shar* of two at the entrance. In 1974, when the yearly *shar* of five was at the entrance and the *shar* of two was at the back, the economy suffered badly after the collapse of the stock market with the Hong Kong index falling to 400 points in December 1973.

In 1983, we again encountered the combination of the *shar* of five at the entrance and the *shar* of two at the back. The year commenced with the Sino-British discussions on the handover of sovereignty. In September, the value of the Hong Kong dollar dropped to 9.8 to one US dollar. The year also saw the collapse of the Carrian group and a typhoon that killed 22 in September. In December 1986, the Governor, Sir Edward Youde, died when the yearly *shar* of two was at the entrance and monthly *shar* of five was at the back. In June 1989, the yearly *shar* of five was at the back of the Governor's house and the monthly *shar* of five at the entrance. The Tienanmen Square tragedy in Beijing shook the confidence of the Hong Kong people. Looking into the future, the next time when the *shar* of two arrives at the entrance and back of the Governor's house is 1992, the Year of the Monkey.

20. The Hongkong Bank Building

The Hong Kong head office of the Hongkong and Shanghai Bank is said to be located at the dragon's lair of Victoria Mountain. *Feng-shui* experts believe that Victoria Mountain is an extension of the Tai Mo Shan mountain range in Kowloon. After crossing the harbour, it rises to form Victoria Peak on Hong Kong Island. Victoria Peak appears to turn its head, looking back towards the Tai Mo Shan. So the configuration is called "dragon turning its head to salute the ancestor". Victoria Mountain descends northwards in two main branches which form two "dragons' dens" before running into the sea. One den, or lair, is found in the backyard of the Governor's house, the other one is the very spot in Central where the Hongkong Bank building is located.

A dragon's lair is the spot where the energy of the whole mountain range concentrates. To qualify as a good dragon's lair, it must be a place well-sheltered on the back and on both sides, and it is best to have water in front to stop the energy from dispersing. The site of the Hongkong Bank is able to satisfy all these criteria. So it is regarded as the heart of Hong Kong, symbolising the place's prosperity.

The physical surroundings of the Hongkong Bank building confers on it good *feng-shui* influence. Besides sitting on the dragon's lair, it has the Statue Square Garden at its front door which constitutes a bright hall to allow the prosperous intangible forces to concentrate. Victoria Harbour and the Star Ferry Pier help to hold the intangible forces in the bright hall and stop them from dispersing. The Bank building is also surrounded and escorted by the old Bank of China, the Chartered Bank, Prince Building and Legco Building, acting as "dragons and tigers" on both sides (guards on the left and on the right). Traffic from Des Voeux Road, going from east to west, flows at a slight slope, meandering slowly through the front door to enhance the benevolent influences. So as far as the physical environment is concerned, the Hongkong Bank building site is well-qualified as a spot of superb *feng-shui*. However, this is only half the story. One also has to examine carefully the distribution of the intangible forces before making any conclusions.

The original Hongkong Bank building was inaugurated in 1935 in the Age of Four. The building sat with its front towards the north and its back against the south. Using this information, we can construct a natal chart of the building showing the distribution of the intangible forces in all directions (Figs. 30 and 31).

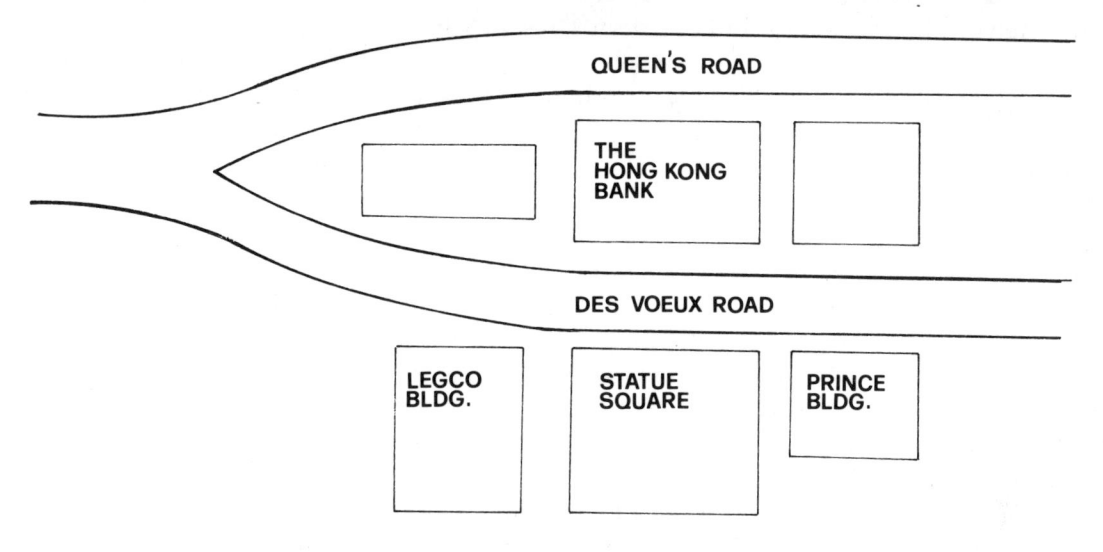

Fig. 30. Location of Hongkong Bank.

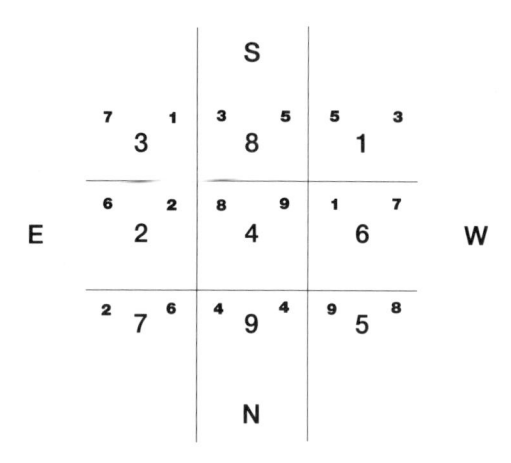

Fig. 31. Birth chart of the old Hongkong Bank building.

    The above flying star chart reflects a prosperous building at the Age of Four with the mountain star and water star four both located at the north and at the front entrance. With the Statue Square Garden and Victoria Harbour in the north forming the bright hall to hold the benevolent intangible forces, one can see that the building is very well placed to enjoy prosperous *feng-shui* influences. The water star five, representing future prosperity in the

46   *Feng-shui and Destiny*

Age of Four, is located at the back in the south. The building's back entrance at Queen's Road is also appropriately placed to welcome such future prosperity from the back. Therefore the twin entrances at Des Voeux Road and Queen's Road guaranteed good fortunes for the Hongkong Bank. So it is not surprising that the corporation continued to grow and expand during the Age of Five, in the period between 1944 to 1963.

After 1963, entering the Age of Six, the benevolent influences of the stars four and five at the front and back entrances faded away and the northeast corner, where the water star six is located, became the most prosperous spot. The Bank was able to sustain the good fortunes as the effect of the water star six was intensified by Victoria Harbour and the traffic flow on Des Voeux Road from the northeast.

The old bank building was demolished in 1981, an appropriate time as far as *feng-shui* is concerned. In the Age of Seven, from 1984 onwards, the old building constructed in the Age of Four could no longer sustain the prosperity as its natal chart shows the prosperous water star seven is in the west location, where no prominent open space or water to enhance its benevolent influence can be found. The flying star four at the front entrance becomes obsolete in the Age of Seven and rebuilding the bank is the only way to regain prosperity. A building's fortune can be changed by reconstruction. To demolish and rebuild, gives a building new life and a new flying star chart.

The new Hongkong Bank building is a celebrated piece of modern architecture. The designer's idea was to construct a building that the Bank and Hong Kong can be proud of, that is flexible and able to adapt to future changes. The construction cost is said to be about 5.3 billion Hong Kong dollars. The new bank building was inaugurated in July 1985, so it is a modern Age of Seven building (Fig. 32).

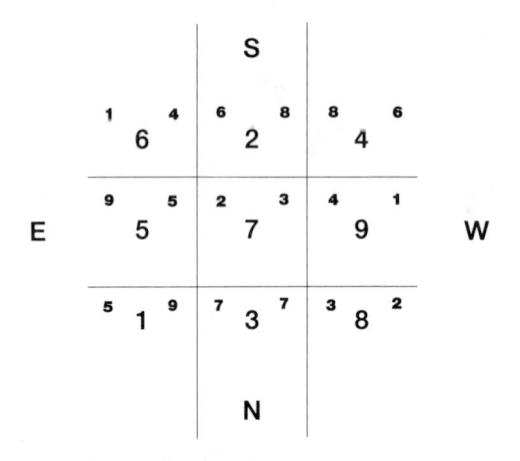

	S	
1 4 6	6 8 2	8 6 4
9 5 E 5	2 3 7	4 1 9 W
5 9 1	7 7 3	3 2 8
	N	

Fig. 32. Birth chart of the new Hongkong Bank building.

The flying star chart is drawn up on the basis of a south-north direction building in the Age of Seven. In the chart, the number seven (meaning current prosperity) is located in the north, at the front entrance. The number eight, representing future prosperity, is found at the back, in the south. The prosperous stars of seven and eight are best placed at the entrance and in open space. In this respect, the Hongkong Bank building appears to be able to exploit good influences with wide entrances both in the north and in the south. At the north entrance (facing the harbour), the prosperity of the water star seven is enhanced by the superb bright hall formed by Statue Square Garden which is also well guarded on both sides by Prince's Building and Legco building. The configuration means that the prosperous intangible forces of the Age of Seven are well-contained and will not disperse quickly.

Good water stars also need movement to activate their benevolent influence. The busy flow of people from the MTR station, the gathering of white collar workers and Filipino maids in Statue Square Garden, the movement of ferries crossing Victoria Harbour to and from the Star Ferry Pier, all create activity right in front of the bank entrance and effectively activate the water star seven to bring in good fortune.

However, a serious drawback is that the ground level plaza of the building appears too empty, with few walls to hold the intangible forces. Also, the hollow and empty base gives the impression of a weak foundation. The new bank, unlike the old one with a solid and broad base, appears not to be standing on firm ground. Imaginative *feng-shui* experts will associate the design with the confidence crisis of the Hong Kong people. Another criticism is the location of the two major escalators leading to the first floor. Instead of drawing up the prosperous intangible forces located in the north, the escalators are placed at the northwest where they only stir up the bad intangible influence of the water star two which is a *shar*, bringing ill influence. Such an arrangement greatly reduces the prosperity of the front entrance.

With the construction of the new Bank of China building on the right of the Hongkong Bank, some experts worry that the sharp edges of the prismatic Bank of China building would impose a *feng-shui* threat and create a *shar* acting on the Hongkong Bank. Fortunately, none of the sharp edges point directly at the Hongkong Bank headquarters. Also, the Bank of China is located in a southeast direction where we find the mountain star one in the flying star chart. The star one, although it does not mean prosperity, is not a *shar* in itself.

Studies have also been made about the position of the Hongkong Bank in relation to the *feng-shui* of the Governor's House. The Governer's residence, sitting on Garden Road, with its back against Victoria Harbour, has derived its past prosperity from its unique "sitting empty, facing solid" configuration. The new tall Hongkong Bank building creates a new "mountain" behind the Governor's House and causes some disturbances to such a good *feng-shui* configuration.

The story of the Hongkong Bank building is not complete without mentioning the famous pair of bronze lions guarding the front entrance. The lions have been a symbol of energy, strength and vigour for the bank and the Hong Kong economy. The relocation of these lions is often associated with misfortune. They were first removed in 1941 when the Japanese invaders took the lions to Tokyo. They were later miraculously recovered from a Tokyo weapons factory and were reinstated outside the bank in 1945 after the war. The second relocation was after the demolition of the old bank building. Some *feng-shui* experts link this recent relocation to the commencement of the Sino-British talks on the 1997 issue and the confidence crisis in subsequent years.

21. *Feng-shui* and the Supernatural

Feng-shui and parapsychology are quite different branches of study, but they are not totally divorced from each other. *Feng-shui* is the study of environmental influences upon human life and this not only involves the physical surroundings but also abstract intangible forces.

Parapsychology deals with the supernatural: paranormal phenomena such as ghosts and spirits which are also abstract beings closely attached to houses and environments. *Feng-shui* experts, when assisting clients in solving environmental problems, may occasionally encounter houses with strange phenomena which can be attributed only to the presence of supernatural beings, thus crossing the borderline into parapsychology. It is generally believed that apparitions and hauntings are the result of bad *feng-shui*.

In the famous *feng-shui* classic written by Master Sum of the Ching dynasty, one can find many cases of haunted houses and the following is one interesting example.

Fig. 33 shows a house with a green tree and river at the back. Fig. 34 is the birth chart of the house. The book recorded that the apparition of a female in a green dress often appeared in the back yard. Master Sum attributed the phenomenon to the physical surroundings (green tree, river, darkness), as well as the concentration of *yin* (female) intangible forces (nine, five, seven, two) at the back yard. The haunting ceased after the entrance of the house was moved to the southwest. The southwest door, with the intangible force 8, *yang*, overcame the *yin* influence and the apparition vanished.

Even in the present day, experienced *feng-shui* experts often have supernatural accounts to relate. The following is said to be a true account of strange events that befell a famous Hong Kong jockey. Mr Jockey's mother died in 1985. In the summer of 1987, Mr Jockey's wife suddenly had a series of bad dreams: her mother-in-law appeared to her and cried, saying that she felt very uncomfortable in her grave and her body must be removed and cleaned. Mr Jockey believed in the significance of such dreams and set out to engage someone to dig up the coffin.

However, no one in Hong Kong was willing to take the job as the woman had been buried for only two years (it usually takes about five years after burial before the skeleton is considered clean enough to handle). The matter was therefore shelved until late autumn when the old woman reappeared in Mrs Jockey's dreams. This time she not only repeated her request but also warned that something bad would happen if it was not met as soon as possible. Mr Jockey then encountered a series of misfortunes. He suffered an injury in a horse race and got into some legal entanglements.

Eventually, an expert was engaged from Taiwan to excavate the mother's coffin. It was found that the corpse was covered with broken glass — the funeral parlour had left a sheet of glass inside the coffin by mistake. This story is well-known in *feng-shui* circles as *yin* house experts were also called in to check the *feng-shui* of the grave site and plan the re-burial.

One famous Hong Kong *feng-shui* expert saw the apparition of a man in Ching dynasty dress warning him: "Mind your own business", when he was evaluating the *feng-shui* of a flat in Mei Foo Sun Chuen. He felt sick and immediately left the house. The next morning,

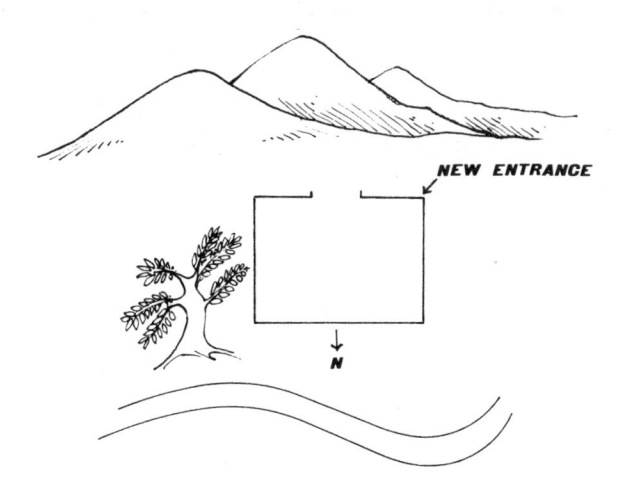

Fig. 33. Layout of haunted house.

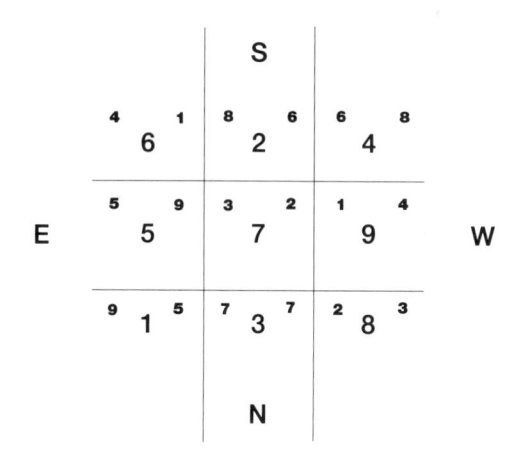

Fig. 34. Birth chart of haunted house in Ching dynasty.

his maid reported to him that she was woken in the middle of the night by a man dressed in Ching dynasty robes standing beside her bed. Knowing that the spirit was at his heels, the *feng-shui* man immediately packed up and moved to a new flat. *Feng-shui* experts in Hong Kong usually have ways of protecting themselves against such encounters. Most of them equip themselves with Buddhist prayers and many carry Buddhist sacred objects such as blessed rings and pendants.

The example from Master Sum's classical *feng-shui* works illustrates one way of detecting the presence of spirits — i.e. the house birth chart shows a concentration of *yin* stars. However, some *feng-shui* experts believe that the *yin* intangible forces constitute only one favourable condition for an uncanny presence. It does not necessarily mean that the house

50 *Feng-shui and Destiny*

must be haunted or that it is psychically "charged". Such an occurence as Master Sum recorded is very rare.

Some *feng-shui* experts believe that the *lo pan* (the Chinese *feng-shui* compass) itself is a ghost detector. When one enters a house holding the *lo pan* and finds the magnetic needle moving wildly and turning circles, it indicates the presence of bizarre magnetic forces.

Another means to check whether a house is "clean" or "not clean", which I believe is the most reliable method, is by way of the *I Ching* oracle. The *I Ching* oracle is considered one authentic way of divination. The most common practice is to toss three coins repeatedly and ask a specific question. By counting the heads and tails of the coins, one can draw up a *kua* which is a combination of two trigrams composed of 6 continuous lines (*yang*) or broken lines (*yin*). Each line of the trigrams symbolises one aspect of human life or a field of events. If one asks about the fortune of a house, lines showing intensive activity in the area of "ghost" may indicate spiritual presence to the degree of "haunting".

The following is a true account of my personal experience with an allegedly haunted house. In early 1988, my friend found a flat in Prince Edward Road. (Fig. 35 shows its birth chart.) The rent was attractive and it had good parking facilities. He asked for my opinion. I made a *feng-shui* study of the flat and found that one room on the north side had a concentration of *yin* stars. The possible presence of some spirit was also confirmed by the *I Ching* oracle. However, owing to the other attractions, my friend decided to rent the house and moved in during the month of July when the *shar* of five also happened to be present in the north, intensifying the *yin* forces.

He phoned me the very next morning after he moved into the flat, saying that his mother, sleeping in the north room, had bruises all over her limbs when she woke up in the morning, for which there was no logical explanation. He therefore invited me to make another visit to his new flat that evening. As his mother is a Buddhist, I taught her some Buddhist prayers and made some *feng-shui* arrangements to reduce the *yin* forces, and left the house after dinner.

When I reached home, I found that two strange things had happened. The magnetic needle of my *lo pan*, normally pointing north, was upside down, pointing south, showing a

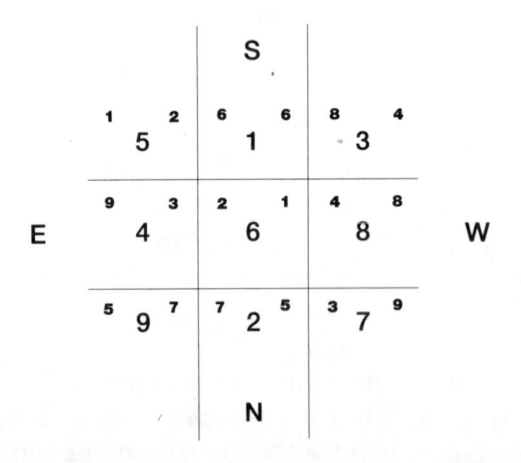

	S	

1 2
  5
	6 6
	  1
		8 4
		  3

9 3
E   4
	2 1
	  6
		4 8
		  8 W

5 7
  9
	7 5
	  2
		3 9
		  7

	N	

Fig. 35. Birth chart of a modern haunted house.

complete reversal of the magnetic poles, so that my *lo pan* was no longer useful. Secondly, the platinum ring on my finger had suddenly become oval-shaped and could not return to a normal round ring.

I was alarmed by the strange phenomenon and discussed the subject with my friend who is a devoted Buddhist and a keen researcher of the paranormal. I lent him my *lo pan* for his inspection. My friend brought the *lo pan* to his house in Mei Foo Sun Chuen on a Sunday afternoon. In the evening he phoned me, urgently asking to return the *lo pan* to me immediately. What had happened was that on the very afternoon he took my *lo pan* home, every member of his family living in the flat, including his father, mother, sister and wife, suddenly fell ill, the symptoms ranging from vomiting and diarrhoea to fainting and palpitations. Naturally, he put the blame on my *lo pan*.

I leave the reader to judge whether this series of bizarre events can be due to mere coincidence.

22. Charting Murder and Mishaps by the Flying Stars

Having seen how the flying star school of *feng-shui* can be applied to evaluate the prosperity of a building and provide references to read the fortunes of houses with the time dimension incorporated, we shall now use the same method to see how numbers can help to describe events in great detail. Classic examples can be found in the great *feng-shui* work by Master Sum of the Ching dynasty.

We should first get acquainted with the flying star table lists and the basic meaning of each number. The first example involves a house in which a lady in a red dress and black vest hanged herself in the sitting position. Fig. 36 is the birth chart of the house which was built in the last Age of Eight (1824-1843).

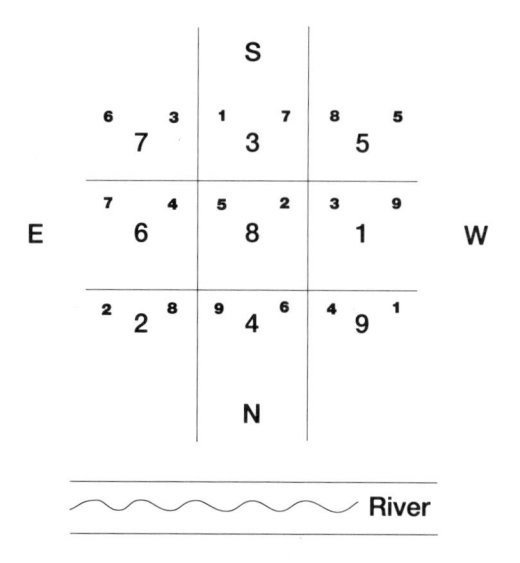

Fig. 36. Birth chart of a house of suicide.

52 *Feng-shui and Destiny*

The house was situated with its back against the southwest and front facing the northeast. There was a river in front of the house covering the directions northeast, north and northwest. As the house was completed in the Age of Eight, we should look for the positions of the number eight first. One is found in the northeast as a water star and one is found in the southwest as a mountain star. So the house is considered a prosperous house with the best water star in front to take in the prosperous intangible forces from the entrance, and the best mountain star at the back to exert good influence on human health. Therefore Master Sum commented that the household enjoyed wealth and good health in the Age of Eight.

However, we note that in the locations north and northwest, we find the numbers four, six, and nine in the north square and the numbers one, four and nine in the northwest square. Previous chapters on the *lo shu* diagram have shown the number six was originally located in the northwest and the number one in the north. Adding these two numbers to the two squares above, the configuration becomes one, four, six, and nine in both the north and the northwest locations.

We can see that the configuration gives us the following information: female, rope — four; head — six; red — nine; black — one. It does not take very much imagination to put together these pieces of the jigsaw and form the picture of a female dressed in red and black who hanged herself with a rope.

Now let us look up the meaning of these numbers from Table 5.

NO.	ELEMENT	PERSON	COLOUR	OBJECT	BODY	SYMBOL
1	Water	Middle-aged man	Black	Blood, Den	Ear	
2	Earth	Old woman	Black	Earth, Ox	Stomach	
3	Wood	Eldest son	Green	Thunder	Foot	
4	Wood	Elder daughter	Green	Rope, Wind	Buttocks	
5	Earth	A *shar*	Yellow	—	—	—
6	Metal	Father	Gold, White	Heaven	Head	
7	Metal	Young girl	Gold, White	Lake	Mouth	
8	Earth	Young son	White	Mountain	Hands	
9	Fire	Mother	Red	Sun, Beauty	Eyes	

Table 5. *Meanings and implications of feng-shui numbers.*

Master Sum went on to explain that the lady must have been in a sitting position when she was found, as the number six, which represents the metal element, was the original background number in the northwest. Metal is heavy, and in the background. The thin rope (four) was not able to sustain the heavy weight, therefore the head (six) could not have been hung up in the air. The manner of the lady's dress can be read from the symbols the numbers represented. Number nine (red dress) is represented by the symbol with an empty space in the centre. The symbol of the number one (black dress) is with a solid centre line to fill in the vacuum of the ☲. So one can picture the black within the red, portraying a black vest on top of a red dress.

One drawback of the example above is that Master Sum only briefly mentioned that this

Charting Murder and Mishaps by the Flying Stars   53

incident happened after the year 1843 in the Age of Nine when the prosperity of the water star eight had substantially faded away. The exact timing of the case was not mentioned. Let us now look at another fascinating example of a homicide case. In this example, the exact month of the incident was also stated and the monthly moving star actually interacted with the house birth chart to bring about the event.

The incident occurred in a certain Mr Chow's house, built in the Age of Eight (1824-1843) with its back against the west and its front facing the east. Fig. 37 shows the birth chart of the house.

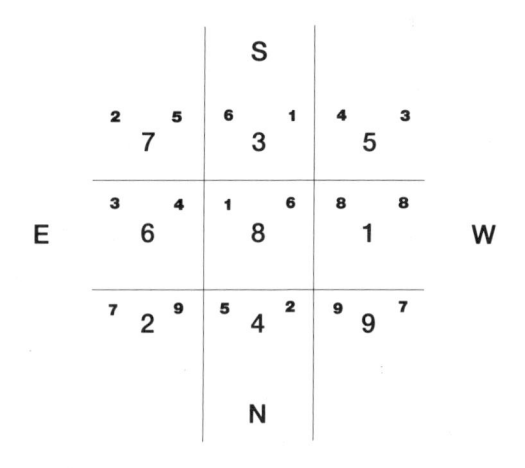

```
                    S
           2   5 | 6   1 | 4   3
             7  |   3   |   5
           ─────┼───────┼─────
           3   4 | 1   6 | 8   8
    E        6  |   8   |   1      W
           ─────┼───────┼─────
           7   9 | 5   2 | 9   7
             2  |   4   |   9
                    N
```

Fig. 37. Birth chart of a house of murder.

There was a well at the back of the place and the study room was at the back near the well. Two homicide cases occurred in 1895 and in 1896 respectively. The cases involved a teacher who murdered two students by hitting the victims on the head with hard wooden objects. The general comment on the house was that it had both eights at the back in the west location, meaning that the "water star went up the mountain". It is not a prosperous house; the well at the back meant the mountain star eight fell into the water (the well); therefore, the house is also not favourable with respect to human relationships and health.

Our attention is then drawn to the locations east, centre and west. The numbers three, four and six are found in the east. If readers look up table 5, they will note that these figures represent the items "wood" and "head". The number six also symbolise an elder person. In the middle square, readers can find the numbers one, six and eight which are respectively associated with blood, head and young man. In the west location, the numbers eight, eight and one also indicate two young men and blood.

Up to this stage, it is possible for us to put together the picture of an old man murdering two young men by hitting their heads with pieces of wood and the bloodshed involved.

Master Sum continued to "calculate" that these two tragic murders occurred separately in two consecutive years. The first was in February 1895 when the yearly moving star, three, and the monthly moving star, four, went to the middle square as shown in Fig. 38.

54 *Feng-shui and Destiny*

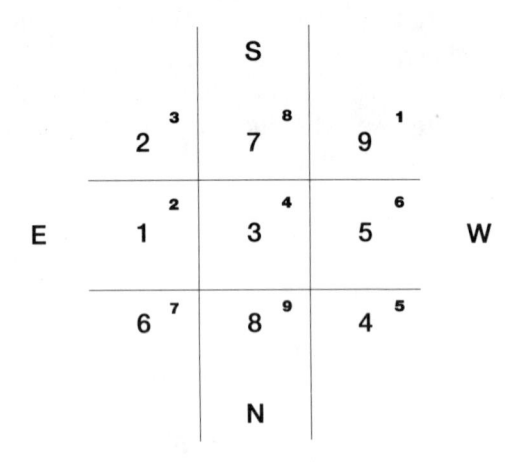

```
            S
      3    8    1
    2    7    9
    ─────────────
      2    4    6
E   1    3    5    W
    ─────────────
      7    9    5
    6    8    4
            N
```

Fig. 38. Star Chart of February 1895 — the first murder incident.

The centre numbers are the yearly stars and the smaller numbers at the corners are the monthly stars. Concentrating on the locations east, centre, and west, the chart shows the numbers three and four meaning wood went to the middle square and wood makes contact with the young men's (eight) heads (six). One, meaning blood, was located in the house entrance at the east, and the *shar* of five meaning misfortune was found in the west where the tragedy occurred at the back. Six also appeared in the west, implying the incident involved the heads of young men. The monthly two, the star of sickness, as well as the "Grand Duke of the Year" in 1895, appeared in the front entrance to intensify the misfortune.

The second incident occurred in February of the subsequent year 1896. Fig. 39 is the relevant yearly and monthly star chart.

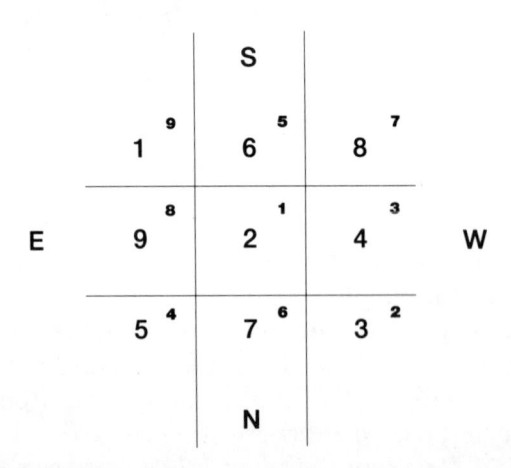

```
            S
      9    5    7
    1    6    8
    ─────────────
      8    1    3
E   9    2    4    W
    ─────────────
      4    6    2
    5    7    3
            N
```

Fig. 39. Star chart of February 1896 — the second murder incident.

Again the numbers three and four show wood concentrated in the west location to destroy the eight (meaning earth and young men). One, depicting blood, was in the centre together with the Grand Duke of the Year, two.

Master Sum was also able to deduce that the two murdered young men were born in the years of the ox and tiger respectively. This can also be explained using the *lo shu* diagram. The wood (three and four) destroyed the young men (eight). If one looks at the *lo shu* diagram, one can see the original number eight was located in the northeast which is the location of the ox and tiger.

As the examples above occurred in the 19th centrury, they may not appear quite "real" to modern readers. We will now discuss a modern real-life case to demonstrate how the same flying star school works in modern cities. The location is a big modern office in Pacific Place in Queensway, Hong Kong. The year is 1988 (around October). Pacific Place was completed only in 1988. So its birth chart is constructed on the basis of the Age of Seven.

The building has the Lane Crawford department store on the Queensway side facing north, but the main entrance with its lift hall to all offices is in fact located in the south. So the building is said to receive intangible influences from the south and the birth chart is drawn up according to its north-south direction.

The office under evaluation belongs to the department head of a sizeable international company located on the upper floors. The manager's office is located in the southeast corner of the building. This high-ranking manager chose the date August 8, 1988, to move into his new office but the lucky date failed to bring him any good fortune. He lost the job in October, only two months after occupying the new position. Fig. 40 is a sketch of the manager's room and Fig. 41 shows the birth chart of the building. Let us now look at the birth chart and see how much misfortune can be explained by the flying star school of *feng-shui*.

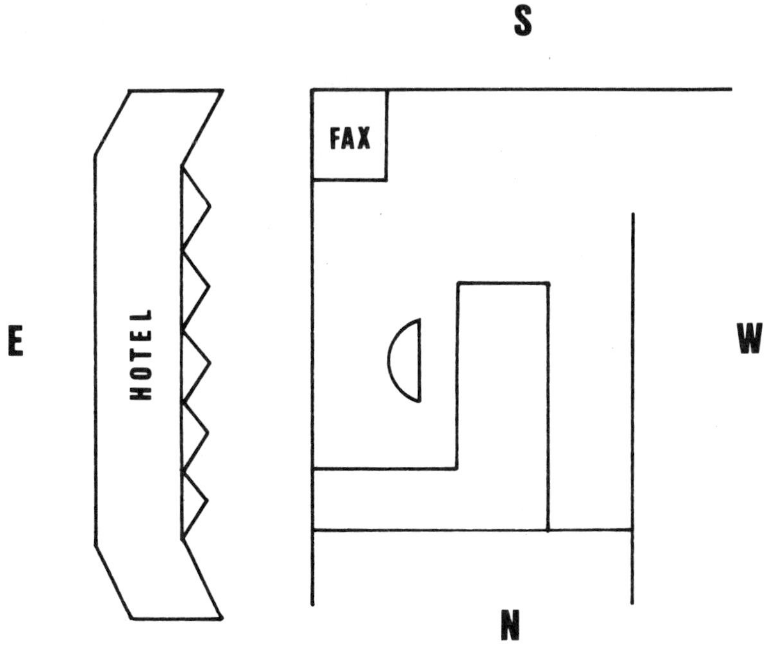

Fig. 40. Layout of manager's office.

56 *Feng-shui and Destiny*

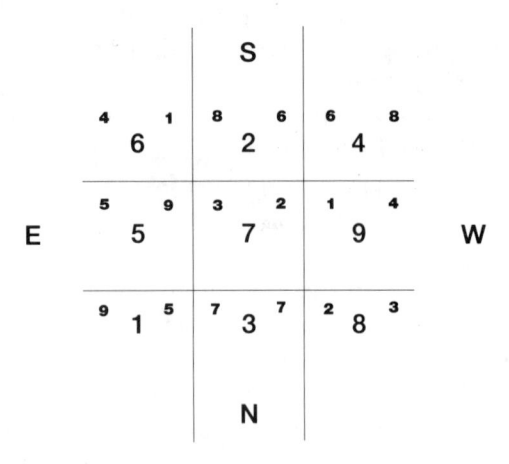

```
              S
      4  1 | 8  6 | 6  8
        6  |  2   |  4
      ----+------+----
      5  9 | 3  2 | 1  4
   E    5  |  7   |  9    W
      ----+------+----
      9  5 | 7  7 | 2  3
        1  |  3   |  8
              N
```

Fig. 41. Birth chart of office building.

As the manager's room is in the southeast location, we can first look at the southeast square of the chart which shows the number four as a mountain star and the number one as a water star. Both are stars belonging to ages of the remote past. So the southeast corner is not a prosperous area of the building. We can then focus our attention on the room where the manager sat and apply the birth chart to evaluate its arrangement. The manager's seat is in the east location of the room where the mountain star five is present. So he is in fact sitting on the *shar* of five which is the worst position for him to sit.

Looking out of the window at his back, we find that there is a new hotel and the design of its windows is like the teeth of a saw with sharp edges pointing towards the manager's back, thus forming a wall of sharp-edged *shars* at the man's back. This intensifies the *shar* of five located in that direction. To add to the misfortune, the three *shars* (see chapter five) of the year 1988 is present in the southeast, so disturbance of this corner should be avoided. However, there is a construction site in that direction, causing a lot of noise and movement. A fax machine placed right at the southeast corner of the room also contributes to more disturbance.

Therefore, one can see that the room has very bad *feng-shui* and any unfavourable yearly or monthly moving star visiting that area will trigger off some mishaps. Such an opportunity arose very soon in October 1988. Fig. 42 is the relevant yearly and monthly star chart.

We can see that the *shar* two and five are concentrated at the southeast, meaning misfortune will befall the manager's room located there. The number three, meaning anger and dispute, has arrived at the southwest which is the direction of the entrance to the room. With all major locations, his room, his seat, his back, his entrance, threatened by unfavourable intangible forces, it is no wonder that the manager had to quit the company after sitting in the room for only two months.

	S	
⁵ 2	¹ 7	³ 9
⁴ 1	⁶ 3	⁸ 5
⁹ 6	² 8	⁷ 4

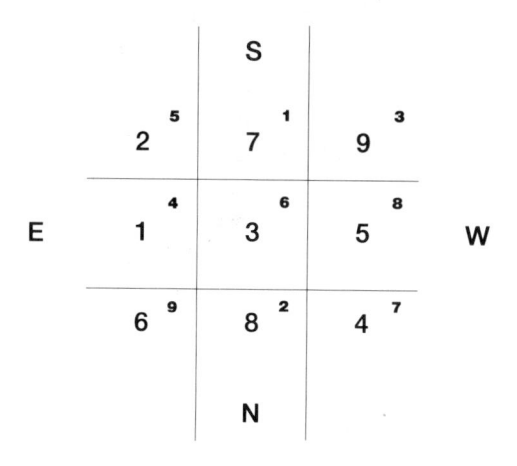

E (left) W (right) N (bottom)

Fig. 42. Feng-shui distribution in October 1988.

23. 8/8/88 and the Art of Selecting an Auspicious Date

In the previous chapter we discussed an example of a manager who chose August 8, 1988 as the grand opening date of his office but who realised to his regret that the auspicious date failed to bring him any good luck. So what was wrong with the date 8/8/88 which was widely believed to be a date of good fortune for everybody?

The answer lies in traditional misconceptions. Certain numbers when spoken aloud sound similar to words which have various connotations. For example, it is commonly believed that the number two is lucky merely because it sounds like "easy" in Cantonese. In *feng-shui,* however, the number is associated with sickness. The number three is customarily regarded as good because it sounds like "alive" and the number four is considered bad because it sounds like "die". In *feng-shui,* these numbers are accorded entirely different meanings. Three represents anger or agitation and four symbolises romance and sex as well as literature and learning.

The date 8/8/88 was considered fortunate only because the number eight sounds like "prosperous" in Cantonese. Aside from this, there is no other reason to support its auspicious significance. Choosing a good date for a grand opening, an engagement, a wedding, or other important event is a branch of *feng-shui* which involves extensive knowledge of the classical Chinese calendar, fortune telling, and *feng-shui* techniques such as numerology. The Chinese calendar incorporates the theory of the basic elements - metal, wood, water, fire and earth.

The birth data of a person (year, month, day and hour) are linked to the five elements which points to a person's destiny. Hence, they are known as the Four Pillars of Destiny. When selecting a suitable date for important events, *feng-shui* attempts to match the five elements with the Four Pillars of Destiny of the person concerned. Therefore, a particular

58 Feng-shui and Destiny

calendar date will have a different impact on different people. This is why it is naive to believe that 8/8/88 would have been a good date for everybody.

The philosophy behind the Four Pillars of Destiny is balance and harmony. A well-balanced relationship between the five elements in a person's birth data is considered benevolent. On the other hand, the absence of balance in the birth data will bring misfortune and disharmony. Therefore a calendar date, carefully chosen, can help balance the five elements, thus bringing good fortune. A date erroneously selected can upset the balance in the birth data and bring misfortune. *Feng-shui* theory can help select a date which can bring harmony and balance.

In our example, the manager's birth data shows that he belongs to the element of strong metal because he was born in autumn when metal is in season and is most prosperous. As the metal element in the manager's birth data is too strong, it is necessary to offset its strength with wood which will provide an outlet for the excess metal energy, and with fire which will keep the strong metal under control. So a calendar date with the elements of wood and fire would have been most suitable for the manager. Unfortunately, in his case, the date 8/8/88 was a date with nothing but metal and earth which is extremely unfavourable to him. It would have upset his balance by generating too much metal in his already excessive metallic birth data.

Another criterion in the selection of a good date is by reference to the moving stars. The task is to select a date when the most favourable moving stars concentrate at the important locations. In our example, the manager's seat and the entrance to his office are naturally the essential locations. Let us now look at Fig. 43 which is the star chart of the date 8/8/88.

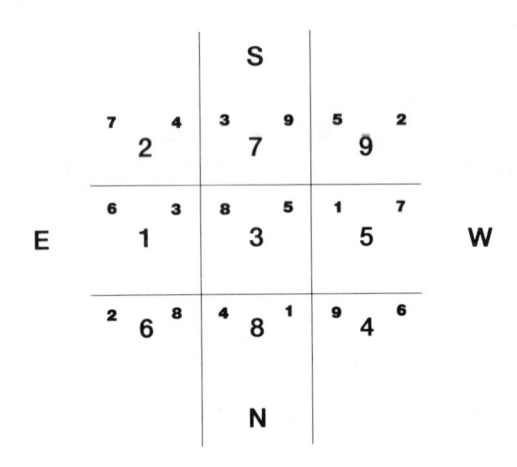

	S	
7 4 2	3 9 7	5 2 9
6 3 E 1	8 5 3	1 7 5 W
2 8 6	4 1 8	9 6 4
	N	

Fig. 43. *Distribution of feng-shui forces on 8/8/1988.*

The figures in the centre are the yearly stars, the smaller figures on the left are the monthly stars for August and those on the right are the daily stars for the eighth day of the month. The entrance of the room is in the southwest location where we can see the group of stars five, two and nine gathered on 8/8/88. The two and five are *shars*, exerting bad influences. They both belong to the element of earth. The nine is not a prosperous star and belongs to the fire element. As fire gives birth to earth, it helped to intensify the bad influence of the two and five *shars*. So it can be seen that 8/8/88 is certainly not a good date for the manager and his room.

The art of selecting an auspicious date is another very important subject. There are many other rules and taboos in choosing a date. For example, one born in the year of the dragon, in principle, should not choose September for any important events as September, represented by dog, will clash with the dragon.

24. Landscape and the Fortune of Hong Kong

The prosperity of a place can be assessed by comparing the location of dragons (mountains) against the *lo shu* diagram. Chinese scholars and philosophers generally believe that the *lo shu* diagram contains the wisdom of their ancestors and the pattern of dots in fact represents the universal order as viewed by ancient Chinese people (see chapter 4).

The *lo shu* diagram is therefore the foundation of the Chinese xia calendar and the *kua* of the *I Ching*. By converting the dots of the *lo shu* diagram into numbers, we get the numerical arrangement which forms the framework of the flying star school of *feng-shui* (Figs. 44a and 44b).

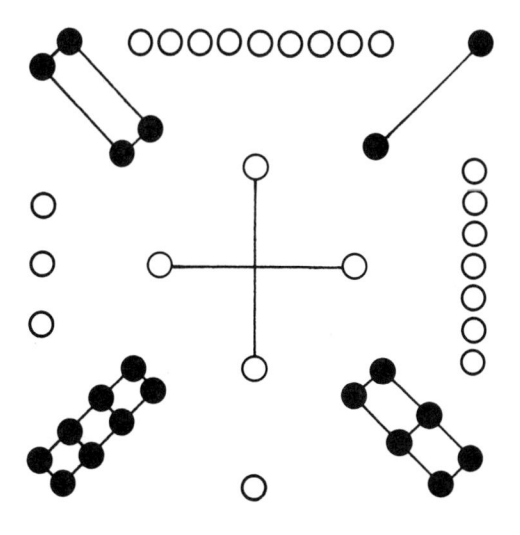

Fig. 44a. The lo shu diagram.

60 *Feng-shui and Destiny*

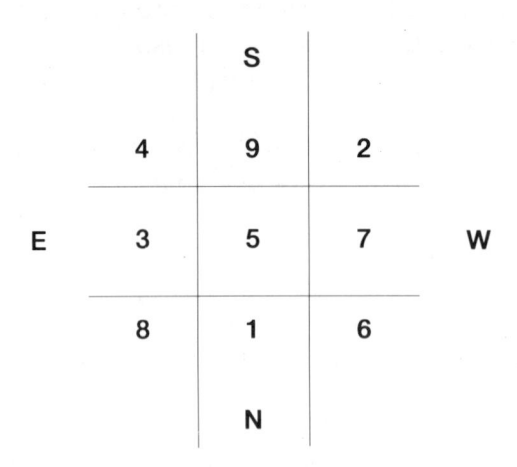

```
                    S
           ┌─────┬─────┬─────┐
           │  4  │  9  │  2  │
           ├─────┼─────┼─────┤
       E   │  3  │  5  │  7  │   W
           ├─────┼─────┼─────┤
           │  8  │  1  │  6  │
           └─────┴─────┴─────┘
                    N
```

Fig. 44b. Lo shu diagram converted to numbers.

The *lo shu* diagram is believed to be a map showing the pattern of movements of the intangible *feng-shui* influences on human fortune. The arrangement of numbers, besides displaying a pattern of changes, has a time and a space dimension. For example, the number six found in the lower right corner of the *lo shu* diagram represents the northwest in terms of space and, with respect to time, it refers to the Age of Six, meaning the sixth 20-year cycle. The last Age of Six fell in the period between the years 1964 and 1983.

The intangible forces of *feng-shui* in the landscape generate benevolent or adverse influences. If there is no landscape, there is no *feng-shui*. A place with good *feng-shui* in fact means that the physical features of the land are in a harmonious relationship with the intangible forces as displayed in the *lo shu* diagram.

Of all the geographical features, there are two important components which generate *feng-shui*. Mountains govern human resources and water and flat land affect economic wealth. A place where mountains feature prominently is often a political centre. On the other hand, places where water is well located are usually financial and economic centres.

In the case of Hong Kong, the main mountain range is Tai Mo Shan which is said to have descended from the huge mountain range of Kun Lun Shan in western China. Tai Mo Shan is located in the northwest of Hong Kong and is 958 metres above sea level. Such a prominent mountain range will certainly bring about human prosperity at the right time, i.e. when the prosperous intangible force arrives at its location: the northwest of Hong Kong (Fig. 45).

If we look up the *lo shu* diagram, we can find the number six in the lower right square, denoting the northwest direction. It means that in the Age of Six (1964-1983), the benevolent intangible influence was situated in the northwest. The presence of Tai Mo Shan in this direction intensified the power of this influence and brought prosperity to Hong Kong. Using the same method, we can see how Hong Kong fares in the present Age of Seven, 1984 to 2003. The *lo shu* diagram shows that the number seven is located in the west. So we need high mountains in the west to create and sustain the prosperous intangible forces in the Age of Seven.

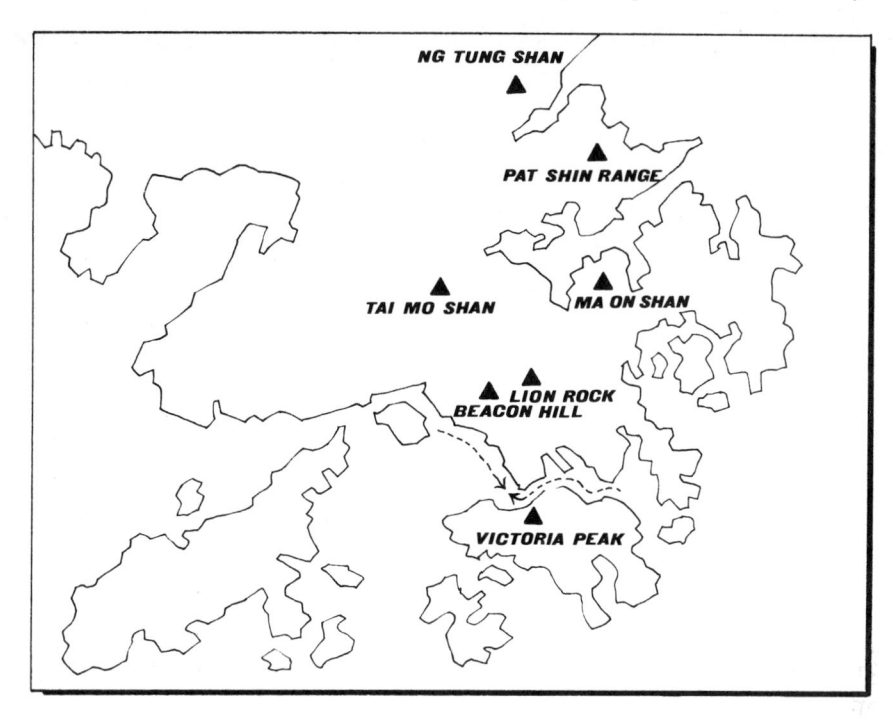

Fig. 45. Map of Hong Kong showing main mountain ranges.

Unfortunately, we only have water to our west. This situation is known as "mountain star falling into water". Although Lantau Island can, to a certain extent, stop prosperity from disappearing quickly, the configuration is very different from the one we experienced in the Age of Six. The obvious effect of "mountain star falls into water" is the loss of human prosperity; in Hong Kong's case it means the brain drain and a crisis of confidence. These are the serious problems we have to face in the Age of Seven. However, a much better situation can be expected in the Age of Eight, the year 2004 onwards. The intangible force number eight is located in the northeast of the *lo shu* diagram, and in our northeast we can find Ma On Shan. Also Ng Tung Mountain in China's Guangdong province enters the New Territories from the northeast. So we can expect prosperity comparable to that of the Age of Six in the Age of Eight.

Fanciful as they may seem, there have been many suggestions to relocate Hong Kong in another part of the world. These stem from the present confidence crisis caused by the imminent return of the territory to Chinese sovereignty in 1997. However, finding a substitute for the good *feng-shui* of Hong Kong presents an insurmountable problem. Hong Kong's good *feng-shui* has been praised by many experts in the field and many appreciate the geographical contribution of Hong Kong's location to the prosperity of the territory.

The Kowloon Peninsula and Hong Kong Island are situated in the dragon's lair of the huge Kun Lun Shan mountain range of Western China. Mountains are called dragons in *feng-shui* and their lairs are where the dragon's benevolent power is believed to concentrate. The mountain is called *yin* (female) and the plain is *yang* (male). Where the mountain descends into a plain *yin* meets *yang* and bears fruit.

62   *Feng-shui and Destiny*

If the landscape at such a junction is well-situated and the surrounding land and water configuration provides protection, such locations are known as the dragon's lair. Here benevolent intangible forces are generated. The Kowloon Peninsula qualifies as a dragon's lair. The huge Kun Lun Shan Range, originating in Central Asia, runs thousands of miles through the mainland and its southern arm enters Guangdong to form Luo Fu Shan. This mountain is 1,281 metres above sea level and it extends into the northeast of the New Territories as Ng Tung Shan, which can be regarded as the nearest ancestor of Kowloon's Tai Mo Shan mountain range.

One arm of Tai Mo Shan ends at north Kowloon to form a plain in front of Beacon Hill and Lion Rock. This plain forms the heart of Kowloon and enjoys the benevolent influences of its far ancestor, the old dragon, Kun Lun Shan. Another branch descends into the sea to the west of Kowloon and re-emerges as Victoria Peak on Hong Kong Island. This again descends to the north to form another dragon's lair at the foot of the mountain. This lair includes Plantation Garden, the Governor's residence and the Hongkong Bank building. As Victoria Peak appears to turn around towards the north to face Tai Mo Shan, this configuration in *feng-shui* is called the dragon turning its head to salute the ancestor.

By "ancestor" we refer to the original dragon from where the Kowloon and Hong Kong mountains descend. In the case of Hong Kong, the "far ancestor" is Kun Lun Shan, one of the largest and tallest mountain ranges in the world. The magnitude of the ancestor determines the intensity of the benevolent forces that the lair can generate. The intangible forces brought to Hong Kong from Kun Lun Shan are certainly massive and long-lasting. As the many arms of Kun Lun Shan form other lairs along the coast of China the question often arises: why is the lair in Kowloon and Hong Kong so special?

The difference is not difficult to see. Lairs generate benevolent forces and they require natural shelters to allow such prosperous forces to concentrate. There is a saying in ancient *feng-shui* books that wind disperses the intangible forces and water stops them from dispersing. Some believe that the name *feng-shui,* meaning wind and water, actually derives from this saying.

So to allow the prosperous forces to concentrate, we need water. Victoria Harbour serves this function well. Besides the Harbour, Hong Kong Island and Victoria Peak together form a natural shield in concentrating the benevolent influences on the flat land on both sides of the harbour. This explains why the dragon turning its head towards its ancestor is considered a superb *feng-shui* configuration.

Feng-shui theories about water are very technical. The most common theory, the *yin* house school of *feng-shui* (evaluation of grave sites), suggests that the direction and location of water flowing near a grave will affect the fortune of the descendents of the deceased. The direction of the grave determines which stretch of water is most desirable. This theory is also applicable to the situation of Hong Kong and Kowloon.

"Near-ancestor" Ng Tung Shan enters Kowloon from the northeast and because of this, the geographical setting of Kowloon is commonly regarded as sitting with its back against the northeast and its front to the southwest. According to the *yin* house theory the best configuration for this setting is water flowing from the northwest to the bright hall (the southwest). Water flowing from the east to the bright hall will also bring money and wealth. Hong Kong is able to satisfy both these conditions. We can thus see that finding a site for a "new Hong Kong" with such good *feng-shui* would be very difficult.

There is, however, a more sophisticated and interesting method of evaluating the *feng-shui* prosperity of a place: using the flying stars school. The procedure is quite similar to that of evaluating *yang* houses, the homes of people. For *yang* houses, the first step is to establish the direction of the building by means of a *lo pan,* but in the case of a city (Hong Kong, for example), its direction is rather difficult to determine as there is no front door or entrance to guide your decision. It is therefore necessary to look at the landscape and make a judgement about the direction on the basis of its mountains, water or flat lands.

In the case of Hong Kong, it is commonly agreed among *feng-shui* experts that the city is sitting with its back to the northeast with its front facing the southwest. The old *feng-shui* concept is that a house must usually have a mountain in the background with water or flat land in front to welcome prosperity. Also, the ancestral mountain of the main Kowloon mountain range, the Tai Mo Shan and Ma On Shan, is part of the Ng Tung Shan range of Shenzhen which enters the New Territories from the northeast.

To set up a flying star chart of a house, we need to know the year in which the house was built. But it is not possible to establish a "formation" date for a piece of land. So we have to apply the primary *lo shu* diagram. The *feng-shui* chart of Hong Kong is shown in Fig. 46.

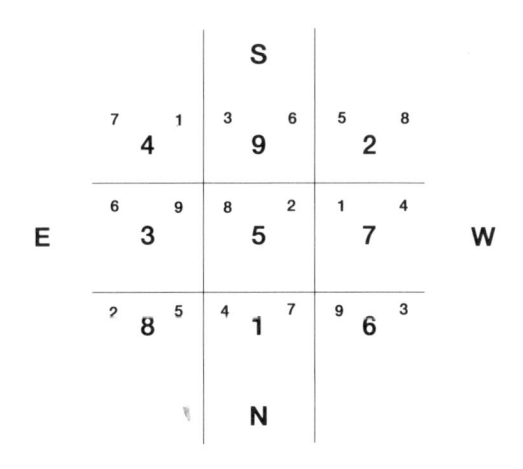

	S	
7 1 4	3 6 9	5 8 2
6 9 3	8 2 5	1 4 7
2 5 8	4 7 1	9 3 6
	N	

E (left) W (right)

Fig. 46. The feng-shui chart of Hong Kong.

The chart shows the distribution of intangible forces in all directions and these *feng-shui* forces will interact with time and space elements to affect our fortune.

Let us first look at the Age of Six, the 20 years between 1964 and 1983. From the *feng-shui* chart we find the number six as a mountain star in the east and another six as a water star to the south. Following the principle that the prosperous mountain star should be placed on the mountain, and the prosperous water star in water, let us check whether the landscape of Hong Kong fits in well with the principles which are supposed to generate and sustain the prosperity of number six. Indeed, we find the sea to the south of Hong Kong, and, to the east, there is a massive piece of land with prominent mountains like the Kowloon Peak, Buffalo

Hill and Ma On Shan.

The good configuration of mountains means human prosperity, while the suitable location of water results in economic gain in the Age of Six between 1964 and 1983. After 1983, we entered a new 20-year cycle called the Age of Seven, and the number seven governs the ruling intangible forces as the number six cycle faded away. The seven is located in the north as a water star and in the southeast as a mountain star. As our north is a mountainous area and our southeast is the sea, the situation is the reverse of the Age of Six. This configuration is described as "the mountain star falling into water and the water star being on the mountain". Such a configuration means failure to sustain prosperity in the Age of Seven.

The Age of Eight, the years between 2004 and 2023, will see the water star eight return to the ocean in the southwest and the mountain star eight going into the centre of the land. So we can predict that there will be another glorious period for Hong Kong in the Age of Eight.

One interesting aspect of this method is that we can also make evaluation on a yearly or monthly basis. Take Fig. 47 which is a star chart showing the distribution of intangible forces in the year 1989. By superimposing this star chart onto the Hong Kong *feng-shui* chart of Fig. 46, one can see a heavy concentration of the *shar* of five, the most unfavourable in the system, to the northeast of Hong Kong. Beijing is situated in the northeast of China and is certainly under the influence of the *shar* of five in 1989. Incidentally, 1989 was the year when the Tiananmen Square incident occured in Beijing.

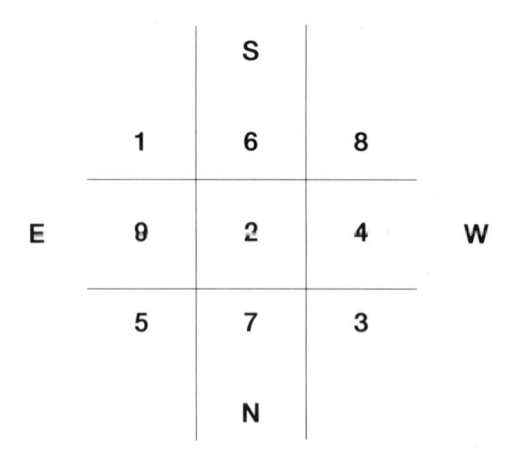

	S	
1	6	8
9	2	4
5	7	3
	N	

E (left) W (right)

Fig. 47. The feng-shui influences in 1989.

25. The Chinese Birth Chart and Your Fortune

Learning to master *feng-shui* can be a very long process as it cannot be isolated from other branches of Chinese fortune-telling. Indeed, there is a vast treasure house of fortune-telling techniques in Chinese culture , many of which supplement and enrich the art of *feng-shui*.

For example, the *I Ching* oracle can be applied to gain clues about the presence of supernatural beings or apparitions in a house. Also, as explained in the homicide cases recorded in Master Sum's *feng-shui* theories, a thorough knowledge about the *kua* of the *I Ching* can help analyse events in great detail. Besides the *I Ching* oracle, another area of study that a *feng-shui* student should master is the technique of reading a person's fortune using his birth data. The commonly used method is the Four Pillars of Destiny.

The Four Pillars refer to the four components of a person's birth data: the year, month, day and hour. Unlike the Western calendar, which is merely a numerical series, the Chinese Xia calendar (which originated in the Xia dynasty in the 21st century BC), is more complex. It not only records the passage of time, but it also incorporates the space dimension showing the interaction of the earth with other planets and constellations in the universe.

Take for example the year 1989. In the Western calendar, the figure 1989 only indicates that it is the 1,989th year after the birth of Christ. In the Xia calendar, however, the year of the snake also indicates that the planet Jupiter is in the southeast direction. This calendar also reflects the position of the earth in relation to the zodiac. In the past, Chinese farmers relied heavily on the Xia calendar to forecast weather conditions for growing crops. There is also much folklore and many traditional beliefs surrounding the important days in the calendar.

Here are a few interesting examples. The first day of the Xia calendar year is called the spring date, and it is held that on this day, eggs can stand on their ends because the universe is considered to be in a state of grand balance. It is also held that we are likely to experience thunder and lightning on the first day of the second month when animals wake up from their hibernation. There will always be rain during the Ching Ming Festival on the first day of the third month. However, it is important to bear in mind that the Xia calendar is not the same as the Chinese lunar calendar which is based on the motion of the moon. The Xia calendar can be regarded as a solar calendar, based on the earth's movement around the sun, and the months are divided according to the position of the earth in orbit.

An important philosophical element behind the Chinese Xia calendar is the theory of the five basic elements — metal, wood, water, fire and earth — which the Chinese believe to be the basic properties of the universe. In the Xia calendar, years, months, days and hours are not expressed in numbers but are written in pairs of Chinese characters representing the five elements. In this manner, the calendar also indicates the life cycle of the five elements.

	Metal	**Wood**	**Water**	**Fire**
Spring	die	prosper	weak	born
Summer	born	weak	die	prosper
Autumn	prosper	die	born	weak
Winter	weak	born	prosper	die

Table 6. Seasonal cycle of the basic elements.

Table 6 shows how the five elements go through the cycle of birth, maturity and death during the four seasons. The earth element is not listed in this table as earth is considered basic and neutral. So its prosperous period is at the end of each of the four seasons which is the third month of each season: March, June, September and December. As the five elements are considered the basic components of everything in the universe, including human beings, reading the life cycle and the inter-relationships of the five elements indicated in the Xia calendar is an accurate method of fortune-telling. The Four Pillars of Destiny developed from such a system is therefore a tool linking human fortune with the universe.

Unlike many other branches of fortune-telling which require the drawing up of complicated natal charts showing the distribution of planets, the Four Pillars of Destiny is unique in its simplicity. You consult the calendar and list the birth data of a person by year, month, day and hour, in the form of eight Chinese characters. Then you evaluate the inter-relationship between the five elements as represented by the eight characters. This method of fortune-telling is therefore known as the eight characters method. In essence, the day when the person is born represents the individual self, and the other seven characters represent his status, health, wealth, character, temperament, family relationships and potential. The information one can draw from the simple eight characters is abundant and accurate.

The philosophy behind the Four Pillars is that a person's nature and abilities are determined by the elements prevailing at the time of his birth. As the individual matures, the five elements as revealed in the Xia calendar come into play and they interact with the person's inborn characteristics to create fortune and misfortune, joy and sorrow. Therefore, you can compare a person's birth data to a motor car. Positive birth data is comparable to an expensive car like a Rolls Royce. The passage through time is like the car travelling on the road. If the road is smooth, i.e. if the five elements are favourable, the good car will have a hazard-free journey.

On the other hand, if the road is rough, i.e. if the five elements in the calendar are unfavourable, even the Rolls Royce may not be able to travel far. The birth data thus reflect life and the passage through time represents luck. The combination of good birth data and good luck will give the best results, and the reverse is equally true.

Nowadays, experienced *feng-shui* practitioners are keen to check the birth data of the household they are evaluating. The reason is that the objective of *feng-shui* is to study how the environment affects human fortune, and how the influences on different people vary in intensity and nature. For example, if a house with three or four dwellers has bad *feng-shui*, the adverse intangible forces do not always affect everyone under the same roof. One explanation for this phenomenon is that not everyone occupies the same room or sleeps in the same location. Those who are situated in the worst spots suffer most. But one factor we cannot ignore is that some houses are particularly bad for certain people as they are especially susceptible to the effects of some houses with bad *feng-shui*. If anything bad happens, such persons will be the ones who suffer most.

The eight houses *feng-shui* school lays great emphasis on a person's year of birth. This school of thought classifies a person into eight different *kua* according to the year of birth. The eight *kua* are again divided into two major groups: east four persons and west four persons. Persons of the east four camp live best in east four category houses and persons of the west four camp should dwell in west four houses.

This division into two camps is not the focal point of the flying star school of *feng-shui*. However, it also takes into account the *kua* of a person which, under some circumstances, will be the paramount factor in determining whether he is compatible with the house. Fig. 48 is the birth chart for an Age of Six house with its front facing west and back facing east.

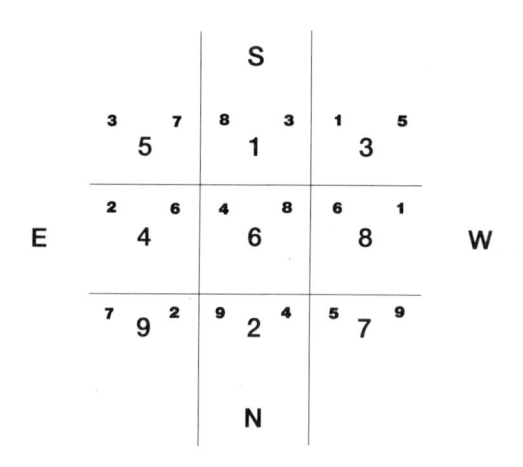

```
                    S
        
        3   7   8   3   1   5
          5       1       3
        
        2   6   4   8   6   1
  E       4       6       8     W
        
        7   2   9   4   5   9
          9       2       7
        
                    N
```

Fig. 48. Birth chart of an Age of Six house.

The small figures four and eight are located in the centre squares. Four represents the wood element and eight represents the earth element. As wood will destroy earth, the four will pose a threat to the eight. So this house is not suitable for persons born under the *kua* of eight or *ken kua*. An examination of Table 3 on page 25 will show that persons of the *kua* of eight are men born in the years 1947, 1956, 1965, 1974 and 1983 and women born in 1945, 1948, 1954, 1957, 1963, 1966, 1972, 1975, 1981 and 1984. *Ken kua* also symbolises a young boy. So if a boy born in 1983 dwells in the house, he will be most susceptible to misfortune.

Another important factor in the birth year of a person is the animal sign of his birth year. Particular animal signs are incompatible or will "clash" with certain house directions. For example, persons born in the year of the rat should avoid living in a house with its back against the south. Persons born in the year of the horse should not live in a house with its back against the north. One other important application of the birth data in *feng-shui* is the determination of suitable colour tones and decorative objects for a person. To make accurate arrangements one must master the technique of the Four Pillars of Destiny.

By listing a person's birth data, one can observe the relationship of the five elements as shown in the eight characters. The day when the person is born represents the individual self. If the day belongs to the element wood, then the person is generally considered a "wood man". Then one should see how the wood stands among the other elements as represented by the year, month and hour.

If the wood man was born in spring when wood is most prosperous (and there are not many metals to threaten the wood, and there is water to give it nourishment), the wood is considered strong. Strong wood needs metal to control it, cut and trim it into useful tools and furniture, and it also needs earth to release its excess energy (wood destroys earth.) So if a person is in the category of strong wood, the suitable colours for him will be metallic, gold, silver, white or earth-yellow. The best decorative objects for the home are metallic or earthy objects such as porcelain ware and pottery. He should avoid too many plants and aquarium tanks at home.

On the other hand, if the wood man is born in autumn, when metal is most prosperous and wood is at its weakest, he then needs water and more wood to support his life. The best colour scheme for him is black, representing water, and green, representing wood. His decorative objects should be plants, wooden furniture and aquarium tanks. He should avoid colours like white and gold and too many metallic objects. Red, representing fire, will also draw away his energy.

The above is a simplified model demonstrating a rough idea of the working of the Four Pillars and how it is employed to supplement *feng-shui* evaluation of a house.

Bank of China building

The Governor's House

Victoria Harbour

World Wide House

Escalators in a shopping arcade

The new Hongkong Bank building

Bronze lions at entrance of Hongkong Bank building

PART TWO

26. The Four Pillars of Destiny

The Four Pillars of Destiny is regarded by many as one of the most accurate means of fortune-telling in the world. The uniqueness of this fascinating system lies in its presentation. Unlike many other branches of fortune-telling which require the drawing up of complicated horoscopes, it only requires the translation of the four components of a person's birth data - year, month, day and hour — each into a pair of Chinese "numerical" characters, each pair called a "pillar". Therefore the method is also commonly known as the Eight Characters besides the Four Pillars.

The origin of this classical technique dates back to ancient Chinese mythology. After thousands of years of using the birth year as the main means of assessment, a genius named Tzu Ping (literally meaning "water in a balanced state") who lived between 907 and 960 re-organised and refined the traditional method into its present form, using the birth date to assess an individual's fortune. It therefore also acquired its present name: Tzu Ping's Eight Characters.

The apparent simplicity in its presentation by no means restricts the four pillars' capacity and scope as an efficient method of fortune-telling. The system is structured on the vast background of the classical Chinese philosophy of the *I Ching* (The Book of Changes), the *tai chi* (the universe), the *yin* and *yang* (the female and the male principles), the principle of the five elements, as well as meteorology and astronomy. By simply listing out the eight characters, an expert in the art will be able to describe, with a high degree of accuracy, a person's character, behaviour, family and social relationships, potentials and achievements, physique, health, etc. Further pairs of characters can also be derived from the basic four pillars to trace the path of fortune. Therefore, as soon as a person's birth data is written down in the format of the four pillars, experts of the art can accurately describe the person's appearance, outlook, and background - like reading a book. He can even forecast his potential achievements and failures, his marriage life, etc. The boundaries of this mysterious technique are yet to be explored.

Expressed in simpler terms, the fundamental theory underlying the four pillars is a matter of balance and harmony. The ancient Chinese believed that the universe is constituted of five basic elements - metal, wood, water, fire and earth. Each character of the four pillars represents an element and good fortune will follow a well-balanced inter-relationship between the five elements. On the other hand, upsetting such balance will bring misfortune and degrade the quality of life.

The value of this ingenious system lies not only in its efficiency and accuracy but also in its intelligent interpretation and revelation of human nature which can always provide guidance for a balanced and harmonious way of living. The technique is therefore treasured and respected by many, not merely as a fortune-telling tool but also as a body of human philosophy, having a profound influence on Chinese culture and traditions.

The process of fortune-telling by the Four Pillars of Destiny involves the following basic procedures. The first step is to put down a person's birth data - year, month, day and hour - and translate them into Chinese characters. To achieve this, the most convenient way is to consult a book called the *Ten Thousand Years Calendar* which is commonly available in Hong Kong and Taiwan book stores. This book contains tables with the Chinese calendar

72 Feng-shui and Destiny

shown against the Western calendar; it is very easy to use.

Having found the Chinese equivalent of a birthday in the Western calendar from this book, we have now 8 Chinese characters in hand, representing the four pillars - year, month, day and hour. The Chinese characters are usually written in four vertical pairs. The upper characters are called "heavenly stems" and the ones underneath are called "earthly branches".

Evaluating the Four Pillars of Destiny is an art of analysing and balancing the strengths of the five basic elements. Therefore, the next step is to find out what elements each Chinese character represents. For readers' quick reference, Table 7 shows the elements as represented by each of the heavenly stems and earthly branches.

Heavenly Stems	Earthly Branches
甲 – *Yang* Wood	子 – Water (Rat)
乙 – *Yin* Wood	丑 – Earth (Ox)
丙 – *Yang* Fire	寅 – Wood (Tiger)
丁 – *Yin* Fire	卯 – Wood (Rabbit)
戊 – *Yang* Earth	辰 – Earth (Dragon)
己 – *Yin* Earth	巳 – Fire (Snake)
庚 – *Yang* Metal	午 – Fire (Horse)
辛 – *Yin* Metal	未 – Earth (Goat)
壬 – *Yang* Water	申 – Metal (Monkey)
癸 – *Yin* Water	酉 – Metal (Cockerel)
	戌 – Earth (Dog)
	亥 – Water (Pig)

Table 7. Heavenly stems and earthly branches.

Readers will note that the five elements are categorised into *yang* and *yin*. In general, *yang* means strong, male and positive, and *yin* means weak, female and negative. The purpose of division of elements into *yang* and *yin* is to distinguish between stronger and weaker characters. For example, *yang* wood is often compared to a tall, thick tree. *Yin* wood is compared to flowers, grass or branches of a tree. *Yang* fire symbolises sunlight and *yin* fire represents candle flame, etc.

With all the elements written down, we can now perform some simple analyses. The essential step is to examine the day pillar. The heavenly stem of this pillar represents the person himself. Fig. 49 shows a sample Pillars of Destiny of a prominent man born on December 26, 1893. As the heavenly stem of the day pillar is *yin* fire, the person is regarded as a "fire man".

Hour	Day	Month	Year
甲	丁	甲	癸
Wood	Fire	Wood	Water
辰	酉	子	巳
Earth	Metal	Water	Fire

Fig. 49. Sample Pillars of Destiny.

Then we have to look at the disposition of the fire element in relation to the other elements. The fire man is born in the winter season, and the year pillar and month pillar show strong water influence. As strong water suppresses fire, we can conclude that the position of the fire is quite weak. Fortunately, there are two wood elements on either side of the day pillar to support the fire. Therefore, the wood will act as life supporters of the fire and will be essential in achieving equilibrium of power between fire and water in this set of Four Pillars of Destiny.

Let us look deeper into the relationships among the elements of water, wood and fire. Water is naturally the destroyer of fire. However, with the appearance of wood, water turns out to be a helpful element to the fire as it supports wood (wood needs water for its growth and survival) which in turn supports the fire person. This means that the fire man is able to keep his enemies — water — under control and win the support of many subordinates (wood). Hence he is a powerful and resourceful man with great talent in manipulating power. He is indeed such a person as this Four Pillars of Destiny belongs to Chairman Mao Zedong of China.

This is an elementary example to show the initial steps of forune-telling by the Four Pillars of Destiny. Readers can see that it is essentially logical deduction on the basis of a simple theory of the five elements explained earlier in this book. If readers gradually get familiar with the technique, they will discover that more fascinating details about human fortune can be exposed from a person's Pillars of Destiny.

The subsequent chapters of this book show readers many more examples and demonstrate in detail how the life and fortune of many prominent persons are accurately reflected in their respective Pillars of Destiny, which is indeed a valid tool enabling us to foresee our future and to make accurate predictions before things happen.

27. Hu Yaobang: The Destiny of a Reformer

The Four Pillars of Destiny is at the root of the whole Chinese system of metaphysics. It reveals the nature of destiny and helps to cast light on the eternal question of human existence. The *I Ching* oracle can be expressed by symbols of continuous or broken lines, the flying star school of *feng-shui* can be expressed in terms of numbers, but the Four Pillars of Destiny can only be expressed by complex Chinese characters called "heavenly stems" and "earthly branches". We shall examine Hu Yaobang's life and see what his birth data, using the four pillars, can tell us about his fortune.

Mr Hu (the late General Secretary of the Chinese Communist Party) was born between 2300 and 2400 hours on November 20, 1915. When expressed in Chinese characters, the birth data can be written as shown in Fig. 50a:

Fig. 50a - 50b. Mr Hu Yaobang's Four Pillars of Destiny.

Hour	Day	Month	Year
丙	乙	丁	乙
子	卯	亥	卯

Fig. 50a.

Hour	Day	Month	Year
丙	乙	丁	乙
Fire	Wood	Fire	Wood
子	卯	亥	卯
Water	Wood	Water	Wood

Fig. 50b.

The upper character is called the heavenly stem; the one underneath the earthly branch. Table 7 on page 72 will enable readers to check which of the five basic elements each of the characters represents. According to the table, we can express Mr Hu's birth data in terms of the five basic elements, as shown in Fig. 50b.

The first step in the reading of birth data is to focus on the day pillar which represents the individual self. In this case the day pillar is 乙卯 and the table shows it is wood on top of wood. The same wood-on-wood configuration is also found in the year pillar, meaning that Mr Hu was a wood person with strong roots and firm foundations.

Hu Yaobang: The Destiny of a Reformer 75

The next thing to check is what season such wood was born in. The month pillar shows that Mr Hu was born in winter when water is most prosperous. Also in the eight characters, one can see that the water element features prominently in the month and hour pillars. As water gives birth and nourishment to wood, such a configuration means the already strong wood is further strengthened by the strong water. So the wood is considered excessively strong.

One thing to note, however, is that such strong wood is of the *yin* (female) category, which must be distinguished from *yang* wood. *Yang* wood (male) is often compared to the trunk of a tree which is stubborn and "unbendable" unless the trunk itself is broken. *Yin* wood, on the other hand, is compared to the small branches of a tree such as the willow, or "bendable" grass or plants. So such configuration of strong *yin* wood shows that Mr Hu had a strong character but was a flexible person. He was not stubborn and would accept opinions and changes. The prominent water element present in the birth data gives him more than sufficient nourishment, implying that Mr Hu was a knowledgeable person and a keen learner.

An examination of the other characters will show two fire elements sitting high on the month and hour pillars. Wood gives birth to fire, so fire releases the energy from the wood: these represent the aspirations of Mr Hu. The presence of some kind of prominent aspiration outlet in a person's birth data means that he is a very intelligent, ambitious and resourceful person with the ability to express himself well.

The birth data can even accurately indicate the physical appearance of the subject. As mentioned above, *yin* wood represents a thin twig or willow which was also an appropriate description of Mr Hu's frail figure. One can also see that the birth data lack the metal and earth elements. Metal symbolises bone and skeleton, earth symbolises fat and muscle. The lack of these elements indicates a person of slight build.

The birth data of Hu Yaobang, a *yin* wood person born in the midnight hours (the hour of the rat), are considered very noble in classical works of the Four Pillars of Destiny. There are many examples in history of such birth data belonging to noblemen and high ranking imperial officials. One example is the birth data of the famous Empress Dowager of the Ching Dynasty, who also belongs to the same category of "*yin* wood born in rat hours". Her birth data are shown in Fig. 50c and readers can observe its startling similarity to those of Mr Hu's.

Hour	Day	Month	Year
丙	乙	丁	乙
Fire	Wood	Fire	Wood
子	卯	亥	丑
Water	Wood	Water	Earth

Fig. 50c. The Four Pillars of Destiny of the Empress Dowager

76 Feng-shui and Destiny

The first step in reading a person's destiny is to express his birth data in four pairs of stems and branches. As demonstrated, the general appearance of Mr Hu Yaobang, the late Chinese Communist Party General Secretary, can be easily seen in such a simple arrangement of eight Chinese characters. After acquainting oneself with a person's innate character and potential by examining his Four Pillars, the next step is to read his fortune by listing out his Luck which is also expressed in the form of heavenly stems and earthly branches. Fig. 50d shows Mr Hu's Four Pillars of Destiny as well as Luck.

	Hour	Day	Month	Year
	丙	乙	丁	乙
	Fire	Wood	Fire	Wood
	子	卯	亥	卯
	Water	Wood	Water	Wood

64	54	44	34	24	14	4
庚	辛	壬	癸	甲	乙	丙
Metal	Metal	Water	Water	Wood	Wood	Fire
辰	巳	午	未	申	酉	戌
Earth	Fire	Fire	Earth	Metal	Metal	Earth

Fig. 50d. Mr Hu Yaobang's full set of Pillars of Destiny and Luck.

The upper lines show the birth data of Mr Hu expressed in the form of Four Pillars of Destiny. The lower line figures are his luck pillars derived from his birth data. The figures on top of each luck pillar show a person's age when he comes under their influence. For example, on the first luck pillar 丙戌 the number four indicates that this pillar governs Mr Hu's luck from the age of four until the age of 14 when the next luck pillar 乙酉 comes into play. A luck pillar will govern a period of ten years. The heavenly stem covers the first five years and the earthly branch covers the period from the sixth to the tenth year. The five basic elements, taken from Table 7, are also listed under each Chinese character for easy reference.

As explained earlier, Mr Hu belonged to the excessively strong wood category as his birth data contained very strong wood and water elements and lacked metal to control the wood energy. Having decided on the strength of a person's birth data, one has to evaluate what element will provide the person the best influence and luck. In doing so, one should bear in mind that the philosophy of balance and harmony is always behind Chinese culture. Anything excessive is against the cosmic order and some actions have to be taken or some other elements have to be employed to restore the balance. In the case of the four pillars, it is a general rule that weak wood needs water and wood to support and assist its survival. Strong wood, on the other hand, needs metal to control it and earth to release its excess energy.

Such rules are generally applicable to ordinary birth data. However, Mr Hu was such a noble person that his birth data were also extraordinary. The wood element in his birth data is excessively strong. To obstruct it with metal and earth would only cause a clash and conflict, hence more disharmony. Therefore, the best treatment is to "follow the trend" and allow the wood to grow and proceed at its full power and avoid any obstructions (metal and earth) on its path. So water and wood would bring good fortune to Mr Hu. And metal and earth were his foes. As fire gives birth to earth and conflicts with water, it is also considered unfavourable.

Hu Yaobang

78   Feng-shui and Destiny

Having examined the configuration of the four pillars and established the favourable and unfavourable elements, we have only got a general picture of the person's appearance and potentials. To further peep into a person's fortune all through his life span, and make predictions about his ups and downs in life, we must see what impact he will receive from year to year. Each year brings about influences of different elements and such influence we can check from the Xia calendar as mentioned on page 72.

Each Chinese character taken from the Xia calendar represents a basic element. As a year is represented by two characters, so a year will bring about influences by two elements. For example, the year 1989 is a year of earth over fire and the year 1991 is a year of metal over earth. These elements have impact on each person's Four Pillars of Destiny and bring about good or bad changes depending on how they react with the person's original set of Pillars of Destiny at birth.

Let us now return to the four pillars of Mr Hu Yaobang and see how the yearly impact caused his ups and downs in the political arena.

Recent events have demonstrated how metal and earth adversely affected Mr Hu's career and brought about his death. In 1967 (a year of fire and earth), when Mr Hu was about 52 and in the luck pillar of fire, he was dragged down and purged by the Red Guards in the Cultural Revolution. During the following two years (1968 and 1969), both years of earth and metal, Mr Hu was forced to live in a cattle shed and suffered tremendous hardship. In 1987 (although a year of fire and wood), the wood element was consumed by the strong fire element. Mr Hu was 62 years of age and in the luck pillar of metal and fire. He stepped down from power in the anti-bourgeois liberalism campaign in January, a month of metal and earth. In 1989, a year of fire and earth, Mr Hu was in the luck pillar of metal and earth. He died in April, the month of earth. And it was on the 15th morning, the day and hour when fire and metal totally engulfed the wood element. It is interesting to note that the Empress Dowager, who had quite similar birth data, met her death in the year 1909 — 己酉 — which was also a year of earth and metal.

28. The Ups and Downs of Zhao Ziyang

To study the Four Pillars of Destiny of VIPs is a very interesting subject as their ups and downs are closely related to the fate of nations. This is especially so in China where power is highly centralised and in the hands of only a few people. There is however a big obstacle: the birth data of Chinese leaders are often hard to find. The only source is their biographies available in bookstores and on magazine stands. But as these leaders are generally over 70 years old and they were born in an age of upheavals and revolutions, the accuracy of their birth data is very doubtful and careful research is necessary before it can be verified.

One interesting example is the birth data of Zhao Ziyang, the former General Secretary of the Chinese Communist Party. Mr Zhao's recorded birthday is October 17, 1919, according to the Western calendar, which when converted into the four pillars, is as illustrated in Fig. 51a.

The Four Pillars of Destiny shows him to be a water person born in September which is the season of earth. As earth destroys water and the prominent wood element in the four pillars also consumes considerable water energy (water gives birth to wood), the configuration shows Mr Zhao is a weak water person. Even if he were born between 9 pm and 11 pm, the hours of metal and water, his water element is still too weak to represent a powerful leader such as Mr Zhao. It is therefore questionable whether this is his true date of birth and it is likely that October 17, 1919, as recorded in his biography, was in fact taken directly from the Chinese lunar calendar. This converts into the four pillars as shown in Fig. 51b.

Hour	Day	Month	Year
辛	壬	甲	己
Metal	Water	Wood	Earth
亥	寅	戌	未
Water	Wood	Earth	Earth

Fig. 51a.

Hour	Day	Month	Year
丁	甲	乙	己
Fire	Wood	Wood	Earth
卯	午	亥	未
Wood	Fire	Water	Earth

Fig. 51b.

Fig. 51a - 51b. The two sets of four pillars of Mr Zhao Ziyang.

This new configuration shows a strongly built and tall wood person with an appearance more in keeping with that of Mr Zhao. There are many points which suggest that this is the more accurate birth date.

A water person, especially weak water, is usually round and fat with weak muscles. Mr Zhao was a tall, sturdy figure, more like a strong wood person. His thick lips reflect the presence of a strong fire element in his four pillars. Fire is absent from the set of four pillars in Fig. 51a, but conspicuous in Fig. 51b. A water person usually has a round or square face. The long, oval shaped face of Mr Zhao reflects a combination of fire and wood as shown in Fig. 51b. The weak water person in Fig. 51a does not portray a strong man. He is a follower, unlike the strong wood person who belongs to the *yang* wood category, much like Mr Hu Yaobang. As mentioned in the previous chapter on Mr Hu Yaobang, *yang* wood is often compared to the trunk of a tree which is stubborn and unbendable.

80 *Feng-shui and Destiny*

One interesting aspect of the four pillars is that it also reveals the person's relationship with his family. It was recorded in Mr Zhao's biography that his father was a rich landlord and Mr Zhao was the only son. At childhood, Mr Zhao received his communist education at the village school and became acquainted with some Communist Party members. He joined the struggle against the Nationalists at a very young age and provided asylum for the communists at his home. This shows that Mr Zhao's father must have been on good terms with his son and gave him his support. This kind of close relationship between father and son is also shown in Fig. 51b.

The year pillar represents the grandfather's generation, the month pillar symbolises the father's and the day pillar is the individual's own pillar. The hour pillar stands for his offspring. The month pillar in Fig. 51b is wood, the same element as the day pillar. So we can deduce that Mr Zhao's father shares his son's ideology. However, in Fig. 51a, the month pillar is wood but the day pillar water. Water gives birth to and supports wood but as the water is weak, the father (wood) is unhelpful to the son (water), as it draws away the already weak water energy. This is not consistent with Mr Zhao's biography and is a good example of how the four pillars of a person can be verified and reconstructed.

Having established the more likely birth data of Zhao Ziyang, we will now go on to check whether the Four Pillars of Destiny can accurately reflect his ups and downs in politics. For such an exercise, we will have to list his luck pillars as well. Each luck pillar governs a person's fortune for 10 years. The upper character usually prevails during the first five years. The lower character takes control during the remaining five years. The full set of Mr Zhao's Four Pillars of Destiny and Luck is shown in Fig. 51c.

	Hour	Day	Month	Year
	丁	甲	乙	己
	Fire	Wood	Wood	Earth
	卯	午	亥	未
	Wood	Fire	Water	Earth

70	60	50	40	30	20	10
戊	己	庚	辛	壬	癸	甲
Earth	Earth	Metal	Metal	Water	Water	Wood
辰	巳	午	未	申	酉	戌
Earth	Fire	Fire	Earth	Metal	Metal	Earth

Fig. 51c. Mr Zhao Ziyang's Four Pillars of Destiny and Luck.

The configuration shows Mr Zhao is a wood person of the *yang* category (male). Wood needs water to support its growth. Born in the winter season when water is in a prosperous phase of its life cycle, the wood is able to obtain sufficient nourishment. On the other hand, readers can also see a prominent fire element present in the four pillars. Such fire draws away the wood's energy.

So weighing the strength of all the elements, we can consider the wood to be fairly balanced with the support of water on the one hand, and fire to release its energy on the other. Such a configuration reflects a very intelligent and resourceful person. A man with balanced four pillars will be susceptible to the influence of his luck pillars which easily tilt the balance and cause the ups and downs in his life. In the case of Mr Zhao, we can see that water brings him good fortune as it gives nourishment to wood. So metal is also favourable as metal gives birth to water. On the other hand, fire and earth have a weakening effect on wood and bring bad luck. Let us pick out some significant years in Mr Zhao's life for examination.

Zhao Ziyang

Mr Zhao got married in 1940, a year of metal when he was 21 years old and in the luck pillar of water and metal. In 1943, a year of water, Mr Zhao was still in the luck pillar of water and metal. He led the Communist soldiers to defeat an army of Nationalist forces and established his firm position in the Communist Party. In the following years, between the ages of 20 and 30, Mr Zhao continued to play an active role in the Communist Revolution. His position was very much strengthened during the civil war years. His career in the Communist Party reached new heights in 1960, a year of metal and water when he was appointed General Secretary of Guangdong province. He was 41 years old at the time and in the luck pillar of metal.

His luck turned in 1966, a year of fire, when the Cultural Revolution broke out. In 1967, another year of fire and earth, he came under severe attack and was purged by the Red Guards. He was detained and later imprisoned in Guangdong. During these dark years, Mr Zhao was in the luck pillar of earth. 1972 was a year of water. During this year, Mr Zhao was reinstated and he was re-appointed General Secretary of Guangdong province. Another period of metal and water (1980 - 1984), brought him to a new peak in his career in the Communist Party. He was appointed to the Politburo Standing Committee in 1980 and worked up the ladder towards the position of General Party Secretary.

In 1989, Mr Zhao was in the luck pillar of fire 乙. The year was 乙乙 (Year of the Snake). The month from May 5 to June 6 was again 乙乙. We note the multiple number of the character 乙 that appeared in May 1989. The character belongs to the fire element and sets out to clash against the water element in Mr Zhao's four pillars. The accumulated power of the snake 乙 was so overwhelming that it destroyed the water's nourishment and upset the balance in the four pillars. Thus May was a disastrous month for Mr Zhao. The four pillars reveal a critical situation for Mr Zhao in 1989. The disastrous events were brought about by a concentration of fire and earth elements.

29. In Search of the Birth Data of Deng Xiaoping

In 1989 there were many rumours surrounding the fate of Deng Xiaoping. With his often prolonged absence from public life, suspicions were bound to arise but they were invariably crushed by his re-appearance with his usual vigour when meeting foreign visitors and delegations.

It is very tempting to check such rumours against Mr Deng's Four Pillars of Destiny which can often cast light on a person's health and luck. However, it is hard to make accurate predictions as his full birth data is not available. It is widely documented that Mr Deng was born on August 22, 1904, but no birth hour is ever mentioned. Many experts and students in the field have evaluated the available data, and opinions about Mr Deng's birth hour are divided. Most people believe he was born in the morning just before noon giving him a four pillars chart as shown in Fig. 52a.

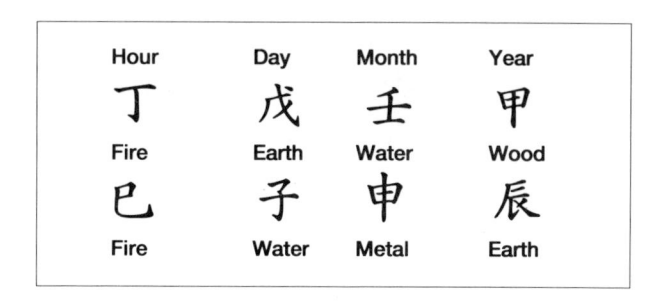

	Hour	Day	Month	Year
	丁	戊	壬	甲
	Fire	Earth	Water	Wood
	巳	子	申	辰
	Fire	Water	Metal	Earth

Fig. 52a. Mr Deng Xiaoping's Pillars of Destiny with birth hour at 9 – 11 am.

The four pillars shows Mr Deng is an earth person born in autumn when metal and water are most prosperous. If we look at the first three known pillars, year, month and day, we cannot see any fire element to support the earth (fire gives birth to earth). So Mr Deng belongs to the weak earth category. Weak earth needs fire to support it. As fire is absent from the first three known pillars, it is logical to assume there should be a strong fire element in the fourth pillar to make Mr Deng such a powerful person. It is therefore generally believed that Mr Deng was born between 9 am and 11 am as these hours provide the fire elements lacking in the first three pillars. On the basis of the assumption that Mr Deng is an "out of season" earth person and needs fire to give him warmth and support, we can expect that the fire and earth elements will bring him good fortune, and the metal and water elements will bring him misfortune.

With such data we can examine some significant years in Mr Deng's past to establish whether this estimated time of birth is correct. For example, the Cultural Revolution years (1966 and 1967) were the most depressing years in his life as he was stripped of all his authority and he and his family suffered extreme hardship. If the above assumption about his birth hour is correct, these years should be characterised by heavy water and metal. However, the years 1966 and 1967 were years of fire and Mr Deng was in the luck pillar of earth and wood. There is a total absence of metal and water elements.

One effective technique often employed to verify a birth date is to check the family background against the month pillar. This often reveals the relationship between the person and his father. In the case of Mr Deng, his month pillar belongs to strong water and metal elements which are supposed to be unfavourable to him. However, the fact is that Mr Deng was from a rich family and spent his childhood in comfort and luxury. So the assumption that water and earth bring him misfortune again fails in this test. Therefore, a birth time of between 9 am and 11 am is not acceptable.

Another school of thought (the minority) considers that Mr Deng was born in the early hours of the same day which gives him a pure water or pure wood hour pillar. Fig. 52b shows the configuration of four pillars drawn on the basis of a 3 am to 5 am birth hour.

	Hour	Day	Month	Year
	甲 Wood	戊 Earth	壬 Water	甲 Wood
	寅 Wood	子 Water	申 Metal	辰 Earth

86	76	66	56	46	36	26	16
辛 Metal	庚 Metal	己 Earth	戊 Earth	丁 Fire	丙 Fire	乙 Wood	甲 Wood
巳 Fire	辰 Earth	卯 Wood	寅 Wood	丑 Earth	子 Water	亥 Water	戌 Earth

Fig. 52b. Mr Deng Xiaoping's Pillars of Destiny (with birth hour at 3 - 5 am) and Luck.

The essential feature of this set of four pillars is the absence of fire to give support to the weak earth, and in its place, there are strong wood elements to suppress and destroy the earth. The theory is that if the day pillar, i.e. the individual self, is extremely weak, it will submit completely to the strongest element and adopt the characteristics of this element. This is called "surrender to the leader". In this case, there is absolutely no chance for the weak earth to survive with the strong wood in the hour pillar, so the earth submits and changes its property to those of metal and water which are the strongest in the four pillars. Anything that assists the earth and stimulates its revival (fire and earth) will bring him bad luck, anything that supports the strongest element (metal and water) brings him good fortune. The birth hour of 3 am to 5 am passes the two tests mentioned above. The years of fire, 1966 and 1967, brought him misfortune during the Cultural Revolution, and the years of metal, 1980 and 1981, put him back in power with the downfall of the Gang of Four. Assuming this latter birth hour is correct, the year of the Snake, when earth and fire are in the ascendancy, represents an uncomfortable year for Mr Deng. The Tiananmen Square incident occurred in this year.

Deng Xiaoping

30. The Rise and Fall of Margaret Thatcher

The Four Pillars of Destiny is generally regarded as a profound yet handy technique of fortune-telling. Its uniqueness lies in the simplicity of its starting procedure and format as one needs only translate birth data from the Western calendar to the Chinese calendar, then convert the Chinese characters into the five basic elements. Many other branches of fortune-telling, such as astrology, require much time in preparing the complicated natal charts or horoscopes, and such a long initialisation process can be rather tiresome. The Four Pillars of Destiny is free from such disadvantages and can be applied to people from any culture.

To demonstrate, let us now focus on former British Prime Minister, Margaret Thatcher. Only her birth year, month and day are known (Fig. 53).

The day pillar represents the individual self. We can see that Mrs Thatcher, the Iron Lady, belongs to the category of metal. Being a metal person born in the autumn season when metal is at its most prosperous phase, her personality reflects these characteristics. Thus the most favourable element for her should be fire which not only controls and dilutes the excessive metal energy but also provides her with power and status. This method will not seem so complicated if we bear in mind that metal needs fire to transform it into useful tools. For example, fire turns iron into steel. The next element favourable to her should be wood. Wood generates fire and also provides an outlet for the excessive metal energy (metal destroys wood). Wood is also her wealth. The basic idea is that the element that one conquers is wealth. Water is also favourable as it is the offspring of metal and it symbolises her intelligence and aspirations. Water also generates wealth as it helps wood (wealth) to grow. (Thus it is easy to understand the common belief that intelligence generates wealth.) A person of strong metal usually dislikes the elements of earth and metal, as earth gives birth to excessive metal and generates severe competition.

Equipped with such data, we can take a closer look at Mrs Thatcher's four pillars and see if they match well with her background. First, we note the prominent presence of the fire element. Fire turns metal into steel. This signifies that she is a powerful lady of high authority and status. The next step is to observe the location of the fire elements. They are very close to the day pillar: one on the month pillar and another underneath the metal (self).

We already know that the month pillar represents the father. There is another, complementary side: the lower character of the day pillar represents the spouse. As both of these locations are occupied by fire, the favourable element, it reveals a very close and harmonious relationship with her father and her husband, and this matches the facts very well.

The four pillars contain only one single metal element (the self). This indicates an

Day	Month	Year
庚 Metal	丙 Fire	乙 Wood
午 Fire	戌 Earth	丑 Earth

79	69	59	49	39	29	19	9
甲 Wood	癸 Water	壬 Water	辛 Metal	庚 Metal	己 Earth	戊 Earth	丁 Fire
午 Fire	巳 Fire	辰 Earth	卯 Wood	寅 Wood	丑 Earth	子 Water	亥 Water

Fig. 53. Mrs Thatcher's Four Pillars of Destiny and Luck.

individualistic character with few close colleagues and friends. The father is the fire on the month pillar and receives the support of wood from the year pillar. Therefore, he is also a strong character (he became a mayor in 1943). Metal is her father's wealth (fire destroys metal). But there is only one metal element in the configuration, so her father is not a very wealthy person and Maggie was not born of a rich family.

The husband, the fire underneath the metal on the day pillar, is a strong fire as it gets the support of wood from the hour pillars. This shows he is not only a respected man of strength, but he is also stronger than the wife in the sense that he is much older in age. Besides reflecting family background, the Pillars of Destiny also accurately reflects Mrs Thatcher's appearence. The strong metal element often gives a person fair skin. The fire element gives bright and piercing eyes, the weak wood element will result in a slightly pointed chin. The prominent earth constitutes a good nose and muscle.

Mrs Thatcher's four pillars also possess two more advantages which could have contributed to her success. A metal person born in the Year of the Ox is a lucky person as the ox is her star of fortune. Fire sitting on the autumn month pillar is a star of virtue. People possessing such a star configuration are good leaders who possess charisma. Chairman Mao Zedong has also such a configuration in his four pillars.

Let us now examine the vicissitudes in Mrs Margaret Thatcher's life by analysing the entire group of her luck pillars. She is a person of strong metal. Her metal is refined and controlled by the presence of a prominent fire element. Her four pillars are quite well-balanced. Fire, wood and water are favourable elements to her, whereas metal and earth may bring bad influences. However, the application of this hypothesis must, of necessity, be flexible for a strong and well-balanced person. The reason is that the impact of the five elements is not so obvious because a person standing on firm ground finds it easier to maintain his or her balance.

The best way to examine a well-balanced set of four pillars is to see how the five elements affect each specific area of life. For Mrs Thatcher, fire represents power, status and her husband. Wood means wealth, while water represents her offspring, aspirations and intelligence. Earth and metal provide support when she is in the weak phases of life but they also generate competition and hinder her achievements when they become excessive. We shall examine Mrs Thatcher's life in these areas and try to explain the events basing our analysis on the interaction of the five elements.

In 1951, a year of wood, the wood element allowed the fire in the four pillars to prosper. Fire is also related to her spouse. So she got married that year. In 1953, a year of water (meaning children, as metal gives birth to water), she gave birth to a pair of twins. She was then 28 years old and was in the luck pillar of water. So the double appearance of water in both the year and the luck pillar brought her two children.

The major breakthrough in her political career was in 1975 when she was elected leader of the Conservative Party. It was a wood year which generated fire, meaning power and status in her four pillars. The year 1979 was the Year of the Ram. In terms of the five elements, the goat is a 'storage of wood'. Mrs Thatcher turned 54 and has just entered the luck pillar of wood. The heavy wood configuration considerably enhanced the strength of her fire and therefore her power. She was elected Prime Minister in May, a month of fire.

Tracing her career as the Prime Minister of Britain, we can see Mrs Thatcher's achieve-

Mrs Margaret Thatcher

ments are somewhat connected with the wood and fire elements which enhance her power and authority. On the other hand, metal, the destroyer of wood, naturally reduces the fire power and is disadvantageous to her. In 1970, a year of metal, her beloved father died. In 1980, another year of pure metal, she faced the problem of the steel workers' strike. The unemployment rate reached 2.5 million, breaking the record since World War II. There were three days of rioting in Liverpool.

The Falklands War broke out in the spring of 1982, a year of water and earth which challenged her fire power. However, the Divine was on her side as strong fire soon came into play when summer came and total victory was achieved in June, a month of pure fire.

In 1983, Mrs Thatcher was still in the luck pillar of wood. The Year of the Pig (meaning water) combined with the luck pillar of wood, resulted in a strengthened wood configuration. She succeeded in the June election which was again a month of strong fire. 1987, another year of fire, brought her victory at the elections held in June. June was again a fire month. In 1989, Mrs Thatcher entered the luck pillar of earth at the age of 64. Naturally the fire power is not as strong as when she was in the wood pillar in the past. But the years 1989 and early 1990 still provided sufficient fire energy to preserve her power. However, the forces of water and metal elements gradually became dominant in the winter of 1990 and eventually she had to step down from the position of Prime Minister when the fire element was besieged by strong water and metal.

At the age of 65, Mrs Thatcher was in the luck pillar of water and earth. So the threat of water was there, but it was in the past years kept under control by strong earth elements.

However, in 1990, a year of metal over fire, the metal element activated the water effect which posed a strong threat to Mrs Thatcher's power — fire. The fatal impact eventually came in winter when the fire element of the Year of the Horse faded away and the metal and water effect took the helm in November.

The dramatic downfall of Mrs Thatcher happened suddenly in November within weeks of Sir Geoffrey Howe declaring his resignation from her cabinet. The month of November, 1990 was a month of fire over water. Fire sitting on water is very weak fire indeed and this month in fact portrayed the end of the fire era. So the weak fire configuration already indicates that Mrs Thatcher was in grave danger of losing her power — fire.

The first onslaught against the weak fire fell on November 13 — a day of water over fire — when Sir Geoffrey Howe made a damaging resignation speech against Mrs Thatcher in Parliament. This was the first wave led by the water element. The second charge of the opposition came on the day of voting on November 20, a day of pure earth. Although the attack was not as fierce as water, the earth element weakened fire as it consumed fire energy. On this day, Mrs Thatcher was short of only four votes to bar her challenger from proceeding to the second round of voting.

The third day was November 22, a day of metal when Mrs Thatcher announced her resignation. The metal element appearing on this day is *yin* metal. Advanced theories of the Four Pillars of Destiny postulate that *yin* metal and *yang* fire are attracted to each other like magnets and once combined, both will change their physical properties to become water. Such a combination effect, or chemical reaction for the sake of simplicity, is devastating as the metal element appearing on November 22 totally snatched away the fire element from Mrs Thatcher's month pillar and that means she was stripped of her power on that date.

31. Paul Chung: Suicide of a Star

The theory of the five elements postulates that the universe is composed of five basic types of matter: metal, wood, water, fire and earth, and everything on earth, including human existence and human fortune, are subject to the interaction of these five elements. The Four Pillars of Destiny constructed from a person's birth data actually reflect the composition of the five elements in a person and so many of his personal characteristics can be revealed: his potential, his social relationships and his inborn merits and demerits.

From the day of birth we can establish which element a person belongs to and what his strengths and weaknesses are. The person's passage through life can therefore be predicted following the five elements cycle. If the person is "favoured" by some element in that cycle, for example a weak fire person getting plenty of wood to nourish him in his life, the person will be fortunate and will achieve success. On the other hand, he will be a miserable man and will have to face many odds when the cycle of fortune turns against him, for example, a weak fire person encountering a strong water year.

As the five elements influence human fortune in a cyclical manner, good luck or bad luck often comes in phases and those who are having bad luck now can look forward to a future phase of good luck when the favourable elements come to lift the troubles away. Unfortunately, the reverse is also true. In our passage through life, we are subject to the influence of two cycles. One is the cycle of the luck pillars, derived from a person's own birth data. The other cycle is the calendar cycle, the yearly, monthly or even daily changes in the influence of the five elements. The calendar cycle has a relatively small impact on a person as these are yearly, monthly or daily influences. However, the luck pillars are more lasting as each pillar governs a period of ten years.

It is not surprising, therefore, that a person under the influence of a bad luck pillar will suffer disastrous failures and may even face problems of survival. This is especially so when a person encounters a bad luck pillar after enjoying life aided by a sustained period of good fortune. This is not difficult to comprehend. A millionaire is often more heavily in debt than an average person when his luck turns against him. So for people who encounter good luck early in life, the very point of leaving a good luck pillar will often be the most dangerous point in the person's life. Fig. 54 shows the Four Pillars of Destiny of Paul Chung, the popular Hong Kong television actor and compere who committed suicide in 1989.

If this is Mr Chung's correct birth data, he was a fire person born in April, the month of spring when the wood element is in the prosperous phase of its cycle. The four pillars contain plenty of wood supporting and intensifying the fire. So it is obvious that Mr Chung was a very strong fire person with abundant energy. Water offers little control as it will be totally absorbed by the strong wood. So the most favourable element should be earth. As fire gives birth to earth, earth represented Mr Chung's intelligence and aspirations and provided the needed outlet to release the excessive power of fire. The single earth element in the year pillar can be compared to the life support of Mr Chung and it represented the wit, creativity and versatility so important to the career of an actor.

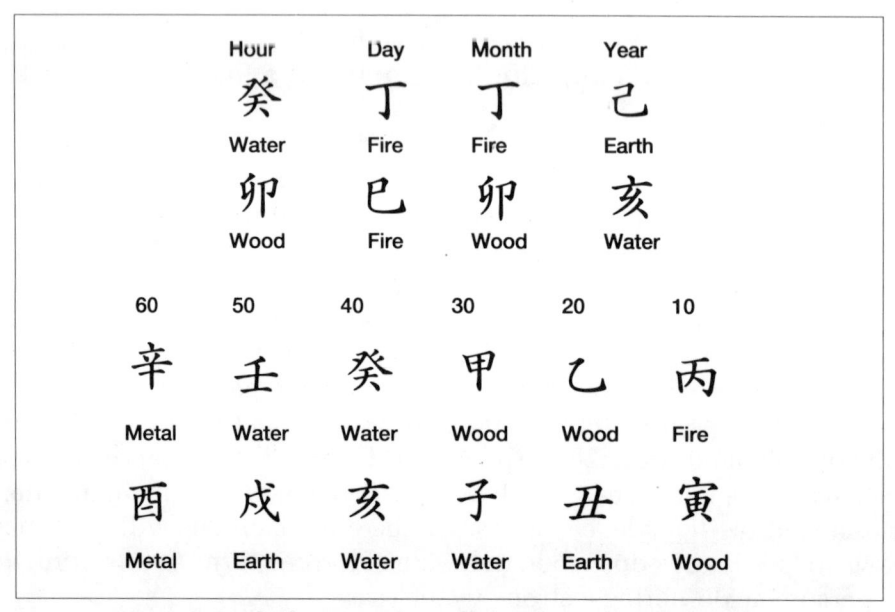

Fig. 54. Paul Chung's Four Pillars of Destiny and Luck.

The most prominent element in Mr Chung's four pillars is wood. It is in a dominant position as wood is not only in season, but also draws strong support from the water elements in the year and hour pillars. Wood can be considered Mr Chung's enemy because it fed him too much nourishment which he was not able to digest. Wood also generates more fire, creating competition. But the worst effect of the wood is that it suppressed the earth element which was so essential to Mr Chung (wood destroys earth). Excessive wood would be an intensive emotional constraint, equivalent to suffocation.

Totally absent from the four pillars is one essential element: metal. Fire destroys metal, so metal represented Mr Chung's wealth. As earth, representing intelligence, gives birth to metal, representing wealth, it means that intelligence should be rewarded with wealth. Unfortunately, the absence of metal in Mr Chung's four pillars indicates that this needed reward does not exist. Earth without metal is like a dead-end street and there would be a burning desire within Mr Chung to find an outlet for his intelligence and this outlet can only be found in metal (money). Frustrated ambition (earth suppressed by wood) and an insatiable appetite for money (metal) are often the two driving forces behind gambling.

Mr Chung's Four Pillars of Destiny belongs to the category of an unhappy artist who has so much to express and to give but so little outlet for the deep emotions to find expression. The strong fire in the four pillars of Mr Chung relies on the single earth element in his year pillar to release his feelings and his talents. So we can consider earth his root of life and anything that weakens or threatens earth his worst enemies.

For example, wood destroys earth. Therefore it is his deadly enemy. On the other hand, fire gives birth to earth, so fire is a favourable element. Water supports wood, so it is in the enemy camp. Also, a man's self control and discipline come from the element which suppresses him. In the case of Paul, as he is a fire person, his discipline comes from water which is the element that controls fire. However, the abundant wood present in the month and hour pillars completely consumes and absorbs the water (discipline). So it is easy to imagine how difficult it was for Paul to exercise self-control.

In addition, the four pillars are totally lacking in metal. Metal meant wealth to Mr Chung. So its absence can be a deep grievance and this stimulated in him an appetite for money. Earth gives birth to metal. So metal consumes earth's energy and weakens its good effect on Paul Chung. This configuration will stimulate hunger for money but money *and* bad luck will come to Paul hand in hand like twins. The stage is set for tragedy.

Good luck came to Paul at an early age as he entered the first luck pillar of fire at the age of ten. The fire, supported by wood, not only provided him a comfortable and stable childhood, but also offered him good opportunity to become a popular disc jockey. His first exposure to the public was in 1978, the year of fire and earth. Paul very soon attracted public attention as a talented young star and he branched out into movies. However, the years of metal and water (1980 - 1984) offset the favourable earth and fire influence of his luck pillar and he was involved in a car accident in 1981, a year of pure metal clashing against his luck pillar of wood.

In 1985, a year of earth, he returned to the spotlight and succeeded in joining Television Broadcast Limited in Hong Kong (TVB). At the age of 26 he had just entered the luck pillar of earth and this led to a successful career as a popular master of ceremonies. The following years, 1986, 1987, and 1988 were years of fire and earth and his popularity climbed new heights just before his death.

Paul's luck changed in 1989 when he entered the luck pillar of wood after his 30th birthday. The fatal blow eventually came in September, the month of water and metal, and on the first day of September, a day of wood, at an early morning hour of wood. To predict death just on the grounds of a bad month, a bad day and a bad luck pillar is simplistic. We need to examine his destiny more closely.

At the age of 30, Mr Chung was just entering the luck pillar of wood and water. Looking beyond, the next luck pillar is water which again enhances the enemy force, wood. So there was absolutely no chance for Paul to have lived through the next harsh pillar even if he had survived this year. So his luck simply expired and this is often the sign that a person's flame of life has burnt out.

The other factor to consider is the year 1989, the Year of the Snake. Mr Chung was born under the Year of the Pig which is not compatible with that of the snake. Furthermore, the more esoteric branches of the four pillars teach that *yin* earth is attracted to *yang* wood. Paul was just entering the luck pillar of the *yang* wood after April. *Yang* wood standing on water is a very strong wood configuration and it attracted away the *yin* earth element at Paul's year pillar. So he lost his only outlet and life supporter and his four pillars tumbled over. It is also worth noting that the Year of the Snake is also *yin* earth so this earth could have come to his assistance. However, the date, September 1, also happened to be a day of *yang* wood, blocking any assistance from the Year. This may have implied that Paul felt very upset on that day and committing suicide was the only way he could release his feelings.

Paul Chung

32. Marilyn Monroe: Murder or Suicide?

Is death predictable? An expert in the Four Pillars of Destiny should be able to answer in the affirmative. The four pillars of a person show inborn potential and weakness, and the accompanying luck pillars reflect his path of life, his ups and downs, brought about by the interaction of the five elements.

As a person travels through the luck pillars, there can come a point when he enters a luck pillar which has adverse effects on him and upsets the balance of his four pillars. In such a critical period, if, by coincidence, or through providence, the person encounters an unfavourable year which intensifies the bad influence, this is often the termination point of life.

Many configurations of the four pillars hinge on one single character to maintain their balance. For example, the four pillars of a weak fire person rely on the single element of wood to provide the necessary "nourishment". So when it comes to a luck pillar of metal, the wood is threatened and suppressed by the metal and fails to give nourishment to the fire. If the person also encounters a year of metal during such a dangerous period, it will be a matter of life and death. Life will expire at the very month and day when the wood, the life supporter, is totally destroyed by multiple attacks from metal.

So a key to looking for signs of death is to establish the compatibility of a person's four pillars. Then one can identify the "hinge", the most essential point in his life and well-being. One should look through the luck pillars to search for a period when such a "hinge" will be under concerted attack. The time of death can often be predicted down to the year, within such a period when the yearly element reinforces the attack and zeros in on the "life supporter" to deliver a fatal blow.

	Hour	Day	Month	Year
	癸 Water	辛 Metal	癸 Water	丙 Fire
	巳 Fire	酉 Metal	巳 Fire	寅 Wood

59	49	39	29	19	9
丁 Fire	戊 Earth	己 Earth	庚 Metal	辛 Metal	壬 Water
亥 Water	子 Water	丑 Earth	寅 Wood	卯 Wood	辰 Earth

Fig. 55. Marilyn Monroe's Four Pillars of Destiny and Luck.

94 Feng-shui and Destiny

The principle itself is not so difficult to comprehend. But when it comes to actual practice, one will find a maze of configurations of the four pillars so the life supporter or hinge is not easy to identify. It requires a great deal of experience and calm, logical analysis to get close to the truth. The four pillars shown in Fig. 55 are those of actress Marilyn Monroe who met her death in 1962 at her home. The circumstances of her death are still a puzzle.

Marilyn was a metal woman born in the hot summer month when fire was most prosperous and sets out to melt the metal. So she was a weak metal person. Let us examine the entire four pillars to identify the role of each element. For a weak metal person, fire is an enemy as it exerts considerable pressure and threatens to destroy the metal. Fire also means male power, male friends or husband. The multiple presence of fire elements in her four pillars shows the very strong male influence which surrounded her life. Wood, the supporter of fire, is naturally unfavourable as it intensifies the fire pressure. But it also meant wealth to Marilyn Monroe as it was something she conquered (metal destroys wood). So there was always the paradox in her life that more wealth brought more pressure. Wood, when it gets out of hand, can be a deadly enemy as it generates more fire to destroy the metal.

Water signalled her aspirations and talent. Two water elements protruding high in the four pillars gave her beauty and intelligence. Water controlled fire and kept it at a distance. So it was a favourable element in the sense that it generated wood (wealth) and protected metal against fire attack. On the other hand, excessive water could have a weakening effect as water releases and consumes metal energy (metal gives birth to water).

As Monroe was a weak metal person, the most favourable element to her would have been earth. This not only supports the life of metal (earth gives birth to metal) but also helps to absorb and reduce the excessive fire power in the four pillars (fire gives birth to earth). However, no earth element is found in the entire four pillars. So it seems the only element Monroe could have relied on in her four pillars was the metal which sits underneath her in the day pillar. We can then consider that the metal in the day pillar was the supporter of her life. Metal was the hinge for the maintenance of a fair balance between the conflict of water and fire in Marilyn Monroe's life.

We have seen that Marilyn Monroe was a weak metal person under strong threat from the fire element — man. Her primary form of life support is the metal element sitting in her day pillar. This provides support to the two water elements to the left and right so that the threat of fire can be kept at a distance. Water represents her thoughts and aspirations. This arrangement clearly shows Monroe to be a talented woman with a strong character and an intelligence which won the admiration of influential males.

The water and metal elements formed a protective shield around her and they worked extremely well. She was surrounded by powerful men from high society, the Kennedys, and they brought her fame and fortune. Metal is the source of water, so the formula worked best from her 29th to her 34th year when she was in her luck pillar of metal. However, after the age of 34, the metal influence faded away. Monroe entered the luck pillar of wood. As wood generates fire, it means that she passed from extremely good fortune into a dangerous phase of her life. The danger was a product of the metal being totally engulfed by a strong flame generated by the wood. Her intelligence, water, was no longer reliable as an effective defence without metal's support.

Monroe died in 1962, a year of water and wood, and at the age of 37, when she was in the luck pillar of wood. The date was August 4, a date characterised by wood, in a month of fire. Her death is believed to have occurred around 7 pm, in the hour of wood. This multiple presence of wood stimulated the power of the fire and clashed against the metal, her support in life. The single metal element was besieged by the wood and fire and it eventually gave way — the four pillars tumbled over.

There have been many accounts of the events of August 4, 1962. Most of them are conflicting. The official version of Monroe's death is that she ingested, either accidentally or on purpose, a fatal overdose of barbiturates. But the conflicting statements about the time and manner of death, and the apparent attempts to cover up the presence of Robert Kennedy at the scene, caused much public speculation.

What type of person commits suicide? Some consider suicide a cowardly act.

Marilyn Monroe

Another view is that it requires considerable courage to terminate one's own life. For example, Hong Kong TVB personality, Paul Chung, who plunged 16 floors to his death, was certainly not a weak man. Chung was a strong fire person desperately in need of earth to release his excess energy. From studying the four pillars of suicidal types, two common elements can be identified: suicides are usually strong people who lack a release for their excess energy.

The four pillars of Monroe do not indicate this. She was a weak metal person with prominent water elements to release her excess energy. She simply was not the type of person to bottle up her feelings. Comparing her four pillars to those of Paul Chung provides several clues to her death. Chung, a strong fire type, killed himself when he found the outlet for his energy, metal and earth, was blocked. The two elements leading to his death, metal and earth, are passive elements in relation to fire, as fire destroys metal and fire gives birth to earth. If the cause of death is "passive", then Chung himself played the active role in ending his own life — he committed suicide. In the case of Marilyn Monroe, the cause of death was fire generated by wood. Fire destroys metal so the fire played an active role in Monroe's death. The four pillars show Monroe to be a passive victim slain by external forces: wood stimulated the strong fire to take her life. It can be argued that this fire which appears in Monroe's four pillars represents a strong and powerful man. In 1962, a year of water and wood, the water was so weak that it failed to control the force of fire. On the contrary, it irritated the fire and stirred up its wrath to devour the weak metal — Marilyn Monroe.

33. John Lennon: Tragic Death of a Great Talent

The Four Pillars of Destiny seems to indicate that life emerges from a bundle of five basic elements interwoven into a human form. Our birthday, expressed in the four pillars, reflects the "chemical formula" of these elements constituting each individual's life. And the various combinations and proportions of the five elements in our body determine our character, strengths and weaknesses.

Humans and all matter in the universe are ultimately traceable to the same basic constituent elements. The five elements in the universe exert influences on human life in a cyclical manner. Cyclical changes of elements in the universe in terms of ages and seasons affect the five elements within man. A balancing influence will bring good fortune, but an upsetting influence will bring about bad luck, or even death.

We now take a look at a tragic death and try to determine how an imbalance between the five basic elements brought about the death of John Lennon, the Beatle who was shot dead by a fan at the age of 40. John's four pillars are set out in Fig. 56.

Hour	Day	Month	Year
庚	乙	丙	庚
Metal	Wood	Fire	Metal
辰	酉	戌	辰
Earth	Metal	Earth	Earth

60	50	40	30	20	10
壬	辛	庚	己	戊	丁
Water	Metal	Metal	Earth	Earth	Fire
辰	卯	寅	丑	子	亥
Earth	Wood	Wood	Earth	Water	Water

Fig. 56. John Lennon's Four Pillars of Destiny and Luck.

The day pillar shows that John Lennon is a wood person born in the autumn season when metal is most prosperous. We note that the wood is surrounded by a number of metal elements and such metals are reinforced by prominent earth elements (earth gives birth to metal). Wood requires nourishment from water, but water is totally absent from the four pillars. So the strength of earth and metal is overwhelming and the wood is extremely weak in this configuration. The wood, being threatened by the strong metal and totally lacking in water nourishment, has no chance of survival. Thus it has to surrender its property to the strongest elements, which are metal and earth in this case. The principle is called "follow the leader".

When the day pillar, representing the self, is too weak to survive, it has to submit totally to the power of the strongest element. Anything which supports the leader (the strongest element) is favourable. On the other hand, anything which supports the weak self (day pillar) will be most unfavourable and will upset the equilibrium.

In the case of John Lennon, as his wood has to submit to the power of earth and metal, these elements brought him good fortune. On the other hand, water and wood would bring about a revival of the weak wood and would upset the equilibrium. The situation is analogous to a helpless man forced to join the Triad Society (a Chinese society of crime). As long as he submits totally and follows the Triad leaders' orders, he is allowed to survive and may be able to share some wealth with the leaders. He is so weak that he dares not object to the leaders. However, if he grows stronger and attempts to get away from the Triad Society, the Triad leaders would consider him a traitor or rebel and punish him severely.

The four pillars of John Lennon clearly reflect such a pattern. Earth and metal brought him good fortune, and wood and water, supporting the day pillar, brought about his tragic death.

John Lennon

Lennon spent his childhood in poverty until he entered the luck pillar of earth at the age of 20. In 1960, the year of metal, the Beatles was formed and the group took the pop world by storm in the following years. Despite ups and downs brought about by the yearly influences, Lennon's good fortune was sustained for 20 years (1960 - 1980) when he remained in the luck pillar of earth. However, he met his assassin immediately after his 40th birthday when he left the luck pillar of earth and entered the luck pillar of metal over the element wood. The wood element in the luck pillar brought about the revival of the "self", wood, and such a revival attempt aroused the antagonism of the metal elements. The wood was immediately crushed by the overwhelming metal power. John Lennon was shot dead on December 8, 1980, a year of pure metal and that day was wood intensified by the month of water. Lennon's last hit *Just Like Starting Over,* incidentally, signified the revival attempt of his weak self, wood, which unfortunately was against the "rules of the game" and he was "killed" by the overwhelming metal power.

34. Karen Carpenter: Death by Uncommon Disease

Remember the beautiful songs *Close to You, Yesterday Once More, We've Only Just Begun?* The soothing voice belonged to Karen Carpenter, who was one of the most talented female singers in the 70s. Her life stimulated interest not only because of her phenomenal success in the world of pop music, but also because of the manner of her death at the young age of 33. She died of a heart attack caused by a disease called anorexia nervosa, a wasting sickness caused by reluctance to eat, resulting from over-consciousness about weight. Such a unique pattern of life and special manner of death must be vividly reflected in Carpenter's birth data. Let us explore her four pillars and examine her destiny to see what brought about her success and ended her life is such a tragic way. (See Fig. 57.)

Carpenter was a fire woman born in early spring when wood is the most prosperous element, as wood generates fire, and there are two wood elements to provide nourishment for one single fire. We cannot say the fire is weak, but it is a little overfed by the wood. So the drawback of her four pillars is that there is too much fuel for too small a fire. She needed to have either more fire to share the wood nourishment, or more metal to keep the excessive wood under control. In other words, both elements, fire and metal, will bring her good fortune. The element wood is something she disliked. Water, the supporter of wood, is certainly her worst enemy as it not only generated the unfavourable wood element, but could also threaten to put out the small fire.

Hour	Day	Month	Year
?	丙	戊	庚
	Fire	Earth	Metal
?	申	寅	寅
	Metal	Wood	Wood

59	49	39	29	19	9
壬	癸	甲	乙	丙	丁
Water	Water	Wood	Wood	Fire	Fire
申	酉	戌	亥	子	丑
Metal	Metal	Earth	Water	Water	Earth

Fig. 57a. Karen Carpenter's Four Pillars of Destiny and Luck.

Karen Carpenter: Death by Uncommon Disease

Karen and her brother Richard's first breakthrough on the pop scene was in 1966, a year of strong fire, when they won the Battle of the Bands at the Hollywood Bowl and were awarded a record contract with RCA. However, the deal eventually fell through as Karen, at the young age of 16, was in the luck pillar of earth which was not her most favourable element. Her good fortune eventually came in 1969, at the age of 19 when she had just entered the luck pillar of fire. The brother-and-sister act was seen by the jazz star Herb Alpert who was attracted by Karen's voice and immediately signed the duo up under A&M records.

The following year, 1970, a year of metal, meaning wealth to Karen, the Carpenters released the immensely successful single penned by Burt Bacharach, *Close to You,* which immediately reached number one in pop charts all over the world and brought them tremendous fame and fortune. The duo then produced a whole string of hits which injected fresh life into the pop world in the 70s. Such good fortune was brought about by the fire in Karen's luck pillar between the ages of 19 to 29.

However, the luck pillar, fire sitting on water, meant hidden danger as the water element in the earthly branch was a threat to her health. Her alarmingly poor health showed its first signs in 1974, a year of pure wood when she collapsed under the spotlight due to exhaustion. Thereafter she was given intensive medication and therapy but these were helpless in the face of destiny. She continued to lose weight and the flame of life slowly drained away from her body and was totally extinguished on February 4, 1983. This date, expressed in terms of the Chinese calendar, is shown in Fig. 57b.

Karen Carpenter

We should also note that Karen, at the age of 33 in 1983, was in the luck pillar of wood over water. So she was already in a dangerous phase of life. On February 4, there was a substantial amount of water and wood to attack her flickering flame and put it out. The prime element contributing to her death was an overwhelming presence of wood. Supported by strong water, the wood provided too much fuel to the small fire. So the fire was overfed and rejected further nourishment. Indeed, refusal to eat was the cause of Karen Carpenter's illness and the immediate cause of death, her heart attack, perfectly matched the configuration as the water accumulated on the date put out her fire, which symbolises the heart in the human body.

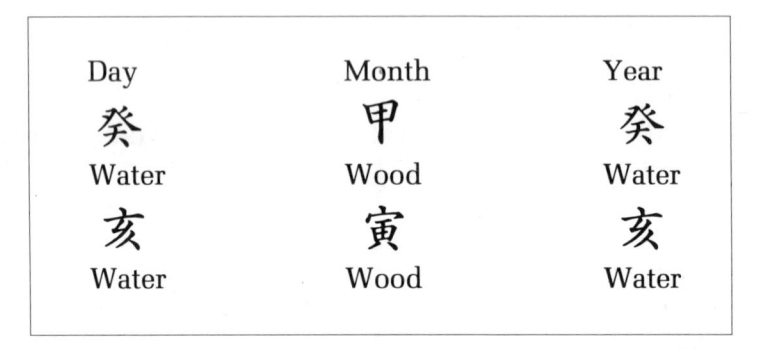

Day	Month	Year
癸	甲	癸
Water	Wood	Water
亥	寅	亥
Water	Wood	Water

Fig. 57b. Pillars of Destiny on February 4, 1983.

35. Bruce Lee's Mysterious Death

Legendary kung fu hero Bruce Lee is regarded as the greatest Chinese international star of the early 70s. His sudden death in 1973 came as a big shock to the entertainment world. In his short career, he starred in some of the best action movies ever made. Did he over-exert himself, with his flame of life burnt out rapidly in the short span of three years' sensational stardom? Let us examine his four pillars and see if we can find some clues to his death (Fig 58).

Lee's Chinese name was "Little Dragon" and he was born in the Year of the Dragon, in the Hour of the Dragon (8 am). His day pillar belongs to the category of wood. He was born in the winter season when water is most prosperous. Water provides nourishment to wood. However, the water is surrounded by walls of earth which hinder the free flow of the water. Furthermore, the earth also supported the metal on the four pillars to threaten the safety of the wood. So Bruce Lee is considered to be a weak wood person.

Earth in his four pillars represents wealth as it is conquered by wood. But too much earth will exhaust the energy of wood. There is a famous Chinese saying: "Too much wealth weakens the health." This proverb applies to Bruce Lee's four pillars. The wood is weakened by the multiple earth elements that symbolise wealth. A person with such a configuration usually finds himself surrounded by wealth but is not able to enjoy it. An appropriate analogy is the situation of a bank teller who handles millions of dollars everyday but only receives a small salary. So in the case of Bruce Lee, the configuration reflected his inability to enjoy his immense riches.

Wood born in a cold winter season needs fire to provide warmth. Fire in November is often compared to the warm winter sun which is essential to prevent plants (wood) from decay. Fire also helps wood to control metal and keep its threat at a distance. So we can consider the fire element in the month pillar as an essential element for the well-being of the wood. It is the hinge, or life support which maintains the equilibrium between metal and wood.

Fire in the month pillar also represents "father". Bruce Lee's father was also a movie star and Bruce was born of a rather wealthy family. His good relationship with his father provides evidence that fire is important to his life. As fire is the offspring of wood, it also symbolises his intelligence and aspirations. Fire governed the manner in which Bruce presented himself to the world. So it was of paramount importance to his artistic life. Anything that supported the fire element would therefore bring him good fortune and anything that suppressed the fire would bring misfortune. As soon as Bruce entered the luck pillar of wood at the age of 28 in 1968, the wood enabled the fire to burn vigorously with heat and light.

Bruce Lee's unique fighting style drew public attention on television. From 1968 to 1973, he conquered the world with one movie hit after another and became many people's idol and hero. However, at the peak of his career, on July 20, 1973, he was found dead at the home of an actress.

Hour	Day	Month	Year
戊	甲	丁	庚
Earth	Wood	Fire	Metal
辰	戌	亥	辰
Earth	Earth	Water	Earth

53	43	33	23	13	3
癸	壬	辛	庚	己	戊
Water	Water	Metal	Metal	Earth	Earth
巳	辰	卯	寅	丑	子
Fire	Earth	Wood	Wood	Earth	Water

Fig. 58. Bruce Lee's Four Pillars of Destiny and Luck.

102 Feng-shui and Destiny

In 1973, at the age of 33, Bruce Lee had just left his luck pillar of wood and entered the luck pillar of metal. So fire, his life support, lost the support of wood and was in a very weak position. Unfortunately, 1973 was a year of water and the water directly clashed with the fire, putting it out on July 20. The fire in Bruce Lee's month pillar, losing the support of wood and threatened by water, could no longer guard against metal in the year pillar. So the metal launched the fatal attack on the defenceless wood and the four pillars tumbled over.

Fire in the heavenly stem (the upper characters) symbolises the brain, the eyes and the nervous system. As Lee's death was caused by the suppression of fire by water, we can postulate that he suffered injury to his brain caused by water. It is not surprising, therefore, that the manner of death suggested in our analysis comes very close to the theory suggested by medical experts in Lee's post mortem. They said that the star died of water ingress into the brain.

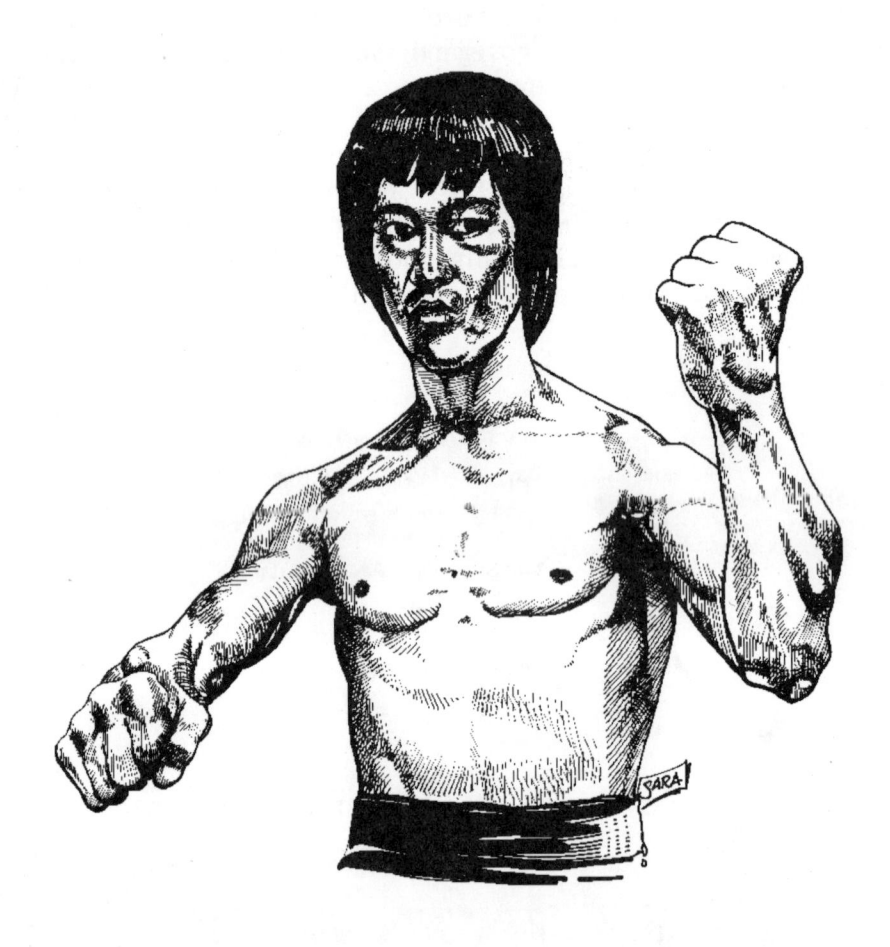

Bruce Lee

36. Richard Nixon and Watergate

Former United States President Richard Nixon was in the limelight again in 1989 when he visited Beijing. Despite the Watergate scandal which resulted in his impeachment in 1973, he is still a well-respected politician. His achievements included the establishment of communications with Beijing and the pulling out of US troops from the Vietnam War.

It is interesting to examine the four pillars of such a great person and see how the interaction of the five basic elements brought about the dramatic ups and downs of his political career. The four pillars show that President Nixon is a metal person born in the winter month, December, which is an earth month (Fig. 59). Although earth can give birth to metal and provide it nourishment, we cannot consider Mr Nixon a strong metal person as there is plenty of water in the year and month pillars to consume the metal energy.

Hour	Day	Month	Year
丙	庚	癸	壬
Fire	Metal	Water	Water
戌	寅	丑	子
Earth	Wood	Earth	Water

79	69	59	49	39	29	19	9
辛	庚	己	戊	丁	丙	乙	甲
Metal	Metal	Earth	Earth	Fire	Fire	Wood	Wood
酉	申	未	午	巳	辰	卯	寅
Metal	Metal	Earth	Fire	Fire	Earth	Wood	Wood

Fig. 59. President Nixon's Four Pillars of Destiny and Luck.

To Mr Nixon, water represents intelligence and aspiration. The prominent water appearing on the heavenly stems gives him quick wit and good power of speech. Another element which features prominently in his four pillars is the fire on the hour pillar. As Mr Nixon is a metal man born in cold winter, the flame of fire is essential as it provides him the needed warmth. To a metal person, fire also represents power and authority as heat can turn metal into useful tools. So anything that helps fire to burn vigorously, such as wood, will intensify his courage and enhance his position.

On balance, Mr Nixon is a weak metal person requiring the nourishment of earth, and earth, in turn, needs the support of fire. So we can conclude that fire and earth are the favourable elements leading to his success. On the other hand, water suppresses fire and exhausts his metal energy, so it is his deadly enemy.

Starting with Richard Nixon's childhood, the month pillar, symbolising his father and family background, is occupied by water which is an unfavourable element. This points to the fact that Mr Nixon was not born into a rich family. In fact, he spent his childhood working hard in his parents' grocery shop. His good fortune began at the age of 29 when he entered the luck pillar of fire and earth. At the young age of 33 in the year 1946, a year of fire and earth, he was elected into the US Congress. In the following 30 years, he remained under the favourable influence of fire and earth with his career peaking in the 10 years between 1949 and 1959. However, there were occasional setbacks brought about by the yearly water influence.

Richard Nixon

In 1960, a year of water, he was narrowly defeated by J.F. Kennedy in the presidential elections. In 1962, another water year, he again failed in the election for Governor of California which discouraged him so much that he announced his retirement from politics to pursue a career in law. However, the water phase soon faded away and the fire power in his luck pillar regained strength in 1964 when he re-entered the political arena and eventually won the presidency in 1968, a year of earth, and at the age of 45, when he was in the luck pillar of fire.

The outstanding achievements by President Nixon during his term of office were the retreat from Vietnam and the re-opening of contact with China. These were done in the water years of 1972 and 1973. Although historians will consider these as great contributions to world peace, one can imagine that the years 1972 and 1973 were hard years when President Nixon was under tremendous pressure, especially since Saigon eventually fell to Communist hands in 1975. So this "achievement" was in fact not a glorious deed to the American public but meant retreat and compromise.

In 1972, the year of water, the Watergate affair blew up from an apparently trivial burglary into a great political scandal which eventually led to the impeachment of President Nixon in 1974, resulting in his resignation. The year 1974 was a year of wood and President Nixon was then 61. He was just leaving the luck pillar of fire. The wood destroyed the earth he needed and brought about loss of reputation. His resignation was announced on August 9, again a day of water. It is worth noting that the very name "Watergate" is an ominous comment on President Nixon's downfall caused by the water element. Should the headquarters of the Democrats have been called "Firegate", it is probable that Nixon would have escaped impeachment.

37. How Ronald Reagan Survived Assassination

On March 30, 1981, former US President Ronald Reagan was shot in the chest by an assassin as he was walking out of the Washington Hilton Hotel. When the news reached Hong Kong, a newspaper reporter interviewed a famous fortune-teller to check whether President Reagan would survive. The fortune-teller asked: "Was it raining at the time of the assassination attempt?" Water is an unfavourable element for President Reagan. The presence of water would be interpreted as an omen of death. Fortunately it was a clear day and President Reagan recovered.

Mr Reagan's day pillar is fire and he was born in early spring, a season of wood. Wood can provide fire with nourishment (Fig. 60a). However, there is only one single wood element which is supportive of fire. The other elements in Mr Reagan's four pillars are metal and earth which all consume fire's energy. On balance, Mr Reagan belongs to the weak fire category. The fire is comparable to candlelight. More fire and wood elements will help him generate strength and allow the fire to burn with heat and light. On the other hand, water will put the fire out and metal and earth will dim the fire as they consume fire's energy.

	Hour	Day	Month	Year
	辛 Metal	丁 Fire	庚 Metal	辛 Metal
	丑 Earth	未 Earth	寅 Wood	亥 Water

81	71	61	51	41	31	21	11
辛 Metal	壬 Water	癸 Water	甲 Wood	乙 Wood	丙 Fire	丁 Fire	戊 Earth
巳 Fire	午 Fire	未 Earth	申 Metal	酉 Metal	戌 Earth	亥 Water	子 Water

Fig. 60a. President Reagan's Four Pillars of Destiny and Luck.

To President Reagan, fire means friendly colleagues and general support. Wood helps fire to burn. So wood is his resource, his life support, and it adds to his strength. Metal will be conquered by fire. So metal is Mr Reagan's reward and his wealth. However, the wealth is favourable to him only if there is a strong fire. Otherwise, the theory that "too much wealth weakens health" will apply and metal will become an unfavourable element. Metal, representing family background, appears on his month pillar and shows that Ronald Reagan was not born into a wealthy family, as metal cannot support his fire. In fact, his father was a shoe salesman and Mr Reagan spent his childhood in poverty.

Fire gives birth to earth. So earth represents his expressions, his intelligence, his power of speech, aspirations and reputation. Water suppresses fire. Being a fire person, water means stress and pressure to Mr Reagan. But it also means authority and power, if he is strong enough to control and manipulate it.

1937, a year of fire on the element earth, was a year he felt an increase in strength and was eager to express himself. In that year, he made a reputation for himself as a movie star. The year 1966 was a year of fire. Supported by the luck pillar of wood, at the age of 55, Mr Reagan was in a vigorous phase of his life. He was elected governor of California.

The year 1981, a year of metal, was certainly the highlight of Mr Reagan's life as he was elected president. He was 69 years of age and was in the luck pillar of 未 which is earth in nature but can also be interpreted as "storage of wood". This supports his fire. Therefore we can say Mr Reagan experienced an energetic phase of life when the strength of fire was enhanced by wood. With such strength, he was capable of manipulating metal (wealth) to his advantage. Metal gives birth to water, which symbolises power. Hence he became the US president and held supreme authority in 1981.

Two months and ten days after Ronald Reagan took office, he was shot by a young assassin who fired six shots, seriously injuring the White House Information Secretary, two body guards and a policeman. He was soon cornered and arrested. Meanwhile Mr Reagan was rushed to hospital. A bullet had penetrated Mr Reagan's chest and lodged under his left lung, only centimetres from his heart. Mr Reagan had an emergency operation which lasted about three hours. Miraculously, he survived and was discharged from hospital on April 11, 1981. Let us now focus on the date March 30, 1981 and see how the five elements interacted with Mr Reagan's four pillars to cause the crisis.

Mr Reagan is a weak fire person who needs the support of wood to enable the fire to burn. On the other hand, the water element, which means power to Mr Reagan, can also suppress fire and so create pressure and stress. Metal generates water, so it enhanced Mr Reagan's power in 1981 when he was elected president. However, metal also has the effect of directly clashing with wood which supports fire. Therefore, the year 1981, a year of strong metal, was a time of real danger for Mr Reagan.

The assassination occurred in March, again a month of metal. This intensified the metal strength so it could launch an attack on the wood. Fig. 60b shows the configuration of the day March 30, 1981, expressed in the four pillars. We note the multiple presence of metal elements on the date of assassination. The metal elements, in terms of the human body, symbolise the respiratory system. The wood element represents the bone. The injury to Mr Reagan's lung and his ribs clearly reflected the clash between the metal and wood elements on that date.

However, Mr Reagan was destined to survive such misfortune. His life was spared for a number of reasons which are also observable on the four pillars. Firstly, his assassination was the result of a clash between metal and wood, but the wood was strong enough to withstand such an attack as Mr Reagan, at the age of 69, was under the influence of the luck pillar 未, which was a storage of wood. Furthermore, to cause death, there should be a direct attack of water to put out Mr Reagan's fire. If any water was present, no matter how little, it would be intensified by the strong presence of metal to launch a fatal attack on the fire and extinguish it, hence causing death. However, there was a total absence of water element on that date. It was also a sunny day, and fate was on Mr Reagan's side.

Hour	Day	Month	Year
戊	丁	辛	辛
Earth	Fire	Metal	Metal
申	未	卯	酉
Metal	Earth	Wood	Metal

Fig. 60b. The four pillars of the day of shooting March 30, 1981.

108 Feng-shui and Destiny

The most fortunate factor is that March 30, 1981 was a day of fire. Fire means colleagues. So Mr Reagan was well surrounded by supporters and his bodyguards and colleagues displayed bravery and loyalty at the critical moment. They were able to shield him from fatal injury. Lastly, the four pillars of destiny postulate that every person has some helpers in life who are called "noblemen". They are a type of guardian angel who come to the aid of a person in trouble. For Mr Reagan, being a *yin* fire, the Year of the Cockerel, 1981, was a year of his nobleman. So Mr Reagan was kept under the wings of his guardian angel in that year.

Finally, at the age of 69, President Reagan was at the luck pillar of 未, a "storage of wood" which is his life supporter. The next luck pillar 午, a fire pillar, is again a very favourable phase of life enhancing his fire strength. So his flame of life should continue to burn vigorously. The assassination was merely one critical point in his life which had only a momentary effect.

President Reagan

38. Corazon Aquino: From Housewife to President

In Chinese metaphysics, time is divided into 20-year periods called ages and each age is represented by a *kua* or trigram of the *I Ching* (The Book of Changes). The 20-year period, 1984 to 2003, is called the Age of Seven which is symbolised by the *tui kua*. The *kua* embraces life in all its complexities. One essential feature of the *tui kua* is that it stands for female and until the year 2003, we can expect more and more prominent women to emerge in politics. Among them, the Philippines President Corazon Aquino is a notable example.

At the end of 1989, Mrs Aquino faced another crisis of political unrest after the rebellion by some factions of the armed forces. President Aquino entered a critical phase of her life in November and her political future and the stability of the country was in doubt. Let us examine her Four Pillars of Destiny to see if the interaction of the five elements can cast light on her past and future.

Mrs Aquino is a metal person born in the winter month of December, when the water element is most prosperous. In her four pillars (Fig. 61a) there are many water elements. As water draws energy from metal (metal gives birth to water), the configuration shows that Mrs Aquino is a weak metal person and so she needs earth to give her nourishment and more metal to support her position. As Mrs Aquino herself is metal, and metal means colleagues, an appropriate amount of metal element will mean additional strength and support. Earth gives birth to metal and nourishes it. So earth should be a most welcome element as it is Mrs Aquino's resource and life supporter.

Hour	Day	Month	Year
庚	辛	癸	壬
Metal	Metal	Water	Water
寅	卯	丑	申
Wood	Wood	Earth	Metal

76	66	56	46	36	26	16	6
乙	丙	丁	戊	己	庚	辛	壬
Wood	Fire	Fire	Earth	Earth	Metal	Metal	Water
巳	午	未	申	酉	戌	亥	子
Fire	Fire	Earth	Metal	Metal	Earth	Water	Water

Fig. 61a. President Corazon Aquino's Four Pillars of Destiny and Luck.

110 Feng-shui and Destiny

Metal gives birth to water, so water represents her intelligence and aspirations. The prominent presence of the water element reflects her intelligence, public appeal and her ability as an eloquent speaker. Mrs Aquino is certainly not an ordinary housewife but a capable leader of high calibre. However, she is a weak metal person. And too much water will exhaust her energy and weaken her power.

Fire suppresses metal. So fire means hard work and pressure for Mrs Aquino. If she is capable of manipulating fire, however, the pressure will turn around to serve her as her power and authority. For a woman, the element that suppresses her also symbolises her husband, who is the centre of power in the family. However, there is a total absence of the fire element in the four pillars. So, to find out about her power and her famous husband, the late Senator Benigno Aquino, we have to examine the wood element instead. This is because wood generates fire, so fire is hidden within the wood which we can find in Mrs Aquino's hour pillar. The fact that Mrs Aquino got married in 1954, a year of wood and fire, proves this point.

Before 1983, she was in relative obscurity, playing her role as a housewife. However, her life pattern changed drastically in 1983 with the tragic assassination of her husband on August 21 at Manila airport on his return from exile in the US. Mrs Aquino had just turned 50 then and she was in the luck pillar of metal. As her husband is fire within wood, the metal was already posing a threat to her husband's life. The tragedy occurred in 1983, a year of strong water, which extinguished the fire. The metal month of August clashed with the wood. The 21st day of that month was of metal, too. So the loss of her husband was predestined.

The brutal murder of Mr Aquino cut deep into his wife's heart. However, the luck pillar is earth on metal. This is not a bad phase after all, as earth and metal gave her support and nourishment. So, instead of burying herself in sorrow, she was able to stand up and continue to fight for her husband's cause; and she triumphed over her misfortune.

August 21, 1983 was a turning point in the history of the Philippines. The killing of Benigno Aquino at the Manila airport sparked off outrage across the country. The tragedy also began the transformation of Mrs Aquino from a housewife to a politician who would ultimately complete her husband's mission, to overthrow the Marcos regime.

In 1985, Mrs Aquino bravely took up the challenge to compete against Mr Marcos in the presidential elections. The subsequent events demonstrated her will and determination. Both sides claimed victory, but the people rose to support Mrs Aquino. She was installed as President and took the presidential oath on February 25, 1986 after Mr Marcos fled in exile to Hawaii.

Let us examine the configuration of Mrs Aquino's four pillars and see how the five elements interacted to bring about her success in 1986. Mrs Aquino is a weak metal person who needs earth to provide nourishment and extra metal to support her strength. Fire suppresses her when she is weak but is transformed into power and authority when she is strong. In line with this hypothesis, February 1986 was the right time in life for Mrs Aquino to seize power from Mr Marcos.

In 1986, at the age of 53, Mrs Aquino was at the luck pillar of metal. The metal gave her strong support and she was in a healthy position to manipulate power (fire). The chance came in 1986, a year of strong fire. Mrs Aquino was elected president on February 25, a day of metal in a month of metal which provided her with more strength to manipulate the fire power. To Mrs Aquino, metal means colleagues. The multiple presence of metal is the source of her strength. This seems to reflect her popularity with the people, her colleagues and friends.

The next year, 1987, was a year of fire and 1988 was a year of earth. These were all favourable years as the earth element provides nourishment to the metal in the luck pillar which added to Mrs Aquino's strength and power. However, Mrs Aquino turned 56 in the winter of 1989 and this affected her fortune in two ways. First, she is leaving the luck pillar of metal which is so essential to her strength. So she is entering a weaker phase. Second, the favourable earth influence for the Year of the Snake (1989) was coming to an end in November which was a month of strong wood, depriving her of the earth influence (wood destroys earth). The loss of the favourable influence of earth and metal in November was bound to result in a crisis situation. The mutiny of the armed troops broke out on December 1, a day of wood in a month of wood, which suppressed her earth support and threw her four pillars off balance (Fig. 61b).

Day	Month	Year
乙	乙	己
Wood	Wood	Earth
未	亥	巳
Earth	Water	Fire

Fig. 61b. The pillars of the day of the coup attempt - December 1, 1989.

The pillars configuration on December 1, 1989 shows that the month pillar was wood and was supported by strong water, and the day pillar was strong wood riding over the element earth. So the strength of wood was overwhelming, and earth was retiring from the scene. But fortunately, fate was still on the side of Mrs Aquino. The Year of the Snake 己巳 was a year of strong earth and the following year, the Year of the Horse, was a year of metal on fire. This means that even though she was nearing the end of 1989, the earth influence, although diminished in strength, still remained, because fire was there to provide additional earth elements. Mrs Aquino still possessed support from earth and metal, reflecting the close support of the people, and distant support from the US.

The month of January 1990, being a month of strong water but weak fire, saw continued unrest and uncertainty. But strong earth re-emerged in February 1990 and the situation became favourable to Mrs Aquino and she resumed full control. However, one should note that Mrs Aquino left the strong pillar of earth and metal at the age of 56 so she is in a weaker position compared with past years. It is logical then to anticipate that she will face more challenges to her authority if she remains in her presidential position in the more critical water year of 1992.

112   Feng-shui and Destiny

Corazon Aquino

39. Nicolae Ceausescu: The Fall of a Dictator

    The dramatic downfall and execution of the Romanian dictator Nicolae Ceausescu on Christmas day 1989, sent shock waves round the world and marked the end of hard-line communism in Eastern Europe. The rapid happenings in Romania in December 1989 and their very quick conclusion took the whole world by surprise. The tragic end to President Ceausescu is the outcome of a maze of political, social and historical factors, the analysis of which will be a task for the historians and political scientists. However, the sudden death of a person is certainly a subject of destiny and fate and the case of Ceausescu again provides an interesting opportunity to demonstrate the workings of the Four Pillars of Destiny.
    Nicolae Ceausescu was born on January 26, 1918 and his four pillars are shown in Fig. 62. The birth hour is not available on record but it is assumed that 1300 to 1500 was his hour pillar. The four pillars show that President Ceausescu is a water person born in the winter month of January when water is most prosperous. Also, there is metal element on the day

pillar to generate nourishment for the water (metal gives birth to water). So he is considered a fairly strong water person.

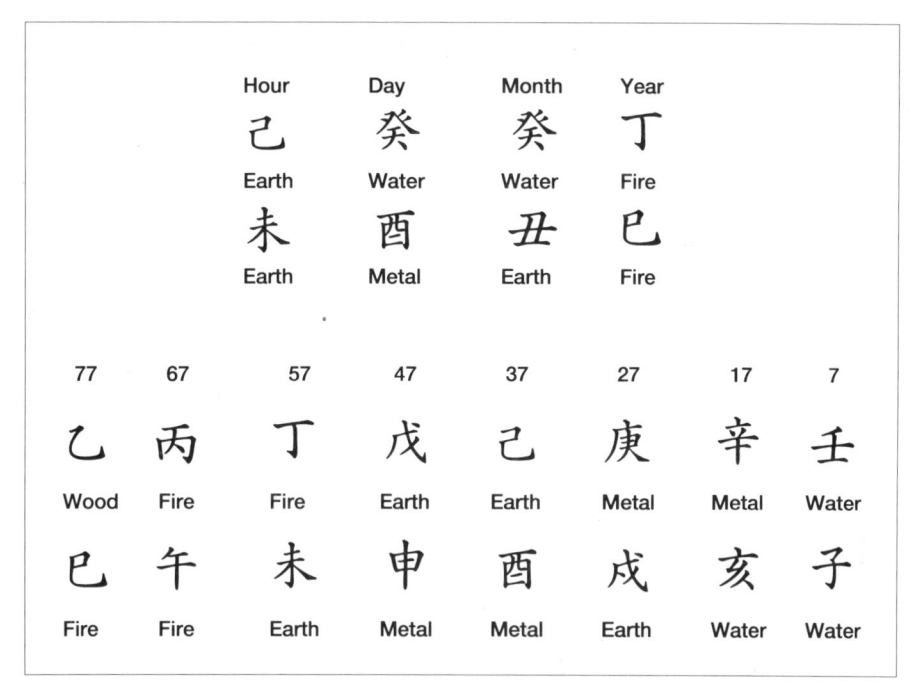

	Hour	Day	Month	Year
	己	癸	癸	丁
	Earth	Water	Water	Fire
	未	酉	丑	巳
	Earth	Metal	Earth	Fire

77	67	57	47	37	27	17	7
乙	丙	丁	戊	己	庚	辛	壬
Wood	Fire	Fire	Earth	Earth	Metal	Metal	Water
巳	午	未	申	酉	戌	亥	子
Fire	Fire	Earth	Metal	Metal	Earth	Water	Water

Fig. 62. Nicolae Ceausescu's Four Pillars of Destiny and Luck.

The element favourable to him would be earth which, in the first place, prevents the water from flooding and overflowing. Secondly, earth gives support to metal which in turn provides sufficient nourishment to the water. However, as earth will destroy water, it was a double-edged sword to Mr Ceausescu. If the water is strong enough to manipulate the earth, the earth will serve as power and control. On the other hand, if the water is weak, the overwhelming earth power will then resume its normal characteristic as the destroyer of the weak water. Such a configuration of the power elements is commonly found in persons deeply involved in power politics.

In the system of the Four Pillars of Destiny, power is represented by the element which destroys the individual self (the day pillar). For example, if the day pillar is in the wood category, meaning that the individual is a wood person, the presence of metal will be the power element as metal destroys wood. By the same token, the power element of Ceausescu was earth as he was a water person and earth destroys water. It is for this reason that the birth hour 1300 to 1500 was assigned to him as this is the hour which provided Ceausescu with the strong earth element (power) to match his position as a dictator.

As power is something that destroys the self, people involved in power politics are in a very delicate position. If the power element is weak, then the person will have little power over others. On the other hand, if the power element is excessively strong, there is the danger of being over-run and destroyed by the power element. Manipulating power is the art of balancing individual strength with the power element. And to help in such a balancing act is another important element, authority, which is the intermediate element in the cycle of birth between the power element and the self.

In the case of Ceausescu, earth is the power element, water the self, so the authority element is metal as the cycle of birth shows that earth gives birth to metal and metal gives birth to water. Metal is called the authority element because it is generated by power, and it is also known as the mother element as it gives birth to the self. So it can be seen that with the authority element standing in between power and self, even very strong power cannot destroy the self as the power energy is absorbed by the authority which transforms it into nourishment to improve the strength of the self.

In the ancient days, the authority of Chinese officials was symbolised by a jade or golden seal assigned to them by the Emperor. The officials could only exercise their power and give orders after presenting their seals, which signified their rank and position, and defined their authority. Therefore, the philosophy in the system of the four pillars is that one can only exercise power properly and wisely with proper authority. Without the authority element to act as a buffer, the power element will launch a direct attack on the self and bring about destruction. This is analogous to a dictator not exercising power wisely. So successful politicians often have well-balanced power and authority elements in their Four Pillars of Destiny and can exercise their power wisely and rise to high positions. The downfall of politicians in history is often brought about by some external force which upsets the balance.

To recapitulate: the Four Pillars of Destiny of a successful politician is often structured in such a manner that the power element, the authority element and the self are well-balanced. So the power generates authority, which in turn supports the strength of the self. In the four pillars of Nicolae Ceausescu, the late Romanian dictator, the strong earth element in the hour pillar is his source of power, and the metal in his day pillar is the authority element acting as buffer and conciliator between the power and himself, the water. The metal element gave Ceausescu the proper authority to exercise his power and protect the water (self) from being crushed by the earth element (power). So in his life, it can be demonstrated that metal and earth are the essential elements leading to his success in politics. Water is an unfavourable element as it weakens the metal and generates competition. Fire enhances the earth power but it could be dangerous as it will destroy metal, the balancing factor in his four pillars.

Nicolae Ceausescu was born into a poor peasant family in a village outside Bucharest. This poor family background is reflected by the presence of an unfavourable element, water, in the month pillar. His childhood was spent in poverty as his first and second luck pillars are all under the unfavourable water influence. It is recorded that he dropped out from elementary school at a young age and was first apprenticed to a shoemaker, before working in a factory. He joined the Communist Party at the age of 15 and even spent some years in jail in the 1930s.

However, his life changed when he entered the strong earth pillar at the age of 32. He became the Deputy General of the Romanian army. In 1965, at the age of 47, he stepped into another luck pillar of strong earth and metal, and it was in this year he became Communist Party Leader after the death of the First Secretary. The Ceausescu epoch of Romanian history commenced in this year. The subsequent years were of strong earth influence which all helped to enhance Ceausescu's power and authority. At the age of 57 (1975), he entered another luck pillar of earth and made himself the President of Romania. In the subsequent 10 years, President Ceausescu ruled Romania with an iron grip. The country was kept under tight control by his secret police force and he turned the Communist Party into his personal instrument.

Why did President Ceausescu degenerate from a great leader into a tyrant and dictator after the age of 57? The four pillars offer an explanation. Before the age of 57, Ceausescu was in the luck pillar of earth on metal, meaning power with authority. The elements earth, metal and water were in a harmonious cycle of birth and regeneration. Hence the configuration of his four pillars was in balance and he was able to manipulate his power wisely in the 10 years between the ages 47 and 57. However, as soon as he entered the luck pillar of fire on earth, fire generated more earth and at the same time threatened to destroy the metal. The implication is that there was a sudden upsurge of power (earth) but a loss of proper authority (metal), symbolising that Ceausescu could no longer exercise his power wisely and he went down the path of dictatorship in the following 10 years.

Without metal to act as the "peacemaker" between earth and water, there existed signs of disharmony in Ceausescu's four pillars in the 10 years from the ages of 57 to 67. But the fire sitting on the earth element was not very strong, as the earth element reduced the fire power. So the metal element, although weakened, was not totally destroyed. The situation continued to deteriorate as Ceausescu entered the next luck pillar of pure fire at the age of

Nicolae Ceausescu

116   Feng-shui and Destiny

67 when the earth element also disappeared and the metal was left in grave danger. It only took more fire generated from the year totally to melt down and devour the metal. Once the metal was destroyed, the water became defenceless against the earth and the four pillars were thrown off balance.

The year of fire, 1990, arrived and President Ceausescu was dramatically dragged down from power. The timing of Ceausescu's death on December 25, 1989, when the year of the fire horse had not yet arrived, is puzzling but can be explained. December 1989 was the month of the rat. As rat and horse are in conflict, the rat woke up the horse of 1990. So the fire horse had already started galloping on its course as early as December 1989 and the effect of the fire horse brought an early end to Ceausescu.

40. Mikhail Gorbachev and the Future of Perestroika

Mr Mikhail Gorbachev, the President and Communist Party Chief of the Soviet Union, is the man now under world focus and the stability of his position has a great impact on world peace. Fig. 63a shows Mr Gorbachev's Four Pillars of Destiny. The birth hour is assumed to be between 9 am and 11 am to fit in with his life as a great leader of power and authority.

	Hour	Day	Month	Year
	癸	丙	庚	辛
	Water	Fire	Metal	Metal
	巳	辰	寅	未
	Fire	Earth	Wood	Earth

78	68	58	48	38	28	18	8
壬	癸	甲	乙	丙	丁	戊	己
Water	Water	Wood	Wood	Fire	Fire	Earth	Earth
午	未	申	酉	戌	亥	子	丑
Fire	Earth	Metal	Metal	Earth	Water	Water	Earth

Fig. 63a. President Gorbachev's Four Pillars of Destiny and Luck.

Mr Gorbachev is a fire person born in the early spring season when the severe cold weather still prevailed in Russia. Therefore, the fire required plenty of wood to help generate more heat and light. Despite the prosperous wood element in the month pillar, the fire is still considered weak in strength. Besides the cold in the circumstance of birth which reduces the fire power, the heat and light of the fire are also dimmed by the presence of metal and earth. It is therefore obvious that Mr Gorbachev's four pillars very much favour the fire and wood elements which help to provide warmth and strength to his fire. As long as he is receiving the support of fire and wood, he is well able to control and manipulate power (water), and water in turn provides nourishment to generate more wood, enhancing the strength of Mr Gorbachev's fire. On the other hand, metal, which destroys wood and consumes fire energy, will be an unfavourable element. Earth gives birth to metal, hence earth is also an enemy to his four pillars, especially when the fire is weak.

Mr Gorbachev was born into a modest family in 1931. His father was a farm machine driver but subsequently became a Communist Party official in the village. It is recorded that a famine plagued the area in the years 1932 and 1933 and many village children died of starvation. The young Gorbachev survived but the years of his youth were uncertain ones for Russia, as Stalin tightened his grip on the country through a series of bloody purges. The Second World War and the German invasion of Russia in 1941 added more hardship to village life.

Gorbachev's family background is reflected by the unfavourable metal elements present in the month pillar, representing parents. Also the childhood suffering is consistent with Mr Gorbachev's first luck pillar of earth which weakened the fire strength by giving birth to more metal. Published information about Mr Gorbachev's youth is very scanty but his four pillars reveal that he entered a better phase of life after he was 17 when he left the luck pillar of pure earth and entered the luck pillar of earth over water. In this luck pillar, the unfavourable earth element was weak as the water provided nourishment to generate wood.

Hence Mr Gorbachev, then a young student and a part-time farm machine driver, was rewarded with the honour of the Red Flag Medal for his contributions in the year 1949. Such recognition also provided him access to the Communist Party and he became a party member in 1952. It perhaps also allowed him the precious chance to enter the renowned University of Moscow as a law student in 1950. Mr Gorbachev graduated from the University in 1955 and took up his first post in politics as an administrator of the Communist Youth Group. At the age of 24 he was under the favourable influence of water in his luck pillar. The subsequent luck pillar was also fire over water. Such favourable elements continued to bring him successes and he worked up the ladder towards party leadership in the Kremlin. At the end of 1962, the year of water and wood, he was promoted to an important position as organiser of the regional party committee, managing the appointment and promotion of party officials and cadres. This was a breakthrough as the position provided him the chance of close contact with central party members in Moscow.

In 1968, entering the luck pillar of fire, he was promoted to Second Regional Party Secretary in charge of agriculture, and was subsequently promoted to First Secretary of the region in 1970. The great success of the harvest in 1977 won for Mr Gorbachev the prestigious Revolution Medal in 1978, a year of fire, and he was eventually appointed as Secretary to the central party committee in the same year.

In Moscow, Mr Gorbachev gradually worked his way into the centre of power in the Kremlin Politburo and became the Party Secretary in 1985, a year of wood, when he just turned 54 and was in the luck pillar of wood over metal. The wood was able to provide him enough strength to manipulate power (water) and the metal, giving birth to water, also enhanced his power. The presence of wood in the month pillar supporting the fire provided him with a strong foundation and showed him to be a resourceful man of knowledge and education. The strong earth elements symbolise his intelligence and aspirations. Their presence in the earthly branches shows that he is wise but reserved. The water element in his hour pillar, strengthened by the prominent metal, exerts appropriate control over the fire, confirming Mr Gorbachev's reputation as a man of discipline. Although the earth element provides him endless reform ideas, his actions are taken with caution and restraint.

However, as the early months of 1990 went by, the Soviet leader appeared to be in a crisis situation caused by armed clashes flaring up in the outlying republics of Azerbaijan and Armenia, and also mounting problems with the Soviet economy. The Western countries were watching developments closely for signs that the pressure on Mr Gorbachev was being exploited by hard-line factions within the Kremlin opposed to reform. The fear was that if Mr Gorbachev's political power began to diminish, there could be a revival of hard-line communism, with serious ramifications for Eastern Europe and the West. The US President George Bush has expressed his sympathy for the Russian leader and his desire that Mr Gorbachev will manage to surmount the crisis and survive as a strong leader.

Let us again examine the four pillars of Mr Gorbachev to see what can be revealed by the interaction of the five elements. Mr Gorbachev is a man of weak fire, requiring wood to generate strength. Since 1979, when he was 48, Mr Gorbachev had been in a luck pillar of wood on metal. The metal served to generate water (power) and the wood provided him strength and put him in a position to manipulate power. Hence he rose rapidly towards the position of General Secretary of the Communist Party in 1985. The four pillars of Mr Gorbachev relied very much on the element of wood found in his month pillar, which acted as his life supporter, maintaining harmony and balance among all elements, with metal giving birth to water, water supporting wood and wood generating fire.

However, once the wood element is removed, the fire will become defenceless. There is the grave danger of metal generating water to extinguish the fire. The wood element served adequately its function as fire supporter until 1989/90 when Mr Gorbachev entered the luck pillar of 甲申 (wood on metal). The difference between this luck pillar and the previous one is that the metal in the present luck pillar is in the *yang* category whereas the previous one was *yin* metal. *Yang* metal, meaning strong and positive, will have a substantial impact on his destiny. Furthermore, the *yang* metal is in direct clash with the *yang* wood in Mr Gorbachev's month pillar. So it directly endangers the position of the life supporter and threatens to upset the balance of the entire Four Pillars of Destiny.

Therefore, entering the luck pillar of wood on metal, Mr Gorbachev moves into a new phase of life when his position will be more fragile and insecure and he will have to face challenges, turmoil and crisis situations. The strong metal poses a strong threat which could remove his foundation of wood and throw him off balance. The configuration of the Year of the Horse (1990) is metal over fire. The metal on the heavenly stem will launch an attack on the wood in Mr Gorbachev's present luck pillar. So he will suffer some apparent challenges and attacks. However, the fire in the earthly branch of the year will come to his aid and strengthen his foundation and he will be able to rally support and continue to stand firm in his position in 1990, despite apparent setbacks.

In January 1990, there were rumours suggesting Mr Gorbachev was about to resign, which he strongly denied, and his subsequent victory over opponents of reform at the plenary session of the Soviet Communist Party Central Committee in early February seemed to confirm this. Each luck pillar governs a period of 10 years and the general principle is that the influence of the heavenly stems (upper character) is more prominent in the first five years and the earthly branches (lower character) will carry more weight in the later five years. As Mr Gorbachev's present luck pillar is wood over metal, the wood influence is stronger in the first five years from 1989. However the dangerous metal effect will gradually intensify yearly from 1989 onwards.

The astonishing events in the USSR in the week between August 18 and 22, 1991 took the world by surprise. The sudden coup and the miraculous return of President Gorbachev to power in Moscow in three days abruptly turned a new page in world history and its impacts and aftermath is comparable to the French Revolution in 1789 and the Bolshevik Revolution in 1917.

We have seen that President Gorbachev is a fire man born in the cold Russian spring and that he is very much in need of the warmth of fire and wood. Therefore he will be able to continue pushing the implementation of pereistroika when fire influence remains powerful. However, his situation will deteriorate rapidly towards 1992 when the element of fire is dying and metal and water will take control.

The wood element is President Gorbachev's supporter and the metal element, especially the *yang* metal symbolised by the Chinese character 申 (monkey), is his deadly enemy as it will destroy his wood support. It is on the basis of such simple theory that Gorbachev is predicted to be entering a more dangerous phase of life as from the autumn of 1991, when fire reaches a very weak phase in its 12-year life cycle and metal gradually takes over the helm in the Chinese almanac.

President Gorbachev, exactly as predicted, had become a victim of the transition from fire into metal on a day of metal in a month of metal in the autumn of 1991. The coup was announced on August 19 but the rebellion actually started with the house arrest of President Gorbachev at his Crimean vacation retreat in the afternoon of Sunday, August 18 at about 4.55 pm. This date is expressed in terms of the four pillars in Fig. 63b. It is obvious that the coup took place at the most unfortunate and darkest hour of President Gorbachev when all the *yang* Metal elements gathered their strength and lauched a massive attack against Gorbachev's life supporter – wood. As readers can see from the above pillars, there are altogether five metal elements on that date and at that particular hour. Three of the earthly branches are *yang* metal represented by the character 申 which is the most dangerous enemy to Gorbachev and comes into direct clash against his wood support. To add to the misfortune, President Gorbachev, at the age of 60, is under the influence of a luck pillar of wood over metal. So there is another *yang* metal in his own destiny which again intensified the metal attack on August 18.

However, President Gorbachev survived this crisis and returned to Moscow on August 22. Political scientists can put forward a thousand reasons to explain the failure of the coup and Gorbachev's returning to power. This can also be clearly explained from the metaphysical angle. As the element of wood is Gorbachev's supporter, the reason for his survival is certainly associated with the wood element. Although the threat of metal is very strong, Gorbachev is still in a luck pillar of wood which took very firm root in his Pillars of Destiny.

120 *Feng-shui and Destiny*

Hour	Day	Month	Year
甲	庚	丙	辛
Wood	Metal	Fire	Metal
申	申	申	未
Metal	Metal	Metal	Earth

Fig. 63b. The four pillars on August 18, 1991.

As such, his wood support is strong enough to resist the metal. Signs of failure of the coup appeared on 21 August – a date of strong water which supported the wood and reduced the metal strength. And President Gorbachev returned to Moscow and resumed office on 22 August which is, of course, a day of very strong wood.

Looking ahead, despite the fact that President Gorbachev has survived this first wave of metal attack and despite the fact that he may appear to be in a stronger position with hardliner elements eliminated, the author is still not too optimistic about his political future in the coming months. The reason is simply that the metal power will gradually become stronger as the Year of the Monkey approaches. It is a strong metal monkey which will again pose a formidable threat to Gorbachev's Wood support. As the impact of the metal monkey

President Gorbachev

is expected to be more fatal, it will not be surprising to see another political storm gathering strength in the Soviet Union which may eventually cause the retirement of President Gorbachev from the Kremlin.

41. Nelson Mandela's 27 Years of Imprisonment

African leader Nelson Mandela was released in 1990 after 27 years of imprisonment. It would be interesting to study his past and evaluate his Four Pillars of Destiny. Being imprisoned for more than one-third of the average human lifespan is grave misfortune indeed and this should be clearly reflected in the Four Pillars of Destiny. We have seen many examples of such a technique accurately revealing a person's rise and fall in politics. Let us put the three pillars of Nelson Mandela to the test and see how the aspect of human freedom can also be read from a person's birth data.

Nelson Mandela was born on July 18, 1918. His three pillars are shown in Fig. 64. He is a fire person born in hot summer in the blazing heat of the African continent. His first three pillars, year, month and day, show prominent fire, wood and earth elements. There is a total absence of water and metal. The dry wood supports the vigorous burning of the fire. Because of this configuration, even without assigning a birth hour for Mr Mandela, it is a reasonable hypothesis that he is a very strong fire person and his fire strength is extreme due to the very hot climate of his birth place.

	Hour	Day	Month	Year
	?	丙 Fire	己 Earth	戊 Earth
	?	寅 Wood	未 Earth	午 Fire

74	64	54	44	34	24	14	4
丁 Fire	丙 Fire	乙 Wood	甲 Wood	癸 Water	壬 Water	辛 Metal	庚 Metal
卯 Wood	寅 Wood	丑 Earth	子 Water	亥 Water	戌 Earth	酉 Metal	申 Metal

Fig. 64. Nelson Mandela's Four Pillars of Destiny and Luck.

For this reason, the normal technique of seeking a balance by restraining fire's energy with water will not work. It is not difficult to see that any amount of water would quickly turn into hot steam with such a strong fire. So it is more appropriate to go along with the fire rather than obstruct its burning. The favourable element for Mr Mandela is therefore earth. As fire gives birth to earth, earth represents Mr Mandela's aspirations and intelligence and provides outlets for his excessive fire energy. On the other hand, water threatens his fire and will cause obstruction in his passage through life. Wood helps to intensify the already excessive fire energy and it will also destroy earth, suppressing his free will and aspirations. So wood can be his worst enemy.

Let us now briefly examine Mr Mandela's background and see if the above hypothesis is consistent with his past. A person's month pillar often reveals information about his parents and the year pillar can reflect the background of his grandparents. Mr Mandela's year and month pillars are both occupied by favourable earth elements. This indicates that he has a strong family background. Indeed, Mr Mandela was born into the royal house of a large African tribe. His great grandfather was a famed tribal king and his father a royal councillor with four wives.

Mr Mandela, although a prince of royal blood, grew up as a herdsman in the pastures by the side of the Bashee river. During his childhood, he assisted with ploughing and looking after cattle. His first two luck pillars of metal show that this was a peaceful, though not very

Nelson Mandela

comfortable, phase in his life. Although metal is not a very favourable element as it generates water, there is no water in Mr Mandela's four pillars to create trouble during this period. He received missionary education which prepared him for legal practice in his later life.

When he was about 24, Mr Mandela entered the luck pillar of water over earth. The water was too weak compared with the overwhelming earth. He entered into a law apprenticeship and subsequently set up his black law office in South Africa. He also joined the African National Congress in 1944.

In the subsequent luck pillar of strong water after the age of 34, his active participation in the struggle against apartheid eventually led to his arrest in 1956 and he was tried for treason. The year 1956 features fire over metal. The metal intensified the water influence in his luck pillar to attack his fire. However, the weak fire in the yearly heavenly stem was still able to come to his aid and so he remained a free man for a few more years.

Let us now focus on the year 1962, the year when Mr Mandela was jailed. He was then 44 years old and had just entered the luck pillar of wood over water. The year 1962 was also a year of water over wood. The combined effect was that water destroyed his fire and wood destroyed his earth. With both favourable elements suppressed, Mr Mandela lost his freedom in August 1962 for incitement and was subsequently sentenced to life imprisonment for sabotage and conspiracy to overthrow the government in 1964, again a year of wood and water.

The elements of wood and water deprived him of freedom (earth) and it was necessary to have the wood and water influence removed or suppressed before he could regain his freedom. So the chance of release from prison should fall in a year of metal and fire, when metal clashes with wood and fire clashes with water. Looking at the Chinese calendar, the earliest year of metal over fire after 1962 occurred in 1990, 27 years after Mr Mandela was jailed.

42. Mike Tyson vs James Douglas

Students of Chinese fortune-telling often find the Four Pillars of Destiny a very difficult subject to master. To start with, they have to memorise a large variety of apparently meaningless Chinese characters. Then they have to try to understand what they symbolise and their complicated inter-relationships. They must go through a lengthy beginner's stage which can be very boring and students may feel they are groping about in the dark for unseen rewards. Many will lose faith in the subject and give up after a few months, searching without seeing the light at the end of the tunnel. As a veteran teacher quite correctly puts it, learning the four pillars is like learning to play the violin. The violin sounds awful in the hands of a beginner, but once he gets past the beginner's stage, he will find endless joy in the beautiful music the instrument can produce.

Those who are persistent in their study of the Four Pillars of Destiny will eventually discover that it is merely a technique of logical deduction based on a simple theory about the interaction of the five elements: metal, wood, water, fire and earth. Once the inter-relationships — the cycle of birth and the cycle of destruction — are well understood, you

124 Feng-shui and Destiny

will find that predicting destiny is relatively simple. And the reward is knowledge of your future and that of other people. You can foresee their ups and downs and see their potential as if you were reading a novel.

So far we have noted that complicated aspects of human life, like suicide, murder, disease, political struggle and tyranny, have been analysed and only simple logic based on the interaction of the five elements has been employed. All one needs in order to master the technique is the courage to imagine, to assume and to have faith in the validity of the art. To demonstrate once again the power of such simple logic, let us examine the four pillars of Mike Tyson and James Douglas to predict their respective fortunes.

Mike Tyson is suitably named Iron Mike, as his day pillar shows he is a pure metal person born in mid-summer when fire is most prosperous. From his four pillars we can see the prominent features, wood and fire (Fig. 65a). Although Tyson has a strong metal foundation as his day pillar is metal on metal, he can only be considered weak metal as he is surrounded by strong fire and wood. Therefore, his favourable elements should be metal and earth which give birth to more metal. Wood and fire will bring him pressure and hardship as wood generates strong fire which threatens to destroy the metal.

	Hour	Day	Month	Year
	?	庚 Metal	甲 Wood	丙 Fire
	?	申 Metal	午 Fire	午 Fire

72	62	52	42	32	22	12	2
壬 Water	辛 Metal	庚 Metal	己 Earth	戊 Earth	丁 Fire	丙 Fire	乙 Wood
寅 Wood	丑 Earth	子 Water	亥 Water	戌 Earth	酉 Metal	申 Metal	未 Earth

Fig. 65a. Mike Tyson's Four Pillars of Destiny and Luck.

The month pillar reflects Tyson's parents and family background. Prominent wood and fire appear on the month pillar indicating an unhappy childhood. Indeed, Tyson was born of a broken family in the urban slums of Brooklyn, New York. The young Tyson grew up in an environment of crime and poverty and by the age of nine, he had acquired a reputation as a pick-pocket. As he grew in age and size, so did his acts of violence and anti-social behaviour. He was frequently taken to police stations after complaints of gang fights and theft. This unfortunate childhood is clearly reflected in Tyson's first luck pillar of wood which exerted a bad influence on his four pillars. Also from the luck pillars we can see Tyson's fate changed dramatically after the age of 12 when he entered the second luck pillar of fire over metal. Fire sitting on metal is often compared to the setting sun with weak light and heat. So it is considered a favourable luck pillar as the metal influence carries more weight than the fire.

At the age of 13 (1979, a year of earth) Tyson met the great boxing coach, Constantine D'Amato who immediately recognised the potential of this stocky young boy and became his manager-trainer. In the following years, Tyson received intensive training and as soon as he came under the influence of pure metal at the age of 17, he was credited with one victory after another, knocking out almost everyone he faced. His iron fists took him from Junior Olympics to the World Championship and at the young age of 20 in 1986, he defeated Trevor Berbick in a technical knockout and won the title of Heavyweight Boxing Champion of the World. All this happened within five years in the second luck pillar of metal which very much strengthened Iron Mike's power. But his luck was soon to change.

February 11, 1990 was a day of catastrophe for Mike Tyson, the man who once boasted: "There is not a soul on this planet who can beat me." But the impossible happened, the undisputed Heavyweight Boxing Champion of the World was knocked out by James "Buster" Douglas in the 10th round of a contest in front of 40,000 screaming fans in Tokyo, Japan. Tyson has vowed to regain the title. What do the four pillars tell us of his chances of achieving this goal?

We have seen that Tyson is a metal man requiring metal and earth to support his strength on the one hand but, on the other hand, wood and fire also reduce his strength as fire destroys metal. Tyson has had a glorious record; before he was beaten by Douglas he had won 37 bouts since he turned 17. Throughout this time he has been guided by a luck pillar of fire over metal, a combination which stayed with him until his 32nd birthday. This combination has two implications. Firstly, the metal element increased Tyson's strength and secondly, the configuration of fire over metal actually reflected his superiority over his opponents.

When evaluating a match between the subject and an opponent one can compare the strength of the subject (represented by the day pillar) against the strength of the competitor (symbolised by the element of the subject appearing in the luck pillar or the dominant yearly configuration). When the subject is Tyson, the metal over metal, as shown by his day pillar, indicates he is strong. His opponents have the combination of fire over metal, Tyson's luck pillars after the age of 17. So Tyson, by virtue of the stronger metal configuration, is at an advantage over his opponents. Therefore it is not surprising that he gained 37 victories. However, the luck pillar is also subject to the influence of the dominant yearly configuration.

1990 was the Year of the Horse and the horse symbolises metal over fire. As the luck pillars, fire over metal, belonged to weaker opponents, it would be logical to assume that in 1990, Tyson would remain unbeaten. However, the Tyson defeat in February shows that although the basic theory of the four pillars is fairly straightforward, it requires much further careful analysis before one can successfully apply the technique with accuracy.

An apparently weak opponent, James "Buster" Douglas, was able to defeat Tyson in February. The moment of truth came at about noon on February 11, 1990. The year pillar of

126 Feng-shui and Destiny

1990, metal over fire, represents the opponent, Douglas (Fig. 65b). If we look at the year pillar alone, he appears to be a weak metal over fire person. However, the entire four pillars reveal many fire and earth elements. Fire gives birth to earth which in turn supports metal. Hence the weak metal, on that particular date, suddenly grew in strength, enabling Douglas to deliver a blow to Tyson's career. On the other hand, the strong fire appearing on this date was most unfavourable to Tyson. The prominent wood elements in Tyson's four pillars intensified the threat of the fire and rejected the favourable earth influences. So through bad timing on Tyson's part, Douglas was able to become champion despite Tyson's being the stronger fighter. However, Tyson's luck pillars, fire and metal, remain strong. If he is able to get a re-match, it would not be surprising if he were to regain his title.

Hour	Day	Month	Year
丙	丁	戊	庚
Fire	Fire	Earth	Metal
午	未	寅	午
Fire	Earth	Wood	Fire

Fig. 65b. The pillars on the day of Tyson's defeat — February 11, 1990.

As February 11 brought catastrophe for Mike Tyson, it marked the beginning of a splendid new life for his conqueror, the new undisputed World Heavyweight Boxing Champion James "Buster" Douglas.

Douglas was born on April 7, 1960. Douglas is a wood person born in late spring when the prosperity of the wood element is phasing out (Fig. 65c). On the heavenly stems of the year and month pillars, strong metal elements are prominent. These threaten and suppress the wood. So Douglas is a weak wood person requiring water for nourishment. Metal is his enemy as it will attack and destroy the wood. Earth is no good either, as it generates more metal and obstructs the flow of water. Fire requires special attention as it weakens the wood on the one hand by absorbing wood energy, and protects it on the other by keeping metal under control. Bearing in mind the intricate relationships among the five elements in Douglas' four pillars, we will now examine how they affect the boxer's life and brought him fame on February 11.

Let us first examine his family background by looking at his year pillar, representing his grandparents; and also his month pillar, symbolising his father. Both are occupied by strong metal, threatening Douglas' wood. Strong pressure from the grandfather and father is consistent with Douglas' background. The family had very high expectations of the young Douglas: his grandfather, William Douglas, was an amateur boxer, and his father Billy "Dynamite" Douglas was also a boxer. They provided him with strict boxing training from a very young age and Douglas was the Golden Gloves Champion of Ohio at the age of 10.

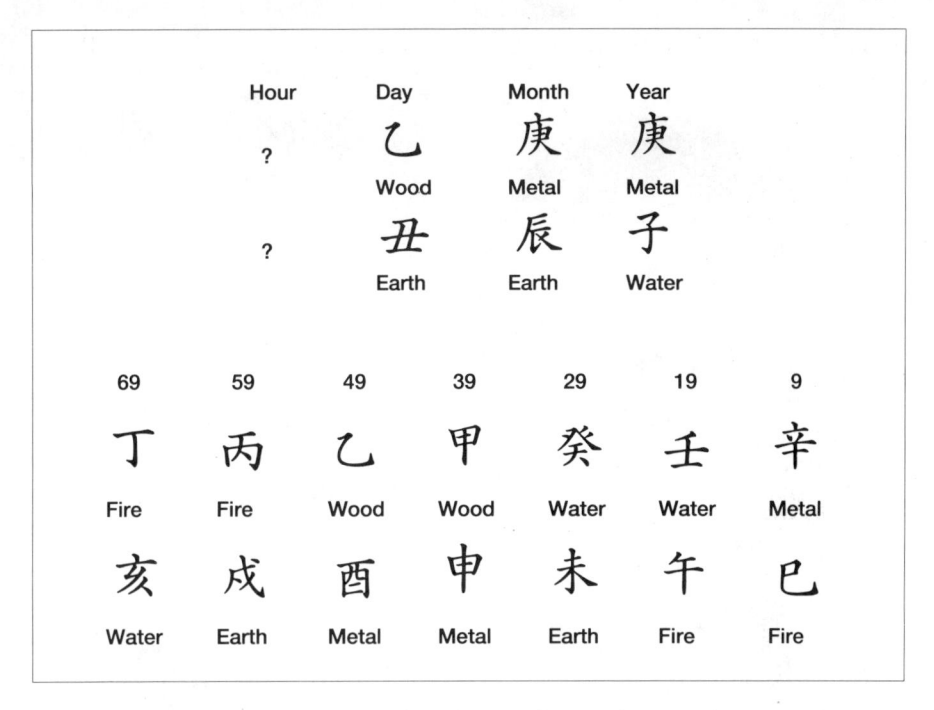

	Hour	Day	Month	Year
	?	乙 Wood	庚 Metal	庚 Metal
	?	丑 Earth	辰 Earth	子 Water

69	59	49	39	29	19	9
丁 Fire	丙 Fire	乙 Wood	甲 Wood	癸 Water	壬 Water	辛 Metal
亥 Water	戌 Earth	酉 Metal	申 Metal	未 Earth	午 Fire	巳 Fire

Fig. 65c. James Buster Douglas' Four Pillars of Destiny and Luck.

Buster Douglas generated interest not only because of his dramatic knockout of Tyson but also because he was able to keep in check his grief caused by the tragic death of his mother only a week before he left for Tokyo. This tragedy was also reflected in the four pillars. As water gives birth to wood, the water element is naturally a symbol of Douglas' mother. At the age of 29, he had just entered the luck pillar of water over earth. Water sitting on its destroyer (earth) must be very weak. So any further earth element appearing in the year or the month will crush the water. This happened in February, a month of earth causing destruction to the water. Thus the death of Douglas' mother was foreseen.

His surprising victory can be attributed to two major factors. Firstly, at the age of 29, Douglas had just entered a very favourable luck pillar of water, providing the necessary nourishment to his wood. Hence he is in a phase of general good fortune. But its magnitude should not be exaggerated as the favourable element, water, is sitting on earth, so it is only of limited strength. Secondly, and I consider this the more important, the day February 11 was a day of strong fire. The fire element is favourable to Douglas as it helps him to keep his deadly enemy, metal, under control. In this case, it was Mike Tyson who was suppressed by the strong fire.

128   *Feng-shui and Destiny*

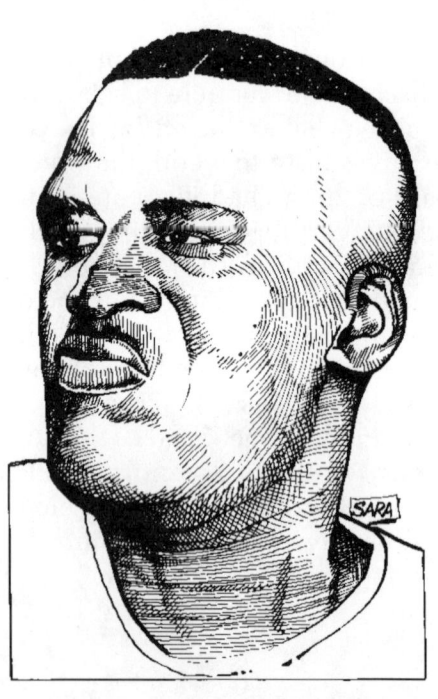

Mike Tyson and James Douglas

43. Stefan Edberg vs Michael Chang

Sports is a very exciting field which can generate many moving stories of human struggle, glory or disappointment. In every match there is a winner and a loser. Victory or failure is the result of complicated factors such as physique, skill, determination and environment. But it seems the majority of athletes admit that luck plays an important role, and luck is commonly regarded as the mysterious unknown factor which may sometimes cause big surprises and bring about totally unexpected results. The overwhelming power of luck often upsets all logic such as physique, skill and experience, and may even allow the underdog to defeat the favourite as in the case of Mike Tyson vs James "Buster" Douglas.

The pattern of luck is traceable through the four pillars of destiny. Theoretically, competitions and match results should be predictable with a high degree of accuracy. The technique is best applied to matches involving only two players, such as in boxing, tennis or chess, as a comparison between the luck of the two opponents will shed light on the match results and victory should be on the side of the player with the better luck. We have already seen how the luck factor helped James Douglas defeat Mike Tyson. Let us now explore the luck factor behind a tennis match, that between Michael Chang and Stefan Edberg, held in Hong Kong on April 6, 1990. The winner was Stefan Edberg. So let us examine his four pillars first (Fig. 66a).

	Hour	Day	Month	Year
	?	戊 Earth	己 Earth	乙 Wood
	?	寅 Wood	丑 Earth	巳 Fire

55	45	35	25	15	5
癸 Water	甲 Wood	乙 Wood	丙 Fire	丁 Fire	戊 Earth
未 Earth	申 Metal	酉 Metal	戌 Earth	亥 Water	子 Water

Fig. 66a. Stefan Edberg's Four Pillars of Destiny and Luck.

Edberg is an earth person born in the winter month of January. The hour of birth is not known. But considering he was born in the cold winter of northern Europe, and that there is a prominent presence of wood threatening to destroy the earth, it is quite certain that he is not a very strong earth person and requires fire to provide him with warmth and nourishment. Besides fire, the element metal is also necessary as it assists to keep the wood under control. At the same time, the element metal also provides an outlet for the earth energy and symbolises his fame and skill. On the other hand, earth symbolises competitors and times of strong earth means he will be facing strong opponents.

Tracing the past success of Edberg, it is not difficult to show that his life runs parallel to the favourable fire and metal elements. His major breakthrough in the field of tennis was achieved after he turned 17 when he was in the favourable luck pillar of fire. His continual success advanced him to the world's number two position in 1987, at the age of 20, in a year of fire. However, he suffered setbacks in the years 1988 and 1989, when he dropped to the number five position and was twice defeated by the teenager Michael Chang. The reason is quite obvious. The years 1988 and 1989 were both years of strong earth, meaning strong competitors appearing on the horizon.

Entering the year 1990, a year of metal over fire, Edberg appears in superb form with renewed confidence. His first important victory was won on March 11. He was rewarded with HK$580,000 and won the Newsweek Cup by defeating Andre Agassi. The day was one of wood on water in a month of earth on wood. As earth appearing in the calendar refers to an opponent, and this opponent is surrounded by wood, it is obvious that it is a weaker opponent, not comparable to the strong earth of Edberg with the fire support. On 6 April, a day of metal in a month of metal, Edberg again displayed great skill and defeated Michael Chang in the Hong Kong Exhibition match. Therefore, as long as Edberg is surrounded by the favourable elements of fire and metal, we can reasonably predict that luck is on his side.

The third victory was on April 15, 1990, again a day of strong metal in the month and year of metal. Edberg is in a very strong position with fire in the year and luck pillar supporting his earth, and the metal in the day pillar to ward off the threat of wood. Hence he won the championship in the Japan Open Tournament in Tokyo with little difficulty. With the combined influence of strong fire and metal in 1990, it is expected that Edberg should maintain his high profile with more victories. But he must avoid the days of earth by all means.

Let us now take a look at the fortunes of Michael Chang, the 18-year-old American Chinese, the favourite star of Hong Kong tennis fans. He won the championship in the French Open Tournament in 1989 and advanced rapidly to the world's fifth seeded player. However, his performance since the start of 1990 has disappointed his Hong Kong fans, who saw him defeated by Stefan Edberg in the Exhibition Match in Hong Kong on April 6. He was subsequently beaten by Aron Krickstein in the Japan Open Tournament on April 14.

On the basis of these match dates, let us see if it is possible to trace the pattern of Chang's luck factor in the year 1990. Chang's Four Pillars of Destiny are shown in Fig. 66b.

Chang is a water person born in the spring season when wood is the most prosperous element. Although the water is not in the season, given the large number of water elements in the three pillars, he can be regarded as a pretty strong water person. He should be strong enough to generate wood, symbolising his skill, aspiration and fame. Also, he should be strong enough to resist the suppression of earth and turn it into useful tools (these represent his social status and position). Therefore, we can assume earth and wood are favourable elements bringing him fame, high status and fortune. On the other hand, water is his competitor and metal, generating more water, will bring strong competition and so is an unfavourable element.

From the age of 14, Chang was in the favourable luck pillar of wood, meaning fame and skill, and he rose rapidly to become the world's fifth seeded player at the young age of 17. Examining Michael Chang's three pillars above, we can see that all three pillars contain water elements. If each pillar symbolises a water person, the year pillar, water on water, is the strongest, and the day pillar, water on earth, symbolising Michael Chang himself, is the weakest.

As water represents Chang's competitors, the configuration of his three pillars shows that he has to face very strong competition all through his life and his competitors, especially the water on the year pillar, are particularly strong. If we view the water on Chang's year pillar as his strongest opponent in any tennis match, then everything that weakens this opponent will improve Chang's chance of winning. On the other hand, an element that strengthens the water will enhance the position of his opponent and lead to Chang's defeat.

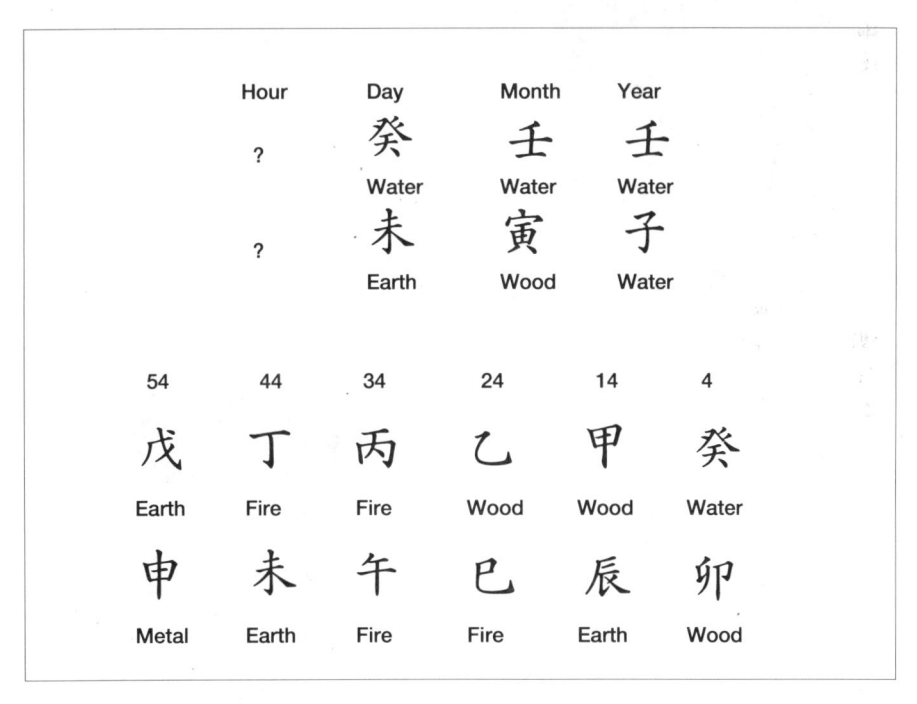

Hour	Day	Month	Year
?	癸 Water	壬 Water	壬 Water
?	未 Earth	寅 Wood	子 Water

54	44	34	24	14	4
戊 Earth	丁 Fire	丙 Fire	乙 Wood	甲 Wood	癸 Water
申 Metal	未 Earth	午 Fire	巳 Fire	辰 Earth	卯 Wood

Fig. 66b. Michael Chang's Four Pillars of Destiny and Luck.

This theory seems to be quite accurate in explaining Michael Chang's past match records. The years 1988 and 1989 were both years of strong earth. The earth element suppressed the water in Chang's year pillar, symbolising the weakening of his opponent. Chang achieved great success, defeated Edberg and won the chanmpionship in the French Open Tournament in 1989.

132   Feng-shui and Destiny

In 1990, a year of metal, the metal element gave birth to water and enhanced the strength of the water element in Chang's year pillar, symbolising the strengthening of Chang's opponents. So Chang did not stand a very good chance of winning. For Chang, the year started off with an apparently encouraging achievement. He won the Chicago Tournament at the end of March, a month of earth suppressing his water opponent. However, the unfavourable metal influence of the year soon came into play. He was defeated by Edberg on April 6 in Hong Kong and beaten by Krickstein on April 4 in Tokyo. Both dates unfortunately fell on a month of metal in a year of metal which generated support for his opponents. The years 1991, 1992 and 1993 are all in the water and metal category. This will mean that more and more strong opponents will appear in Michael Chang's life and he will have to fight harder and harder to maintain or advance his position.

Stefan Edberg and Michael Chang

44. President George Bush's Victory in the Gulf

At the beginning of 1990, I made some brief remarks about a few prominent persons' Four Pillars of Destiny in an article appearing in the *Hong Kong Standard* on January 26, the eve of the Year of the Horse. I commented briefly on President Bush: "On balance, the year is a turbulent and eventful one for President Bush with heavy work pressure and travels. President Bush was born in the Year of the Rat, which is in conflict with the fire horse. Hence it will be a hard and active year and President Bush will face strong challenges and critical situations." The activities of the President in 1990 seem to bear out these predictions.

After the controversial military operation to capture General Noriega in Panama earlier in the year, President Bush was again driven by destiny into another crisis situation in the Middle East. The scale of US commitment and military involvement this time was the largest since the Vietnam War. A more detailed evaluation of President Bush's Four pillars of Destiny at this time, therefore, should be most appropriate.

As usual, his exact birth hour is not known and we can only make an assessment on the basis of three pillars (Fig. 67).

	Hour	Day	Month	Year
	?	壬 Water	庚 Metal	甲 Wood
	?	戌 Earth	午 Fire	子 Water

68	58	48	38	28	18	8
丁 Fire	丙 Fire	乙 Wood	甲 Wood	癸 Water	壬 Water	辛 Metal
丑 Earth	子 Water	亥 Water	戌 Earth	酉 Metal	申 Metal	未 Earth

Fig. 67. President Bush's Four Pillars of Destiny and Luck.

President Bush is a water person born in the mid-summer month of June when the most prosperous element is fire. So the water element is not "in the season". Furthermore, the water is sitting on earth, its destroyer. So although the water has taken root in the year pillar and has the close support of metal in the month pillar, on balance, we can conclude that

President Bush is a weak water person relying on the support of metal and water elements for survival. So, metal and water are his favourite elements whereas earth and fire could be his deadly enemies.

As our assessment is made only on the basis of three pillars instead of four, further checks should be made to test the hypothesis to make sure that the birth hour, which is unknown, will not substantially change the effect of the first three pillars. To verify the predictions about President Bush's favourable and unfavourable elements, the usual method is to check the month pillar against the person's family background. The heavenly stem of the month pillar symbolises a person's father, so a favourable month pillar will usually reflect a good family background and good support from the father. In the case of President Bush, the metal element in the month pillar provides him strong support. Indeed, his father, Mr Prescott Shelton Bush, is a prominent banker and a respected Senator. Such a wealthy family background matches well with the father-and-son relationship as reflected by the three pillars.

Another effective test is to check on some major events in the person's past to see if its year of occurrence can support the prediction. Let us look at President Bush's marriage. He got married to Lady Barbara Pierce in 1944 when he was 20 years old and was in the luck pillar

President George Bush

of water on metal. Also, the year 1944 was again a year of metal, hence the heavy metal influence brought him a happy and lasting marriage. As our predictions successfully pass the two tests, it can be firmly established that metal and water elements can bring good fortune to President Bush, and such predictions also provide the basis for forecasting the development of the Gulf crisis.

President Bush was 66 years old in 1990 and in the luck pillar of water which was certainly a favourable phase in his life. The Year of the Horse was metal over fire. The fire element was in conflict with the water and caused some challenges and turbulences but the metal element of the year was still supportive of President Bush.

Now let us look at the date August 2 when the Iraqi troops invaded Kuwait. It fell in a month of water over earth. Water symbolises President Bush's colleagues. Water sitting on earth, its destroyer, shows a friend is in trouble. From August 8 to October 8, the Chinese almanac passes into a period of wood over metal. The wood is weak and the metal influence is dominant. So President Bush was in high profile and his status and power will be enhanced in these two autumn months. However, after 8 October, there comes a month of fire on earth, when we can expect President Bush to suffer some temporary setbacks.

In the long run, the years 1991, 1992 and 1993 are all years of water and metal which are all favourable. Therefore it is quite safe to predict that the Gulf crisis will eventually turn out to be a victory for President Bush.*

* The predictions made here and elsewhere in the book about the Gulf War and the role of key figures like President Bush and Saddam Hussein appeared in the author's weekly column in the *Hong Kong Standard* throughout 1990 as the Gulf crisis made front page news worldwide. Many of the predictions have proved amazingly accurate. See also *Chapter 46: Operation Desert Storm*, and *Chapter 52: The I Ching View of the Gulf Crisis*.

45. The Destiny of Saddam Hussein

Iraq's sudden invasion of Kuwait in August 1990 stunned the world and quickly developed into the greatest crisis facing the US and Arab countries. Tension increased throughout the Middle East with the build-up of military forces in the Gulf and the international embargo on, and naval blockage of, Iraq. However, over a month went by and there was still no sign of a quick solution to the crisis. The state of affairs kept the world in suspense and people were wondering when the first shot would be fired and how long the war would last if it did break out.

To try to forecast the development of the Gulf crisis, one possible way is to check on the fortunes of the key persons involved in the conflict. Having examined President Bush's Four Pillars of Destiny for a prediction of his fortune, let us now turn to the man at the centre of the conflict — President Saddam Hussein. His three pillars are indicated in Fig. 68.

136   Feng-shui and Destiny

	Hour	Day	Month	Year
	?	乙	甲	丁
		Wood	Wood	Fire
	?	酉	辰	丑
		Metal	Earth	Earth

68	58	48	38	28	18	8
丁	戊	己	庚	辛	壬	癸
Fire	Earth	Earth	Metal	Metal	Water	Water
酉	戌	亥	子	丑	寅	卯
Metal	Earth	Water	Water	Earth	Wood	Wood

Fig. 68. Saddam Hussein's Four Pillars of Destiny and Luck.

President Saddam Hussein is a wood person born at the end of the spring season when the power of wood was fading away. Also, there is no water element in the three pillars to support the wood, but we see the prominent presence of metal and earth which together have a weakening effect on the wood. So on balance, President Saddam Hussein is a weak wood person in need of water and wood support for survival. Metal can cause harm to the wood and so could be his deadly enemy. Earth gives birth to metal and destroys the water he needs; earth is therefore his foe. Fire, although it consumes his wood energy, can turn out to be favourable as it will help to keep the threat of the metal under control and so can defend the wood against any attack from metal. Let us put our assessment to the test and see if it matches President Hussein's past.

Saddam Hussein was born in 1937 in the small town of Tikrit. He came from a landless peasant family and his father died before he was born, and he was entrusted to the care of his uncle — Khayr Allah Talfah — an army officer who took part in the unsuccessful Rashid Ali coup against the pro-British government in 1941. This uncle Talfah had strong influence over Saddam in his political ideas, and the favourable wood element on the heavenly stem of his month pillar obviously reflected the support of his uncle, rather than his father who died before his birth.

In 1959, a year of earth, Hussein took part in an unsuccessful coup against the Qasim regime and was shot in the leg on October 17, 1959, a day of metal in a month of earth, and he fled in exile to Egypt and Syria. In 1964, another bad year of earth, he was arrested and sent to the central prison in Baghdad for smuggling firearms. The years of hardship were also accurately reflected by his luck pillar of metal between the ages of 28 and 33.

The Destiny of Saddam Hussein

The success of another coup in 1968 led by Al Bakr put Saddam in power. But he soon got himself involved in severe party struggles and lived in permanent fear of arrest, imprisonment and death. However, with the support of the strong water influence in the favourable luck pillar after the age of 38, he gradually worked his way to the presidency in 1979 at the age of 42.

An examination of the turn of events in the eight-year Iran-Iraq War also leads to the same conclusion. It appears that Iraq was victorious in the early years (1982 to 1984) which were consecutive years of water and wood and so were totally in Saddam's favour. However, Saddam soon left the strong luck pillar of water and entered the unfavourble luck pillar of earth in 1985 when he turned 48. Iran launched a massive counter-offensive in 1986 and compelled Iraq to bargain for peace in 1988, which was again a year of earth, an element unfavorable to Saddam Hussein.

On the basis of the above prediction, we can see that the conflict in Hussein's Pillars of Destiny is basically a struggle between the two groups of elements — water, wood, fire against the power of metal and earth. And such a conflicting relationship between the two groups of elements will provide us with more insight into the role of President Hussein in the Gulf crisis. A brief explanation of each of the five elements are given below:

Wood — Saddam Hussein himself, also his colleagues
Metal — Threatens to destroy wood, so it symbolises any threat to Saddam's position, his opponents, enemies, the US.
Water — It helps the wood to grow, so it symbolises support to Saddam and his resources.
Earth — It generates metal and destroys water, so it is a real threat, the enemies' supporter. It is deadlier than metal as it deprives him of his resources (water).
Fire — It is generated by wood to destroy metal. It therefore symbolises Saddam's army and weapons.

The Year of the Horse, 1990, is a year symbolised by metal over fire. As fire represents Saddam's weapon to attack his enemy, metal, the strong fire in the year reflected his expansion of military power and preparation for war. The month of July/August is a month of water over wood. Encouraged by the favourable water support, Saddam launched a blitz invasion into Kuwait in early August. However, after the date August 8, the Chinese almanac went into a phase of strong metal. So he faced strong opposition led by the US in the form of sanctions, blockade, and deployment of US military forces to the Gulf. The phase of metal will last from August 8 until October 8. During this period, President Hussein will be under the hard pressure of metal. He will see the loss of his former friend and ally as the wood elements in these two months have to submit to metal and turn against Saddam. However, if he can survive and hold out against the metal pressure until after October 8, he should have a chance to gain some control and may even launch an offensive in the month of October/November when the last flames of the fire horse will emerge again. The following winter months of December and January will see the strong presence of the water influence which will have the effect of putting out Saddam's fire and at the same time consuming the metal energy of the US. This may be interpreted as another period of stalemate.

1991, the Year of the Ram, is a year of strong metal over earth and there will be concerted attack against President Saddam Hussein's wood element. The heavy clashes between metal and wood, reflecting fierce fighting or disturbance surrounding Saddam, will occur in early 1991. The heaviest clashes could be seen in February and March, both months being metal over wood. April 1991 is an interesting month to watch as the water emerges on the heavenly stems to extinguish the fire in Saddam's Year Pillar. This probably symbolises a ceasefire or peace talk.*

It is important to remind ourselves that the prediction above is made purely on the basis of one individual's Pillars of Destiny. However, the fate of a world leader, although it can affect the nation, may not exactly coincide with the fortune of the nation. So the clash between wood and metal in Saddam's Four Pillars may perhaps only reflect his own personal conflict rather than a war of the nations.

* These predictions were made before the Americans' victory in the Gulf. See footnote on page 134.

Saddam Hussein

46. Operation Desert Storm

In September 1990, when the majority view was still very optimistic about the outcome of the Gulf crisis, the author analysed the Pillars of Destiny of President Bush and President Sadam Hussein and it was predicted that war will eventually break out in early 1991, and that it will last for a few months until around April 1991. The forecast was accurate but unfortunate for the thousands of war victims. The following paragraph appeared in the author's column on October 8, 1990 in an article entitled *Pillars Point to Saddam's Own Conflict:*

"The heavy clashes between metal and wood, reflecting fierce fighting or disturbance surrounding Saddam, will occur in early 1991 if the Gulf crisis is not resolved by then. The heaviest clashes could be seen in February or March, both months being metal over wood. April 1991 is an interesting month as the water emerges on the heavenly stems to extinguish the fire in Saddam's year pillar. I hope this would symbolise a ceasefire or peace talks."

It is the author's custom to prepare an article well in advance, usually a few weeks before it appears in his column. So this paragraph was in fact written in early September, very soon after the invasion of Kuwait took place in August. At the time, the majority opinion was that the conflict was not likely to develop into a war as the superpowers seemed to unite against Saddam. Even if there was a war, it would be swift and short, given the extreme imbalance in military strength between the coalition forces and isolated Iraq. However, destiny does not necessarily follow human logic. The world was eventually driven to war. The decision to go to war was apparently made by President Bush or Saddam Hussein. But as the destiny of war is well written in their respective birth data, one can also interpret that they are driven on to the path of war, not by their will, but by destiny or fate.

To thoroughly understand the mechanism of this war, viewed from a metaphysical angle, it is worthwhile to explain once again how the five elements provide hints regarding its outbreak and developments. The Pillars of Destiny of the key figure, Saddam Hussein, as well as the configuration of the spring day of the Year of the Ram produce a picture of conflict between the opposing elements wood and metal (see Fig. 69a). As Saddam is a wood person, it is logical to regard metal, the allied forces, as his enemy. Besides the clash between wood and metal we can also bring another pair of opposing elements into the picture. They are fire and water. Fire is generated by Saddam the wood and fire will destroy metal. So we can use fire to symbolise Saddam's weapons, perhaps the Scud missiles and other weapons. On the other hand, metal generates water which can put out the fire. So the stronger the water, the easier it would be for the allies to suppress and neutralise Saddam's weapons.

Operation Desert Storm erupted on January 17, a day of strong water configurations when Saddam's fire defence seemed the weakest. Indeed the spectacular air strike on Baghdad by the allied air forces seemed almost too easy and Iraq seemed almost defenceless. Reproduced in Fig. 69b is the Pillars of Destiny drawn up on basis of the time when the operation commenced.

The overwhelming metal and water totally overpowered the weak flickering fire, the symbol of Saddam's defence. The apparent air supremacy and the hi-tech war gear displayed by the coalition forces on that day generated optimism that the war would be over

140   *Feng-shui and Destiny*

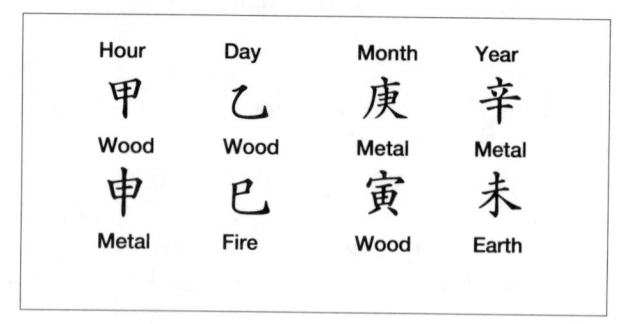

Hour	Day	Month	Year
甲	乙	庚	辛
Wood	Wood	Metal	Metal
申	巳	寅	未
Metal	Fire	Wood	Earth

Fig. 69a. Spring day, February 4, 1991, expressed in terms of the four pillars, shows heavy clashes between metal and wood – a sign of war.

Hour	Day	Month	Year
庚	丁	己	庚
Metal	Fire	Earth	Metal
子	亥	丑	午
Water	Water	Earth	Fire

Fig. 69b. Pillars of Destiny on January 17, 1991.

Feb. 1991	March 1991
庚	辛
Metal	Metal
寅	卯
Wood	Wood

Fig. 69c. Configurations of February and March, 1991.

in a few days. But Saddam's Pillars of Destiny revealed this was not to be the case. Subsequent events show that it was almost naive to expect a short war. Saddam appeared to try to preseve his power and drag the allies into a long war. Indeed, February and March were the months of Spring when Sadam's wood element was in the season, symbolising Saddam's tendency to fight in these two months. The configurations of the months February and March are shown in Fig. 69c.

Both months in the Chinese almanac present metal over wood, again symbolising fierce clashes between these two opposing elements. So it is logical to deduce that the heaviest fighting will take place in February and March. After the Ching Ming Festival on April 5, the Chinese almanac went into a month of water over earth. The water which assisted the allies to suppress Saddam's fire emerges again to put out the remaining fire. This perhaps indicated the exhaustion of Saddam's weapons.

This is the general picture that can be derived from the available birth data of the key figure in the conflict. Again we must be prepared for surprises which may arise from Saddam's birth hour which is an unknown factor.

47. The Destiny of Wars

The Gulf War has been described as a struggle between the elements wood and metal with fire defending the wood. Interestingly enough, there was a war in Chinese history (in the Ching Dynasty) which bears startling resemblance to the Gulf War. It was the Boxer Rebellion with the Empress Dowager against the Allied Forces of Eight Powers.

The last years of the Ching Dynasty were under the undisputed authoritarian rule of the Empress Dowager. It was a period of great turmoil when foreign powers intensified their aggression to exploit the weak Chinese Government. The Sino-Japanese War of 1895 brought disgrace to China and exposed the corruption of the Ching Court and the greed of the foreign powers. The anti-foreigners sentiment in China developed to the point of explosion and the Boxer Movement broke out against foreign imperialists. The Boxers were a group of religious people practising martial arts. They were anti-foreigners. The movement won enthusiasm and support among the masses. The Empress Dowager, seeing in this a chance to expel the foreigners, decided to recognise the legal status of the Boxers and allowed them to enter Beijing where the Boxers attacked foreigners and set fire to churches. Very soon, the anti-foreigners movement swept through the country and this eventually led to the famous invasion of Beijing by the Eight Powers Allied Forces in June 1900.

There are interesting parallels between the Boxer Rebellion and the Gulf War. Both wars were fought between the East and the West with a dictatorial Eastern regime against a coalition of Western powers. Furthermore, if we compare the two wars from a metaphysical angle, in terms of the pillars of destiny, the similarities are even more remarkable.

Firstly, the key persons involved, the Empress Dowager and Saddam Hussein, were both born on a day of wood. So they are both wood persons as defined by the Pillars of Destiny. Secondly, both wars broke out in a year of metal. The Boxer Rebellion occurred in 1900, a year of metal over water, and the Gulf War started in the Year of the Horse, a year of metal

142 Feng-shui and Destiny

over fire. Metal is the natural enemy of wood, threatening its safety, therefore the years of metal brought war to both wood persons, the Empress Dowager in 1900 and Saddam Hussein 90 years after (Fig. 70).

Fig. 70. Comparison of the Pillars of Destiny of Saddam Hussein and the Empress Dowager.

Hour	Day	Month	Year
?	乙	甲	丁
	Wood	Wood	Fire
?	酉	辰	丑
	Metal	Earth	Earth

The pillars of Saddam Hussein.

Hour	Day	Month	Year
丙	乙	丁	乙
Fire	Wood	Fire	Wood
子	丑	亥	卯
Water	Earth	Water	Wood

The pillars of Empress Dowager.

It is also interesting to point out that among the five basic elements, wood also symbolises the east direction, and metal, on the other hand, symbolises the west. So it seems the struggle between metal and wood also demonstrates a clash between the West and the East. As metal is the natural destroyer of wood, so wood is in a weaker position and the only weapon wood can employ to resist the metal is fire, symbolic of the Empress Dowager's Boxers and Saddam Hussein's Scud missiles, Republican Guards, etc.

An even more interesting parallel is that the elements at play in both wars are exactly the same. It was a war between the Empress Dowager, the wood person, against a coalition of metal, the Western powers. The war broke out in a year of metal in 1900 when the metal threat to the wood intensified. However, without the help of fire, the wood cannot resist the metal. Hence the war broke out in June in a month of fire and the Boxers won some initial victories as fire was in a prosperous season. But as soon as the fire power started to fade towards July 1900, a month of water over earth, the Boxers suffered serious casualties in the face of Western superior firearms and the 20,000 strong Allied troops captured Beijing in August forcing the Empress Dowager to bargain for peace. August was a month of strong metal and wood was at its weakest.

The Empress Dowager had to surrender to the metal power in the autumn of 1900 when there was no more fire to defend her. Looking back at the Gulf War today, it seems the clash between wood and metal, and the use of fire against metal, falls exactly into the same pattern as the Boxer Rebellion in 1900. Although a ceasefire was declared on February 27 it appears the clash between metal and wood was not yet over. There would be continued struggles surrounding Saddam Hussein, either in the form of military operations or diplomatic or political skirmishes in March with Saddam really losing his fire defence in around April when his fire is totally extinguished by water.

Indeed, on April 13, 1991, Saddam formally accepted the United Nations Security Council's resolution which required Iraq to destroy all its chemicals, biological weapons and long range ballistic missiles as the terms for a permanent ceasefire.

48. The Collapse of the Stock Market, October 13, 1989

On October 13, 1989, Wall Street plunged 191 points and triggered off another crisis on the global stock market. The interesting fact is that a similar but more serious crash occurred exactly two years ago in October 1987. Looking further back in history, a big stock collapse of similar magnitude also took place in October 1929. Everyone notices the ominous coincidence that October is usually an unstable month for the stock market. Let us see if the Four Pillars of Destiny can offer an explanation.

The stock market works on a very complicated mechanism with a vast number of variables and uncertainties. So there is a lot of room for speculation and no financial expert can make forecasts with 100% certainty and human fortune and luck play an important role. In the past four years, it has become more and more evident that the interaction of the five basic elements which affects the luck of the individual on a micro scale also contributes to stock market fluctuations, at least indirectly, through human fortune.

The phenomenon is not difficult to comprehend. As the luck of individual speculators is governed by their own Four Pillars of Destiny, if most of these individuals enter into a period of good luck, in theory, they should be able to win and gain money on the stock market. So the "macro" outcome is that there must be a boom with share prices soaring. On the other hand, if the majority of speculators are subject to the influence of an unfavourable element, the aggregate result will be a big collapse with most of the people losing money.

The Chinese name each year in terms of a series of two characters, one on top of another. The character on top is called the heavenly stem and the one underneath is called the earthly branch. Each heavenly stem and each earthly branch symbolises an element. For example, the year 1989 is named 乙巳. The heavenly stem 乙 symbolises the earth element. The word 巳 is an earthly branch representing fire. The two characters therefore indicate that the elements earth and fire are the reigning and prevailing influences in the year 1989, so human fortune is generally subject to the effect of earth and fire in this Year of the Snake.

If a person's Four Pillars of Destiny favour more earth and fire, then he will run into good luck in 1989. However, a person who favours earth and fire elements cannot expect to enjoy fortune all the year round. He is also subject to monthly ups and downs brought about by seasonal changes. Put simply, we need only remind ourselves that, in general, spring is a season of wood, summer is a season of fire, autumn is a season of metal and winter is a prosperous season for water. So the summer season intensifies the power of earth and fire (fire gives birth to earth), and the autumn and winter seasons, on the other hand, will hamper the effect of earth and fire as they are collectively a season of water and metal which will put out the fire and exhaust the earth power (earth gives birth to metal).

According to this theory, those who enjoyed prosperity in life in the summer time in 1989 may encounter a change of luck with setbacks in October which is in the autumn/winter season when the effect of metal and water comes into play and the fire power totally loses its vigour. This explains the fluctuations on the stock market in October. However, one may ask: "Why doesn't the market collapse occur every October?" To determine whether there will be a big collapse in October, we need also to examine the heavenly stem and earthly branch of the subsequent year. Take for example the year 1986, a year of fire on wood. In October 1986, the seasonal metal and water effects also threatened the yearly fire and wood. However, the next year, 1987, was also a year of fire and wood. So there was continuity of fire power and the stock market remained strong (see Fig. 71).

In October 1987, the yearly fire power came to an end as the following year, 1988, was a year of earth which exhausts fire energy. As the fire effect totally expired and submitted to the seasonal water force in October 1987, the good fortune of speculators in the preceding two years also expired and this resulted in the big stock market collapse in October 1987. In the same way, the year 1988 was a year of earth. The earth power was able to last into 1989 as it was another year of earth and fire, so the continuity of earth power was able to overcome the attack of seasonal water influences in October 1988. Thus, no Wall Street plunge occurred in 1988. But in October 1989, the earth power arrived at its termination point with the next year, 1990, being a year of metal on fire. So a stock market crash in October 1989 was inevitable. However, the changeover from earth and fire to metal and fire was not as drastic as the transition from fire to earth in 1987. Hence the crash of 1989 was not of very serious magnitude.

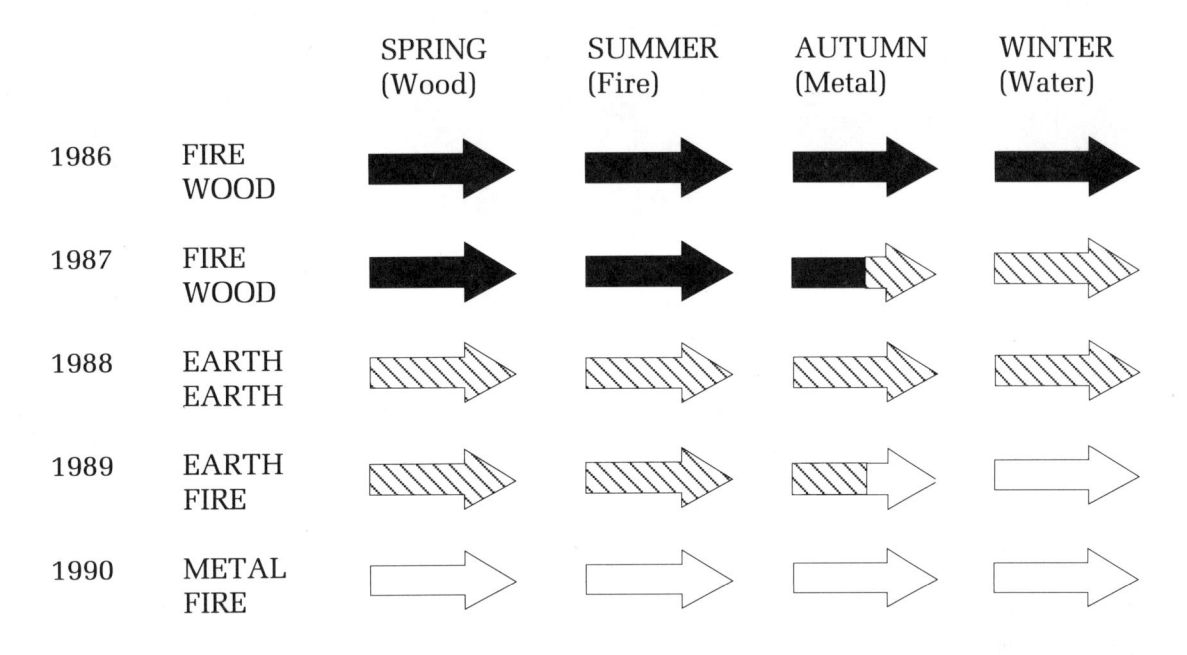

		SPRING (Wood)	SUMMER (Fire)	AUTUMN (Metal)	WINTER (Water)
1986	FIRE WOOD	██▶	██▶	██▶	██▶
1987	FIRE WOOD	██▶	██▶	▓▶	▓▶
1988	EARTH EARTH	▓▶	▓▶	▓▶	▓▶
1989	EARTH FIRE	▓▶	▓▶	▷	▷
1990	METAL FIRE	▷	▷	▷	▷

Fig. 71. The influence of the five elements 1986 - 1990.

49. The *I Ching* Oracle and Chinese Politics

Of the various branches of Chinese metaphysics, the *I Ching* (Book of Changes) seems to be drawing the most attention from Western scholars and intellectuals, perhaps because of its vast store of ancient cultic wisdom. Unlike other Chinese fortune-telling techniques such as the Four Pillars of Destiny, books on the *I Ching* are easily available in English. Much of the literature concentrates on the historical and academic aspects. Many give detailed explanations of the 64 *kua* (hexagrams) but very few provide adequate examples of its application as a tool for divination.

The origins of the *I Ching* is lost in ancient history and Chinese literature cites Fu Hsi, a legendary figure, as inventor of the linear symbols or *kua* of the *I Ching*. The system is known to have existed as early as the Xia Dynasty of the 21st century BC as the *kua* appeared prominently in the Xia calendar, an accurate calendar system still popularly used among the Chinese people.

The main feature of the *I Ching* is the eight *kua* which are represented by continuous and broken lines. The fundamental philosophy is that the universe is a world of opposites. Everything that exists has a *yang* and a *yin* side. *Yang* is positive, light, male. *Yin* is negative, dark, female. *Yang* is represented by a continuous line and *yin* by a broken line. Three such lines form a symbol called the trigram and there are a total of eight trigrams formed by various combinations of the three continuous and broken lines as shown in Fig. 72.

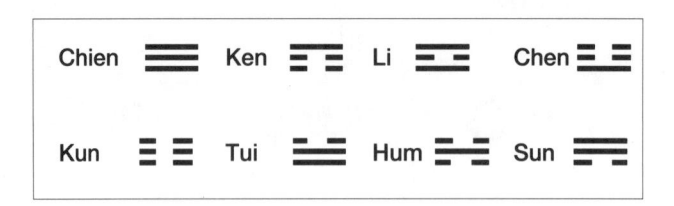

Fig. 72. The eight kua or trigrams.

A combination of two such trigrams into one set, one on top of another, forms a hexagram, or a *kua*. So each kua means a symbol of six continuous or broken lines. Using various combinations of the six lines, 64 hexagrams, or *kua*, are formed. So the original *I Ching* is believed to be just a book of line signs. (The various explanations, commentaries and foot notes were added in the subsequent ages by Emperor Chou [about 1,000BC] and Confucius.)

The *I Ching* linear symbols are believed to contain the *tao* or universal order. As everything in the universe follows rules and patterns, theoretically the future can be predicted by tracing the *tao* or course of events. Also, the process of obtaining a *kua* for divination makes it possible for the subconscious in man to become active and synchronise with the universe. So the book is a valuable tool for casting light on uncertainties about the future for which one needs guidance.

The first step in consulting the *I Ching* is to formulate your question properly. The question should be as specific as possible. After some practice one will learn that vague and broad questions will only cause difficulty in interpreting the meaning of a *kua* and so a clear answer cannot be obtained. For example, in June, 1989, people were concerned about the political crisis in Beijing. Such questions as "Will the Chinese people achieve democracy?" are too broad and have no single key point and no time reference.

After formulating a "good" question in one's mind, the second step is to obtain a *kua*. A common and easy method is to cast three coins six times to get six lines so as to formulate the *kua*. The lines, whether continuous or broken, are determined by casting three coins on the ground and observing the combination of heads and tails. Fig. 73 shows how to draw continuous or broken lines by counting heads and tails.

The three heads and three tails configuration represents an active line, meaning a continuous line (*yang*) changes to a broken line (*yin*), or vice versa. Such action lines indicate an area of motion and often provide an indication of the key message of a *kua*. Fortune-tellers usually put three coins in a tortoise shell, concentrate and then mentally ask a well-formulated question. Then he will shake the three coins in the tortoise shell for a short while and cast them on the floor. After casting six times, six lines are drawn up to form a complete hexagram.

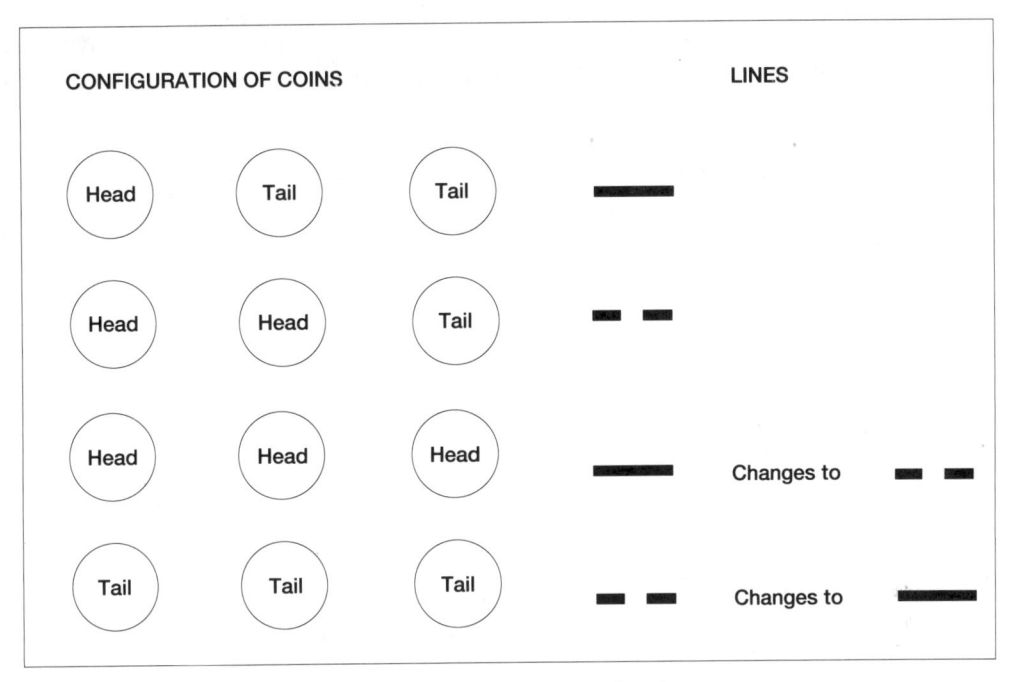

CONFIGURATION OF COINS			LINES		
Head	Tail	Tail	▬▬▬▬		
Head	Head	Tail	▬▬ ▬▬		
Head	Head	Head	▬▬▬▬	Changes to	▬▬ ▬▬
Tail	Tail	Tail	▬▬ ▬▬	Changes to	▬▬▬▬

Fig. 73. Configuration of coins.

Consulting the *I Ching* for revelations about the future can give startlingly correct answers. However, as mentioned above, to employ the *I Ching* Oracle successfully, one must note the following:

1. Formulate the question in a clear and specific manner;
2. Concentrate hard when asking the question; and
3. Choose a quiet location for the exercise.

After establishing a *kua* by casting the three coins, One comes to the difficult task of interpretation which requires patience and extensive practical experience.

Two methods of interpretation are commonly employed. One can be regarded as the Academic school which emphasises the explanations attached to the *I Ching* by the Duke of Chou and Confucius. Most of the *I Ching* books available in English follow this method. The drawback is that the ancient explanations are very abstract, so there is high risk of misreading a *kua* as interpretations are often highly personal.

Fortune-tellers usually employ a different method which is quite similar to the Four Pillars of Destiny and employs the theory of the Five Elements. The merit of this method is that the information revealed by the *kua* can be narrowed down to five major areas: wealth, power, status, colleagues and subordinates, and they embrace most questions one would need to ask.

A good case in point would be the widely conflicting rumours concerning the fate of Zhao

148 *Feng-shui and Destiny*

Ziyang in China on May 24 1989. Many reported that he had won a quick victory in the power struggle but others said he was bitterly criticised as counter-revolutionary and was deprived of his authority. To determine the relative merits of the rumours, an *I Ching* oracle was consulted. The *kua*, shown in the table was obtained on May 25. The specific question asked was: "What is the current political status of Zhao Ziyang?"

The *kua* is named "pushing up" with the active line on the third level (counting from the bottom upwards). This *kua* is of the wood category. So wood is called the *kua* element, and each line is also assigned one basic element as shown in Fig. 74.

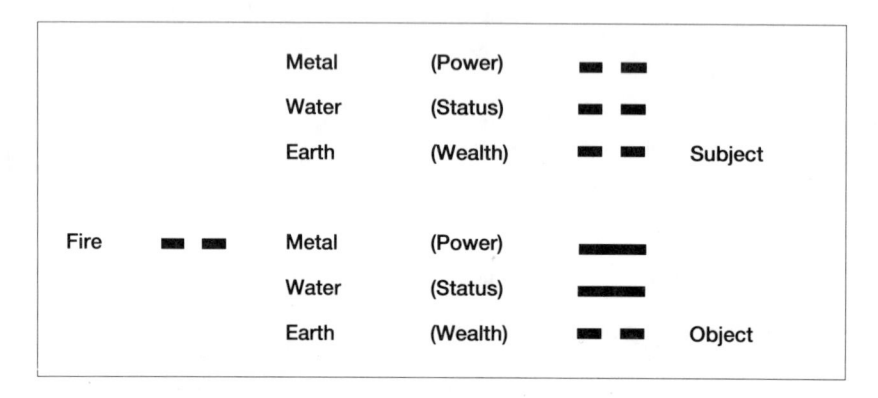

```
                Metal    (Power)     ▬▬ ▬▬
                Water    (Status)    ▬▬ ▬▬
                Earth    (Wealth)    ▬▬ ▬▬   Subject

    Fire  ▬▬ ▬▬  Metal    (Power)     ▬▬▬▬▬
                Water    (Status)    ▬▬▬▬▬
                Earth    (Wealth)    ▬▬ ▬▬   Object
```

Fig. 74. Kua shows Zhao Ziyang's downfall in 1989.

Each of the lines has its respective element, and is related to human fortune, wealth, power, status, colleagues and subordinates. The elements of each line can be translated into these five areas of human fortune. Translating the lines is a little complicated but the following rules should help beginners.

Kua element: the basic element of the whole *kua*, in this case, wood.
Power: this is the element that destroys the *kua* element. In this case it is metal, as metal destroys wood.
Status: this is the element that gives birth to the *kua* element. Here it is water, as water gives birth to wood.
Wealth: the element destroyed by the *kua* element. Wood destroys earth, so earth is wealth in this case.
Colleagues: the same as the *kua* element in this case, wood.
Subordinates: spawned by the *kua* element. It is fire in this case, as wood gives birth to fire.

The Five Areas of Fortune are also listed in Fig. 74.

As the focus is on Mr Zhao's political fate, the area of fortune, we should concentrate on his power, i.e. his position in the government. The line of power is found on the third level. It is an active line, changing from *yang* (continuous line) to yin (broken line). This clearly indicates there will be activity and change in Mr Zhao's position in government. The third line shows that it changes from metal to fire. As fire destroys metal, the change will be unfavourable, threatening his power.

The I Ching Oracle and Chinese Politics 149

Also, this line of activity is located in the lower trigram, or "internal" trigram. This implies that the destructive forces are generated from within the government. This *kua* also shows that the destruction will not come about until June as this oracle was consulted in May when the fire element which imposed the threat was not yet at its peak of activity. The fire element will be in its full power in June to inflict damage on the metal, Mr Zhao's power in government. We should, however, remember that the question asked in this instance is merely the current status of Mr Zhao as at the end of May 1989. Any long-term changes will not be shown by this *kua*.

The *I Ching* is so versatile a fortune-telling instrument that it can be used to provide clues to answer any questions in our minds. Let us now take a look at two other prominent Chinese leaders: Mr Li Peng and Mr Deng Xiaoping. The question of Mr Li Peng's political future was raised on May 25, 1989.

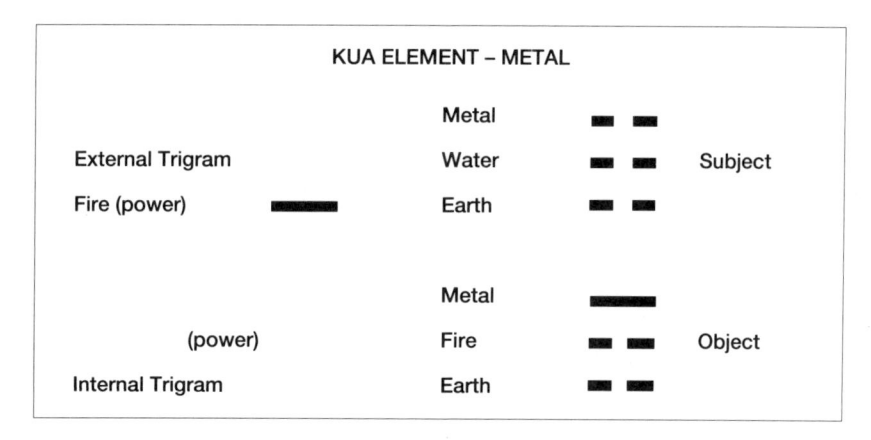

```
                      KUA ELEMENT – METAL

                           Metal       ▬▬  ▬▬
    External Trigram       Water       ▬▬  ▬▬    Subject
    Fire (power)    ▬▬▬▬▬  Earth       ▬▬  ▬▬

                           Metal       ▬▬▬▬▬▬
         (power)           Fire        ▬▬  ▬▬    Object
    Internal Trigram       Earth       ▬▬  ▬▬
```

Fig. 75. Kua shows Li Peng's political position in 1989.

Fig. 75 was obtained by casting three coins. The "subject" line represents the person involved in the question, Mr Li Peng. The element of this line is water. Immediately underneath is earth "in action" and as earth destroys water, an active earth line means Mr Li's position is threatened by external forces. The active line shows earth changing into fire (fire gives birth to earth and strengthens its power). This indicates that the threat is real and intensive. Also, fire is the power of the person or his position in the government in this case. Fire on an active line in the external trigram means that there are external forces threatening his position in the government. The power line in the internal trigram also poses a threat, but as it is an inert line, the danger is not from within the government.

Then we have to evaluate to what extent the external threat will bring about changes to Mr Li's position. As Mr Li's power is symbolised by the fire element, and the *kua* was consulted in the summer when fire was in a prosperous phase of its life cycle, the political position of Li Peng remains strong. It appeared that such power would be further strengthened in June when the fire element would be at its peak.

Fig. 76 represents the political status of Deng Xiaoping revealed by the *I Ching* oracle on the same day, May 25, 1989. The unique feature of this hexagram is that there is no active line, implying all is quiet and there will be no immediate threat, action or change to

Mr Deng's position. However, despite the lack of an active line, we can observe that some struggle was going on in the background as the subject line, representing Mr Deng, belongs to the metal element and immediately underneath is a wood line. Metal destroys wood, so there is a sign of conflict. However, the diagram shows that metal is very much in the ascendant as there is earth next to metal intensifying its strength. Therefore the diagram clearly shows Mr Deng is in control.

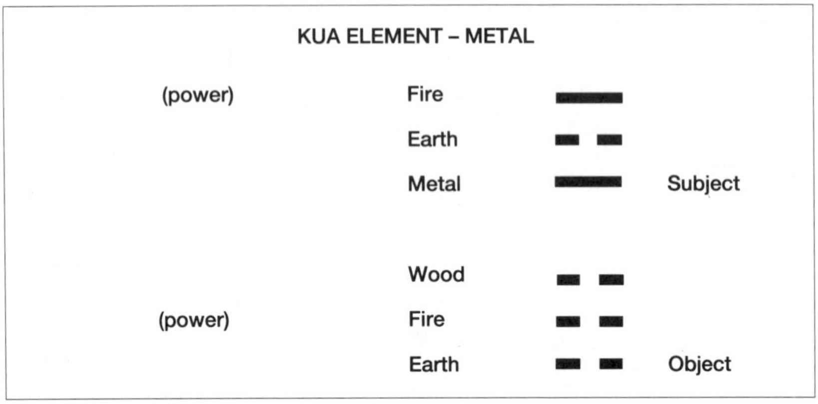

```
                    KUA ELEMENT – METAL

       (power)         Fire       ━━━━━━
                       Earth      ━━  ━━
                       Metal      ━━━━━━      Subject

                       Wood       ━━  ━━
       (power)         Fire       ━━  ━━
                       Earth      ━━  ━━      Object
```

Fig. 76. Kua shows Deng Xiaoping's political position in 1989.

In interpreting the hexagrams we have so far not resorted to the *I Ching* to check the explanations and commentaries and have only employed the interaction of the five basic elements to analyse the essence of the *kua* to get appropriate answers. However, it is recommended that one should also check the meaning of the *kua* from any *I Ching* book for comparison. One can often find enlightening messages to enrich one's understanding. For example, the above hexagram about Mr Deng Xiaoping is named "progress" in the *I Ching*. The upper trigram *li* symbolises fire, the lower trigram *hun* symbolises earth. The image is the sun shining over the earth. The commentary by the Duke of Chou on this hexagram is that "a powerful sovereign rallies his feudal lords to come around him to pledge loyalty and the sovereign rules with strengthened power". This implies a strengthening of Mr Deng Xiaoping's power.

50. The Kua of Hong Kong's Economy

In the second half of 1989, the burning question on most people's minds was the future of Hong Kong. For the majority of the population who have to stay behind to face the uncertainties, it may be worthwhile to refer to the *I Ching* to determine what the future holds. In order to do this we need to prepare ourselves mentally to adopt the correct attitude about fortune-telling. There is a Chinese saying about this: "By knowing one's future, one should feel contented and at peace and accept Heaven's will." So the purpose of fortune-telling is not to stir up emotion, be it fear or optimism, but to point to the right way of preparing for the future. If a dark and unpleasant future is forecast, then one should be prepared to face it boldly so that one will not feel shocked and desperate when adversity actually strikes. On the other hand, if a rosy future is revealed, one should feel more confident and continue to work hard to accomplish better success and satisfaction.

Such an attitude is necessary if we want to exploit fully the valuable predictive power of fortune-telling and make it a useful tool for creating a brighter future. The degree of adversity and misfortune depends to a great extent on subjective perception. Getting psychologically prepared for the worst scenario will actually reduce the feeling of desperation when one actually goes through difficult times. Let us now then try to answer a specific question: "What will happen to the Hong Kong economy in the next six months?" The question was asked on June 22, 1989, with Fig. 77 showing the *kua* obtained by casting three coins. The striking feature of this *kua* is that it has three active lines. A large number of active lines usually indicate a high degree of change or fluctuations. In our case, it shows the lack of stability over the six months following June 22. As our question refers to the economy we should focus on the earth element which signifies money.

The fifth line from the bottom is the subject, meaning Hong Kong. Hong Kong astride a money line (earth) simply means that we have wealth. Fire gives birth to earth, and the money line needs fire to support its growth. But there is only one fire element in the entire *kua* and this fire lies on the bottom line which is too far away from the subject to provide any firm support. Instead, there are ample water and metal elements. Earth destroys water and gives birth to metal. So water and metal are there to consume the earth (money). Such a configuration suggests we are exhausting our wealth and lack an injection of fresh investment.

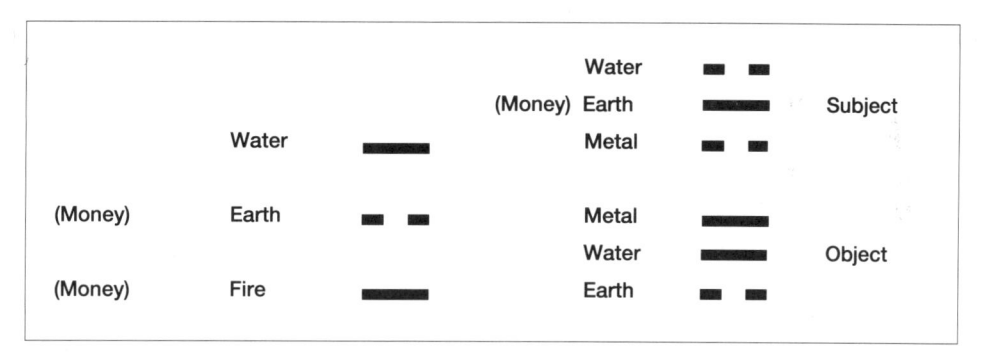

Fig. 77. Prediction of Hong Kong's future economy. The kua element is wood.

Let us also examine other signs of money (earth) in the *kua*. The bottom line is optimistic as the earth (money) changes to fire which provides support to the earth, a sign of internal efforts to support the economy. However, next to it is a water line which immediately extinguishes the fire. The third line from the bottom also shows active money but it is again consumed by the metal element as earth gives birth to metal. The fourth line too is a metal and water line which consumes the money and threatens the economy.

The whole *kua* is a picture of instability and lack of support to the economy. There is too much money flowing out and a shortfall of fresh investment. One interesting aspect of this

152 *Feng-shui and Destiny*

kua is the absence of the wood element from the scene. As wood destroys earth, we can interpret the absence of wood to mean that we are safe from external interference. So any disappointment will be self-inflicted, brought about by our own actions.

The *kua* was obtained in June, a summer month when fire was most prosperous. As fire supports earth (our money) we can expect the economy to sustain a reasonable growth in the summer season. But when autumn arrives with fire fading away and metal and water influences coming into play, we have to prepare ourselves for some disappointment. However, the commentary by the Duke of Chou on the *I Ching* provides words of comfort. This *kua* is called the "well". The image is water on top of wood or a deep-rooted plant drawing water nourishment from the well and the water is inexhaustible. Hong Kong is such a resourceful place (it has the best *feng-shui* in Asia), so there is no reason to be overly pessimistic about the future.

51. The I Ching and Perestroika

The art of the *I Ching* oracle is often employed to provide answers to specific questions. It is regarded as a reliable tool which will provide guidance in case of doubt and uncertainty about the future. Let us have a look at the political future of Soviet President Mikhail Gorbachev. Again we begin with a specific question: "What is the political status of President Gorbachev in the next three months?" This question was asked on January 23, 1990. By tossing three coins, the *kua* (trigrams) reproduced in Fig. 78 was obtained.

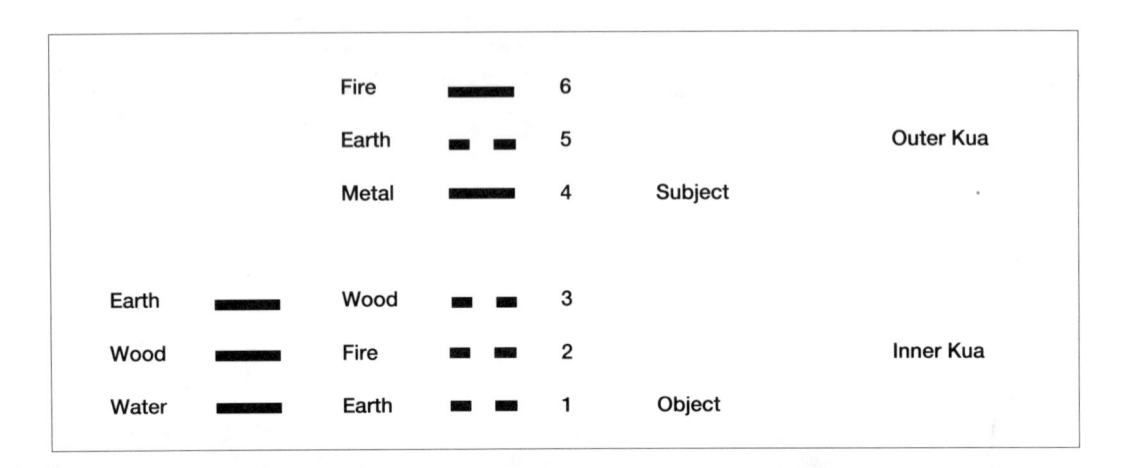

	Fire	▬▬▬	6		
	Earth	▬ ▬	5		Outer Kua
	Metal	▬▬▬	4	Subject	
Earth ▬▬▬	Wood	▬ ▬	3		
Wood ▬▬▬	Fire	▬ ▬	2		Inner Kua
Water ▬▬▬	Earth	▬ ▬	1	Object	

Fig. 78. Kua shows prospect of Perestroika.

The prominent feature of this *kua* is that all three lines in the inner kua are active lines, transforming from broken lines (*yin*) to continuous lines (*yang*). Active lines in the inner *kua* symbolise internal activities. This is a clear indication of internal unrest and turmoil within the Soviet Union. The line marked "subject" represents President Gorbachev, and the bottom line marked "object" symbolises the matter in question. In our case, it is his political status. Let us now examine each line in relation to the subject, Mr Gorbachev, and see what more can be revealed.

Line 1

The bottom line belongs to the element of earth which provides support and nourishment to Mr Gorbachev (the line of metal). So it is a favourable line. This is also an "object line". The object supporting the subject is interpreted as a good omen pointing to success in one's goals. However, earth in this line transforms to water which will consume Mr Gorbachev's metal energy. Therefore this configuration reveals that there is support for his position and reform policy , but the strength is limited.

Line 2

This belongs to the fire element which will destroy Mr Gorbachev, the metal. The fire element transforms into wood which again reinforces the fire power. So this line is a real threat to Mr Gorbachev's position. We can interpret this line as rebel forces, or the political enemies of Mr Gorbachev.

Line 3

A line of wood transforming into earth. The wood is not helpful to Mr Gorbachev. On the contrary, it supports the fire in line 2, the opposition forces.

Therefore, the *kua* provides us with a picture of unrest, clashes and conflict within the Soviet Union in the three months from January 23, 1990 onwards. The restless lines 2 and 3 in the inner *kua* indicate rebellion or opposition occurring in at least two areas, one reinforcing another. Line 3, being wood lying underneath metal, will be easily kept under control by the strong metal in line 4, but line 2 is the most dangerous enemy, receiving reinforcement from line 3 and threatening Mr Gorbachev.

So what is his chance of survival through this crisis situation? To find clues to this question we have to examine the outer *kua* and the configuration of the date when the oracle is consulted. Usually, the outer *kua* symbolises external influences. The three lines starting from the top (lines 6, 5 and 4) appear to be in harmonious relationship as fire gives birth to earth and earth in turn gives birth to metal. This represents the moral support and sympathy of Western leaders. However, when interpreting a *kua,* the date and season of the consultation carries much weight. In this case, the element of the season is a determining factor in assessing Mr Gorbachev's chance of survival.

The *kua* was obtained on January 23. This day, if expressed in terms of the five elements, is a day of water in a month of earth. Earth supports metal (Mr Gorbachev) and water suppresses fire (the rebels and opposition). So the seasonal influences are totally in favour of Mr Gorbachev. The *kua* gives a picture which is quite in line with the indications from Mr Gorbachev's Four Pillars of Destiny discussed earlier. Despite apparent setbacks and crises, his foundation is unshaken and he will be able to continue to pursue his policy of perestroika in 1990. His success in breaking the Communist Party monopoly in early February 1990 appears to prove the accuracy of this *kua*.

52. The *I Ching* View of the Gulf Crisis

For the analysis of the development of the Gulf War, I have not only experimented with the Four Pillars of Destiny but also engaged the *I Ching* oracle to check the results. The *I Ching* oracle, being the most respected art of predictions and the mother of all Chinese metaphysical studies, can always provide revelations and insights into the future with startling accuracy. Reviewing the note book I kept about the Gulf crisis, I find almost all oracles performed on the war matched the actual events well. Here I will describe some interesting examples.

To get clues about the outcome of the Gulf conflict, two simple questions were asked and two hexagrams or *kuas* obtained by tossing three coins. The oracles were performed back in August. The first question was asked on a day of water: Can President Bush succeed in driving Iraqi troops out of Kuwait in the next three months? The following *kua* was obtained (see Fig. 79). It is called the *kua* of oppression or exhaustion.

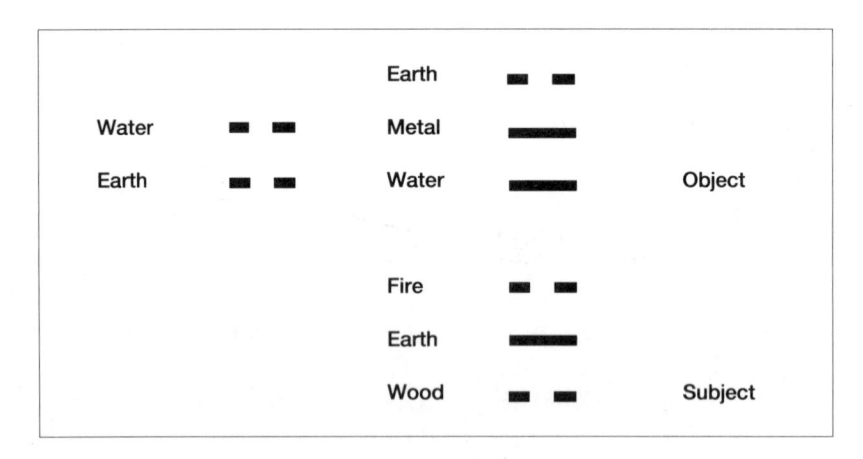

Fig. 79. Kua showing President Bush's success in the Gulf.

The bottom line is the subject, representing President Bush. The fourth line from the bottom is the object, symbolising the objective. In our case, it is the Iraqi troops which Bush wished to expel from Kuwait. Let us compare the strength between the two lines. The US sits on a line of wood, which is supported by the water element on the date of performing the oracle. This means that President Bush is in high profile and with strong support behind him. However, it is a static line, showing no movements.

Next we should look at the object line, symbolising Iraq. It is an active line transforming from water into earth. So Iraq is the one which made the attack and invaded Kuwait first, but the move turns into earth which destroys water. So such a move aroused strong reaction and opposition against itself. We can see that the fifth line of metal is also an active line. As metal generates water, this symbolises some support to back up Iraq. However, such support is weak as the metal line transforms into water which exhausts the metal power. The key to this

154

The I Ching View of the Gulf Crisis 155

kua is that the US is symbolised by an inert line, reflecting a stalemate situation in the short term. But Iraq's aggression was kept under control.

The question is then reversed and projected further ahead, on a date of metal in August. The second question is: Can Iraq succeed in this confrontation in the next six months? The coins produced the following *kua* which is called "deliverance" (see Fig. 80).

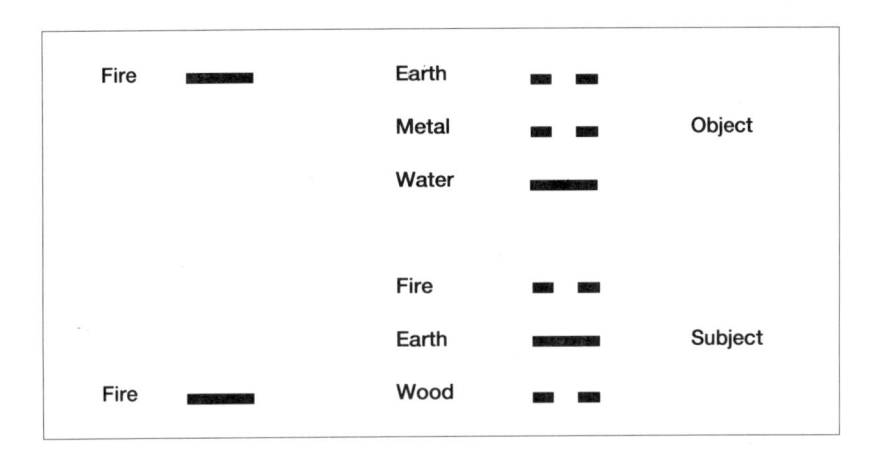

```
Fire    ▬▬▬▬    Earth   ▬▬ ▬▬
                Metal   ▬▬ ▬▬   Object
                Water   ▬▬▬▬▬

                Fire    ▬▬ ▬▬
                Earth   ▬▬▬▬▬   Subject
Fire    ▬▬▬▬    Wood    ▬▬ ▬▬
```

Fig. 80. Kua showing Saddam's failure in Kuwait.

This time the subject line is Iraq and the object line is the US. The subject line falls on the second line from the bottom. It is a line of earth, which is considered weak for two reasons. Firstly, the metal of the day and on the object line exhausts the earth energy. Secondly, the bottom line immediately underneath the subject is an active line of wood which moves to destroy the earth. As the bottom line is in the "inner" *kua,* this may indicate internal turmoil within Iraq.

The next thing to examine is the object line of metal symbolising the US. It is in a strong position supported by the metal of the day and the month of August, reflecting the strong international backing behind the US military operation. Furthermore, the top line of earth is an active line and it moves to support the metal. So the US will remain strong and in high profile. It is obvious that this *kua* points to US victory in the long term.

When President Gorbachev and Mr Tariq Aziz met in Moscow to formulate a peace deal and there was general optimism that a ground war could be avoided, I performed an oracle and asked the question: "Will the allies start the ground assault in the next 30 days?" and the following *kua* was obtained on February 21 by tossing three coins in the *I Ching* manner (see Fig. 81).

The prominent feature of this *kua* is that the upper trigram, symbolising the allies, is a *kua* of metal; the lower, or inner *kua,* representing Iraq, is a *kua* of wood. The two are in a clashing position with metal threatening to destroy the wood. So the hexagram already portrays a picture of fierce clash and conflict.

The next step is to evaluate the disposition of the subject line and the object line. The subject line, representing the allies, is a line of fire. The object line at the bottom, symbolising Iraqi troops, is a line of water. Fire and water are again in a clash position. So the overall

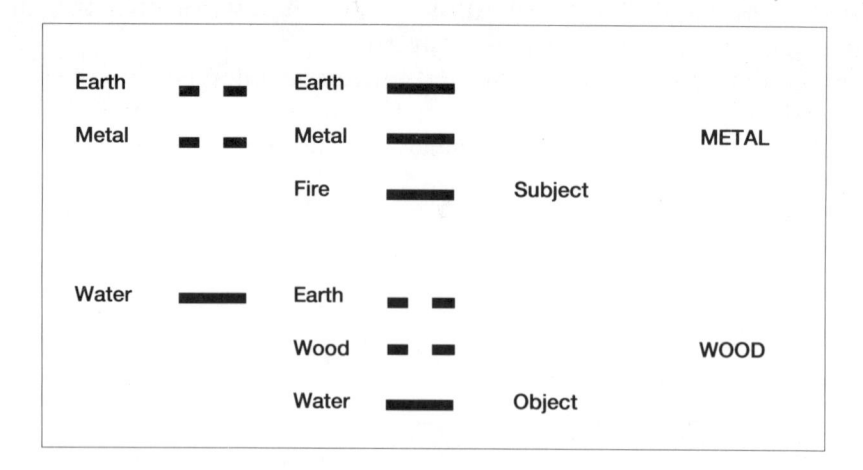

Fig. 81. Kua showing the day of the alllies' ground assault.

picture is one of conflict and it is very obvious that the ground war would start within 30 days from February 21.

To retrieve more detailed revelations from this *kua,* we can go on to examine each line one by one. Special attention must be paid to the active lines, which are lines changing from continuous to broken lines (*yang* changes to *yin*) or vice versa, as these lines give more insight into the areas of action and focus.

The *kua* has three active lines. Such a large number of active lines again display considerable war activities. Let us now examine each line on the upper *kua* which represents the actions of the allies.

Sixth line (top) — earth

It is an active line of earth and reinforcing itself by transforming into earth. Earth is destroyer of water. So this line clearly portrays the allies' strong offensive against the Iraqis which is represented by the water line at the bottom.

Fifth line (second from top) — metal

It is an active line of metal transforming into metal. Metal will exhaust earth energy and will support water. So this line appears to represent Mr Gorbachev who made an attempt to save Iraq, the water line, by dissolving the earth offensive.

Fourth line (third from top) — fire

This is the subject line representing the allied forces which is in direct clash with the object water line, symbolising Iraq. This line of fire also keeps the metal on the fifth line under control and prevents it from saving the water. This symbolises the allies' rejection of the Soviet peace plan.

To avoid making this discourse too lengthy, I must stop here and leave wise readers to make their own assessment of each line in the lower *kua*. However, I must not finish here without pointing out the most important and striking revelation of this *kua* - the dates of the ground war. The object water line at the bottom not only symbolises Iraq, but also represents the object of the question which is the ground war. The object falls on a line of water, revealing to us that the ground war would take place on a day of water. Indeed, the ground offensive actually started on February 23 - a day of water. Furthermore, the third line from the bottom shows an active earth line transforming into water. As earth is the destroyer of water (Iraq), earth transforming into water means that the earth no longer threatens Iraq at that stage. This is an indication of ceasefire on a day of earth. Again, the allies eventually declared ceasefire on February 27, which is indeed, a day of earth.

54. Conclusion: Destiny and Free Will

Destiny or free will? This question has haunted philosophers and great thinkers since the beginning of human history. With great advances in science and technology, improvements in communication and transportation have removed many restrictions and there seems to be no boundary to the intelligence and power of man. The current view is that man is the supreme master and conqueror of nature. Thus any idea about destiny and limited free will is no longer held "fashionable". However, as we grow older and become more mature and experienced, we gradually feel we are not totally in control and the question of destiny or some kind of "fate" begins to bother us. One fact which stares us in the face is human inequality. We have different abilities, potentials, talents, etc. and all these play an important role in a person's well-being and development. So to what extent are we free? Then there is the mystery of "luck", something which we encounter in our daily life, whether losing or winning in a game of chance or major matters of life and death such as the miraculous survival of some "lucky" ones in a plane crash.

Destiny and luck are ever-present in our lives and it would be simplistic to discard them as mere superstition. Throughout human history, and in many nations, there exist various traditions and techniques related to the exploration of destiny or fortune-telling: tarot cards, astrology, crystal ball, the reading of tea leaves, etc. These explorations into the unknown represent man's ambition to master his own fate, and the accumulated knowledge in this field deserves more serious study.

The study of destiny and luck has been a long tradition with the Chinese and the ancient art of The Four Pillars of Destiny, *fung-shui* and the *I Ching* Oracle may be regarded as an accumulated store of wisdom and discoveries of the ancient Chinese. Such techniques were refined and found wider applications through the ages and a more systematic, formal theory of life, fortune and destiny became part of Chinese culture. Until the end of the Ching Dynasty, fortune-telling and metaphysics were an essential part of the daily life of the Chinese and almost every family kept a Chinese almanac which they consulted for occasions big and small. And, historically, experts in *feng-shui* and destiny were important consultants on matters of state. The Ching Emperors contributed much to this field by ordering the editing of many classical books on Chinese metaphysics and included them in the *Complete Books of the Four Libraries.*

The various examples given in this book, especially the analyses of the Pillars of Destiny of prominent people and world leaders, demonstrate that there is a traceable pattern of destiny, in one or the other methods of fortune-telling. A very good example would be the author's analysis of the Gulf War. The analysis was made long before the events took place. It may be broken down into five main points:

1. A war would break out in the Gulf in early 1991.
2. Fierce fighting would take place in around February 1991.
3. Fighting around Saddam would last until April 1991.
4. The Gulf crisis would last until April 1991.
5. President Bush would achieve the final victory.

The predictions were startlingly accurate. The war eventually broke out in January 1991 with the ground assault of the Allied Forces launched in February. Although the ceasefire occurred in February, civil struggle and rebellion against Saddam Hussein continued until April 1991 when the opposition forces were put down and suppressed by troops loyal to Saddam.

If the future is so accurately predictable, can we then conclude that we are all subject to destiny and that everything is predetermined? Is there no place for free will? For example, it may be argued that both Presidents Bush and Saddam Hussein were reluctant to go to war but were eventually driven into war by their respective destinies. As the signs of war are traceable to their birth data or Pillars of Destiny, we may even argue that the decision to fight is not a result of free will but predetermined by their destiny. So where is free will? If the future is already there, fixed, does it mean that we are powerless to alter it?

To advocate that everything is destined and unchangeable seems fatalistic. It is a negative attitude and has been rejected by many, even in the field of metaphysics and fortune-telling. Experts in Chinese metaphysics tend to take a neutral view — that destiny and free will can co-exist. This view makes fortune-telling meaningful and can have positive effects on our lives.

It is held that the Four Pillars of Destiny determines a life profile: its drawbacks, its potential, its ups and downs. However, they may not determine the "standard", or the vertical level of achievement. So whether a person can achieve greater success is still subject to factors other than destiny. These include *feng-shui,* philanthropic deeds, and of course free will.

The effect of *feng-shui* on human fortune has been discussed in the first section of this book. Though *feng-shui* may not be able to totally save a person from grave misfortune, it can at least reduce its intensity or help the person to achieve some degree of success. Experts in the Four Pillars of Destiny believe that there a number of "down" phases or danger periods in a person's life and some of these may threaten life. Such mishaps could be fatal to some people but others may survive them without harm. The deciding factor is believed to be a person's or even his ancestor's philanthropic deeds.

Two persons born with exactly the same Pillars of Destiny should have quite similar life patterns in terms of "up" and "down" luck profiles but their respective intensity of success or failure in life may not be identical. If both men are destined to become rich, one could be a billionaire while the other could be just a millionaire. The difference may be attributable to factors of *feng-shui,* philanthropy, or even the influence of geographical locations and the environment in which each person is born. However, many believe that free will also plays a role in placing a person's achievements on a higher or lower plane.

Let us again take Saddam Hussein as an example. His Pillars of Destiny showed fierce struggle around him in early 1991. However, the exact scale of the struggle could not be clearly defined from his four pillars alone. Perhaps if he did not exercise restraint and refrained from using chemical warheads, the war could have had catastrophic consequences. He might already have exercised some free will in order to avoid a bigger disaster. His free will, though, did not prevent him from going to war. So it is very difficult, perhaps impossible, to alter one's destiny profile (the general pattern of ups and downs) but free will, to a certain extent, may be able to control the intensity of the ups and downs and have a moderating influence on the misfortune.

The positive value of fortune-telling is that it enables us to understand ourselves and realise our goals. The Pillars of Destiny shows us our potentials and weaknesses, and ups and downs, and such knowledge can be valuable guidelines when developing our potentials and planning the best time for achieving our objectives. Even if the four pillars indicate misfortune ahead, they allow us to make preparations in advance, and even if we cannot do anything about it, we can at least face misfortune with a calm and philosophic mind. This positive aspect of fortune-telling is confirmed by the ancient Confucian adage: "He who does not know his destiny is by no means a wise man."

This book is a record of the author's personal experience and exploration of the techniques of Chinese fortune-telling. This is an important field of study, and at present, research is limited. It is hoped that more systematic studies will be conducted into the true nature of life, fortune and destiny, to open up this vast treasure to a wider public.

Glossary

Ages
To assess change of *feng-shui* influence over time. A twenty-year period of time is called an age. Each age is symbolised by a number from 1 to 9. For example, the period 1964 to 1983 is the Age of Six. The current period from 1984 to 2003 is the Age of Seven.

Bright Hall
The open space in front of a building to hold benevolent *feng-shui* forces.

Dragon's Den
Mountain ranges are called dragons. A dragon's den is a spot of land where the configuration of the landscape allows the benevolent natural forces of the dragon to concentrate and is a good site for houses and graves, bringing prosperity to the people living there as well as their descendants.

Dragon Arm and Tiger Arm
Objects on both sides of a building to help hold *feng-shui* forces and to prevent them from dissipating quickly. Object on the left is called dragon arm and that on the right is called tiger arm.

Eight *Kua*
A set of eight trigrams drawn up in the form of various combinations of continuous lines and broken lines. They originate from the ancient *Book of Changes*, the *I Ching*. The eight *kua* or trigrams are believed to reflect the universal order.

Five Basic Elements
One basic principle behind all schools of Chinese metaphysics is that everything in the universe, including human beings, is composed of five basic forces, called the five elements. They are metal, wood, water, fire and earth. These elements are related to one another by the relations called the Cycle of Birth and the Cycle of Destruction.

Flying Stars
The term refers to the intangible *feng-shui* influences which change over time and space. They are usually symbolised by the numbers 1 to 9, each number occupying a square in the nine-square chart.

Four Pillars of Destiny
An art of assessing human fortune by expressing a person's birth data in the form of four pairs of Chinese characters taken from the Chinese almanac. Each pair of characters representing year, month, day and hour, is called a pillar. The day pillar symbolises the individual self while the other pillars show his relation with other people and his circumstances.

Grand Duke of the Year
The Chinese animal sign of a year actually represents a direction where the planet Jupiter is located. The direction is called the Grand Duke of the Year and has serious *feng-shui* implications. For example, it is recommended not to disturb the earth in the direction of the Grand Duke.

Heavenly Stems and Earthly Branches
A pair of Chinese characters taken from the Chinese almanac form a Pillar of Destiny. The two characters are written vertically one on top of the other. The character on top is called heavenly stem and the one underneath is called earthly branch.

Lo Pan
A complicated Chinese compass for measuring *feng-shui* direction and influences.

Lo Shu Diagram
This refers to a special pattern of dots found on the shell of a legendary tortoise which emerged in the River Lo in China. The pattern is usually presented in the form of a nine-square chart. Each square contains a number symbolising the flying star influences. The *lo shu* diagram is considered the origin of *feng-shui,* revealing the pattern of change of *feng-shui* influences.

Luck Pillars
The Four Pillars of Destiny only shows a person's character, potential, relatives and circumstance. The fortune he encounters throughout his life is represented by another set of pillars called the luck pillars. The luck pillars are derived from the person's Four Pillars of Destiny and they show a person's passage through life. Each luck pillar contains two Chinese characters and governs ten years of a person's life.

Mountain Star and Water Star
The pair of numbers found in each square of a nine-square chart. The one written on the left is the mountain star, associated with health; the number on the right is the water star, which is associated with wealth.

Nine-square Chart
The common drawing representing the *feng-shui* influence which comes from all directions to a house or place. It is like a horoscope of a house and is drawn up according to the birth year and the direction of a house. Each square symbolises a direction and the number contained in each square shows the *feng-shui* influence that the house will receive from that direction.

Shar
This refers to bad *feng-shui* influence. They are either tangible or intangible influences. For example, a sharp edge of a building is a tangible, physical *shar*. The direction related to the opposite side of the Grand Duke is known as the three *shars*.

Yin and Yang
The basic principles of dualism in Chinese philosophy. The universe is seen as composed of two opposing yet complementary principles, the *yin* and the *yang*. *Yin* refers to the negative, female, the moon, dark, low, etc. *Yang* refers to the positive, male, the sun, bright, high, etc.

Yang House
Houses for living people.

Yin House
Graves for the dead.

The 120 Years Basic Element Components Table

Animal Signs	Heavenly Stems										Earthly Branches
子 Rat	庚 Metal 1900	壬 Water 1912	甲 Wood 1924	丙 Fire 1936	戊 Earth 1948	庚 Metal 1960	壬 Water 1972	甲 Wood 1984	丙 Fire 1996	戊 Earth 2008	Water
丑 Ox	辛 Metal 1901	癸 Water 1913	乙 Wood 1925	丁 Fire 1937	己 Earth 1949	辛 Metal 1961	癸 Water 1973	乙 Wood 1985	丁 Fire 1997	己 Earth 2009	Earth
寅 Tiger	壬 Water 1902	甲 Wood 1914	丙 Fire 1926	戊 Earth 1938	庚 Metal 1950	壬 Water 1962	甲 Wood 1974	丙 Fire 1986	戊 Earth 1998	庚 Metal 2010	Wood
卯 Rabbit	癸 Water 1903	乙 Wood 1915	丁 Fire 1927	己 Earth 1939	辛 Metal 1951	癸 Water 1963	乙 Wood 1975	丁 Fire 1987	己 Earth 1999	辛 Metal 2011	Wood
辰 Dragon	甲 Wood 1904	丙 Fire 1916	戊 Earth 1928	庚 Metal 1940	壬 Water 1952	甲 Wood 1964	丙 Fire 1976	戊 Earth 1988	庚 Metal 2000	壬 Water 2012	Earth
巳 Snake	乙 Wood 1905	丁 Fire 1917	己 Earth 1929	辛 Metal 1941	癸 Water 1953	乙 Wood 1965	丁 Fire 1977	己 Earth 1989	辛 Metal 2001	癸 Water 2013	Fire
午 Horse	丙 Fire 1906	戊 Earth 1918	庚 Metal 1930	壬 Water 1942	甲 Wood 1954	丙 Fire 1966	戊 Earth 1978	庚 Metal 1990	壬 Water 2002	甲 Wood 2014	Fire
未 Ram	丁 Fire 1907	己 Earth 1919	辛 Metal 1931	癸 Water 1943	乙 Wood 1955	丁 Fire 1967	己 Earth 1979	辛 Metal 1991	癸 Water 2003	乙 Wood 2015	Earth
申 Monkey	戊 Earth 1908	庚 Metal 1920	壬 Water 1932	甲 Wood 1944	丙 Fire 1956	戊 Earth 1968	庚 Metal 1980	壬 Water 1992	甲 Wood 2004	丙 Fire 2016	Metal
酉 Rooster	己 Earth 1909	辛 Metal 1921	癸 Water 1933	乙 Wood 1945	丁 Fire 1957	己 Earth 1969	辛 Metal 1981	癸 Water 1993	乙 Wood 2005	丁 Fire 2017	Metal
戌 Dog	庚 Metal 1910	壬 Water 1922	甲 Wood 1934	丙 Fire 1946	戊 Earth 1958	庚 Metal 1970	壬 Water 1982	甲 Wood 1994	丙 Fire 2006	戊 Earth 2018	Earth
亥 Pig	辛 Metal 1911	癸 Water 1923	乙 Wood 1935	丁 Fire 1947	己 Earth 1959	辛 Metal 1971	癸 Water 1983	乙 Wood 1995	丁 Fire 2007	己 Earth 2019	Water

The 120 Years Basic Element Components Table

How to use this table:

The table shows the basic element components in each year from 1900 to 2019. Each year is represented by two basic elements - the heavenly stem and earthly branch. For example, for the year 1990, the basic element components are:

Heavenly stem – metal 庚
Earthly branch – fire 午

The table also shows that it is a Year of the Horse. The elements mean that metal and fire are the prevailing influences in 1990. But as fire destroys metal, the fire influence can be regarded as relatively stronger.

As for the year 1991, we can see it is the Year of the Ram, and the following element components are found from the table:

Heavenly stem – metal 辛
Earthly branch – earth 未

So metal and earth are the prevailing influences in 1991. As earth gives birth to metal, the metal influence can be relatively stronger.